75

PRIVACY
RIGHTS

Adam D. Moore

PRIVACY RIGHTS

MORAL AND LEGAL FOUNDATIONS

The Pennsylvania State University Press
University Park, Pennsylvania

Library of Congress Cataloging-in-Publication Data

Moore, Adam D., 1965–
Privacy rights : moral and legal foundations / Adam D. Moore.
p. cm.
Includes bibliographical references and index.
Summary: "Provides a definition and defense of individual
privacy rights. Applies the proposed theory to issues
including privacy versus free speech; drug testing; and
national security and public accountability"
—Provided by publisher.
ISBN 978-0-271-03685-4 (cloth : alk. paper)
1. Privacy, Right of—United States.
2. Data protection—Law and legislation—United States.
3. Public records—Access control—United States.
4. Freedom of speech—United States.
5. Drug testing—Law and legislation—United States.
6. Intellectual property—United States.
I. Title.

KF1262.M66   2010
342.7308'58—dc22
2009053062

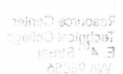

For Amy, Alan, and Kimberly

CONTENTS

Acknowledgments   ix

1
Introduction   1

2
Defining Privacy   11

3
The Value of Privacy   33

4
Justifying Privacy Rights to Bodies and Locations   57

5
Providing for Informational Privacy Rights   81

6
Strengthening Legal Privacy Rights   99

7
Privacy, Speech, and the Law   133

8
Drug Testing and Privacy in the Workplace   153

9
Evaluating Free Access Arguments: Privacy,
Intellectual Property, and Hacking   175

10
Privacy, Security, and Public Accountability   189

Select Bibliography   216

Further Readings   225

Index   234

ACKNOWLEDGMENTS

Much of the work on Chapters 2 through 4 of this manuscript was completed while I was a fellow at the Social Philosophy and Policy Center, Bowling Green State University, in the summer of 2002. A shortened version of Chapter 4, "Justifying Privacy Rights to Bodies and Locations," was presented at the fellows summer colloquia series. I would like to thank Fred D. Miller Jr., Ellen Frankel Paul, Jeffrey Paul, Travis Cook, and the other summer fellows Edward Feser, Richard Timberlake, and George Selgin for their suggestions and comments. I am grateful to Kim Moore for editing Chapters 1 and 2; Jay Hester for offering comments on Chapters 1 and 10; Scott Fields for editing Chapter 5; Peter Winn for providing suggestions on Chapters 6, 7, and 10; and Sarah Bosarge for helping with the bibliography. I would like to thank Judith Wagner DeCew, James Stacey Taylor, and William Kline for reading and commenting on the entire manuscript—the critiques and suggestions offered by these reviewers have helped immeasurably.

During the summer of 2004 and again in the fall of 2007 much of the material found in this work was presented and discussed in an upper-division undergraduate/graduate course at the University of Washington. I would like to thank the students who attended these classes for their astute comments and suggestions. Kris Unsworth and Elizabeth Jones deserve special mention.

Chapter 5, "Providing for Informational Privacy Rights," benefited significantly from being presented at the American Philosophical Association Meetings (March 23–27, 2005) and at the Conference on Informational Privacy, April 27–28, 2007, University of San Diego Institute for Law and Public Policy. I am grateful to Judith Wagner DeCew, James Griffin, Amitai Etzioni, David Brink, Larry Alexander, Daniel Solove, Kenneth Himma, Richard Arneson, Don Dripps, Adam Kolber, Evan Lee, Orly Lobel, and Sam Rickless for providing criticisms and suggestions. Chapter 10, "Privacy, Security, and Public Accountability," was presented at the American Philosophical Association's Mini-Conference on Secrecy, March 22–26, 2006. Thanks to Tom Grassey, David Woolwine, Don Fallis, Kenneth Himma,

Alasdair Roberts, David Resnik, Philip Doty, Mark Alfino, and the other conference participants for their comments and criticisms.

Parts of Chapters 2 and 3 appear in "Privacy: Its Meaning and Value," *American Philosophical Quarterly* 40 (2003): 215–27; "Values, Objectivity, and Relationalism," *Journal of Value Inquiry* 38 (2004): 75–90; and "Defining Privacy," *Journal of Social Philosophy* 39 (2008): 411–28. Sections of Chapters 3 and 4 and the conclusion of Chapter 7 draw from material published in "Intangible Property: Privacy, Power, and Information Control," *American Philosophical Quarterly* 35 (1998). Parts of Chapters 5 and 10 were published in "Toward Informational Privacy Rights," *San Diego Law Review* 44 (Fall 2007). I would like to thank the editors of these journals for allowing me to present this material here.

With homage to the genius of Lee, Lifeson, and Peart—these three started me thinking about philosophical topics, and they continue to inspire. I would also be remiss if I didn't thank my hockey buddies on the Fossils, who have provided the sorts of diversions necessary for productive academic life—Brian Basset, Jeff Caso, Brodie Klenk, Mark Megathlin, David Galloway, Johathan Suga, Dan Laronde, Gordon Trifts, Michael Tremblay, Ted Gay, Cameron Smith, Lorne Berns, Justin Richey, Steve Grant, John Putnam, Bill White, and David Mohr. Special thanks as well to my friends and loved ones who have supported me throughout the writing process—Walter James, Claus Pörtner, Bill Kline, Jay Hester, Scott Rothwell, Mark Van Hook, Ashley Hoyle, Nancy Moore, Scott Moore, Julie Moore, Alan Moore, Amy Moore, and Kimberly Moore.

Finally, I would like to thank the editors at Penn State University Press—Sanford Thatcher, Laura Reed-Morrisson, and Andrew B. Lewis.

1

Individuals have privacy rights. We each have the right to control access to our bodies, to specific places, and to personal information. Beyond controlling access, individuals should, in large part, also determine how their own personal information is used. While control over access to bodies and places appears to be on firm ground, informational privacy is everywhere under siege. Corporations large and small engage in data-mining activities that capture massive amounts of information. Much of this information is about our daily activities—what was purchased, when, where, and for how much. Our mail boxes and e-mail accounts are then stuffed with an endless stream of advertisements and solicitations. Even more alarming are tele-marketers, who intrude upon our solitude. Financial information, phone numbers, and personal addresses of all sorts, whether accurate or not, are captured in databases and bought and sold to individuals, corporations, and government agencies. Beyond data mining, video surveillance, facial recognition technology, spyware, and a host of other invasive tools are opening up private life for public consumption.

Physical or locational privacy, on the other hand, seems to enjoy stronger protection. Forcibly entering someone's house or touching that person's body without just cause is considered a serious moral and legal violation. Strengthened by property rights to houses and land and by walls, fences, and security systems, our physical selves appear quite secure—at least compared to our personal information. In any case, individuals are more willing to trade informational privacy for security or economic benefits than physical privacy.

The underlying assumption is that in relation to human well-being or flourishing, control over our bodies, capacities, and powers is more important than controlling who has access to facts about ourselves. I do not deny this—to be able to "create" the facts of my life I must first be in exclusive control of my body, capacities, or private locations. It does not follow from any of this, however, that personal information control does not deserve protection. Similarly, a right to life, crudely defined as the right not to be killed unjustly, may be more essential or fundamental than physical property rights, yet we should not hastily conclude that lives deserve robust protection while property does not. In fact, without the moral authority to control physical objects in arrangements that support our lifelong goals and projects, a life may not be worth living. A similar point can be made with respect to our physical and informational selves. Being captured on video, audio, and financial data streams is almost as threatening to individual autonomy and well-being as losing physical control of bodies, capacities, and private spaces.[1]

Consider the following thought experiment. One day we are told that the earth is dying—in a few weeks some event will deprive us of oxygen or sunlight. However, we are not to worry. Two advanced humanoid societies have been discovered and are willing to take us in. We have a once-and-for-all choice to go live with the Fencers or the Watchers.

In Fencer society technological improvements, including advances in cryptography and outerwear, have produced near perfect privacy protections. Each individual may wear an antimonitoring suit that completely shields him or her from the prying eyes and ears of others. Court-enforced contracts along with near unbreakable encryption algorithms protect informational privacy. The separation between one's physical self and one's informational self is nearly unbreachable.

But one might ask, "What of security, criminals, and terrorists?" Not a problem. The antimonitoring suits do not make one invisible—suspected criminals can still be questioned and taken off to jail if necessary. Moreover, court-issued warrants override secrecy agreements and allow for encrypted

---

1. James Stacey Taylor and others have challenged the view that there is an essential connection between privacy and autonomy. See J. S. Taylor, "Privacy and Autonomy: A Reappraisal," *Southern Journal of Philosophy* 40 (2002): 587–604. I discuss many of the issues taken up in the Taylor article in later chapters.

codes to be broken and information gathered. Informants, incarceration, plea bargains, as well as other law enforcement tools are still available: "Taken from a Fencer Immigration Advertisement: *Come join the Fencer society—a society of privacy and security. Feel free to engage in new experiments in living without becoming someone else's news story. Relax, think, and meditate without an endless stream of solicitations pursuing your every free moment. . . . With privacy enshrined, solitude, tranquility, and peace of mind are secured.*"

In the Watcher society technological improvements, such as advances in facial recognition technology, video miniaturization, data mining, and nanotechnology, have opened up all private domains for public consumption.[2] Every movement and sound made by each individual is recorded, stored, and uploaded for public consumption to the Watcher database. Security is complete, and criminal activity is nonexistent. Total information awareness has been achieved.

But what about pressures to conform, restrictions of autonomy, and Big Brother worries? In the Watcher society individuals have learned to cast aside shyness and enjoy total openness. Moreover, given that transparency is universal, governmental officials are truly accountable to public concerns. At the same time, information overload or superabundance assures anonymity for average law-abiding citizens: "Taken from a Watcher Immigration Advertisement: *Come and be a part of the open society. Cast aside your inhibitions to conform when being watched and embrace total information access. . . . What do you have to hide? Transparency is liberating! Accountability ensures security!*"

Thinking about these two fictitious societies raises multiple questions. Would the bonds of community break apart in the Fencer society? Would total information access in the Watcher world include real-time access to one's thoughts, and would such surveillance lead to social conformity of thought and action? Could average citizens really hide—unmonitored—in the mountain of data being captured by the Watchers? If we had to choose one of these alternatives, which would be better, all things considered?

While we are not faced with these stark possibilities, our policy choices may lead us toward them. For example, according to one estimate there are over four million surveillance cameras in Britain.[3] One concern is that the

2. See Arthur C. Clarke and Stephen Baxter, *The Light of Other Days* (New York: Tor Books, 2000), and Isaac Asimov, "The Dead Past," in *The Best of Isaac Asimov* (New York: Doubleday, 1973), for two science fiction treatments of "Watcher" societies.

3. Michael McCahill and Clive Norris, "CCTV in London," Urbaneye Working Paper 6 (June 2002): 20; cited in Jeffery Rosen's *Naked Crowd* (New York: Random House, 2004), 36.

rich, powerful, and connected will live in a world closer to Fencer society, while the poor and disenfranchised will inhabit something close to the Watcher society. Privacy has always been a commodity secured, more or less, on the basis of wealth, power, and privilege.[4] Nevertheless, a hundred years ago privacy concerns were not so important because of technological barriers related to information gathering and control. The digital and computer revolution, along with numerous other advances in technology, have changed the game.

OVERVIEW OF A THEORY

In the most general terms, my goal is to provide a philosophically rigorous defense of privacy rights while addressing numerous important applied issues that surround privacy such as free speech, drug testing, hackers, public accountability, and national security. While other applications and issues could have been taken up, such as the feminist critique of privacy,[5] I think that the issues discussed herein are important and worthy of consideration. Informational privacy is typically viewed as less important than free speech and a free press. Physical or bodily privacy is too easily traded for national security and for economic values such as workplace productivity. Many digital natives, those who have grown up with digital technology, have been advocating "free access" views that would undermine legal protections for privacy. I would like to reverse these trends.

In Chapters 2, 3, 4, and 5 I provide the theoretical foundations for the analysis and conclusions contained in Chapters 6 through 10. Many, perhaps most, books and articles on privacy simply assume that privacy is valuable and that individuals have privacy rights. Another often used strategy is to hold that privacy is entailed by some other, higher-level concept or theory like autonomy.[6] Without an analysis or justification of the back-

---

4. For an analysis of the cultural and historical roots of privacy, see Barrington Moore Jr., *Privacy: Studies in Social and Cultural History* (New York: M. E. Sharpe, 1984); Judith Wagner DeCew, *In Pursuit of Privacy: Law, Ethics, and the Rise of Technology* (Ithaca: Cornell University Press, 1997); Ferdinand D. Schoeman, *Privacy and Social Freedom* (New York: Cambridge University Press, 1992); Alan F. Westin, *Privacy and Freedom* (New York: Atheneum, 1967); and Paul Veyne, ed., *A History of Private Life*, vols. 1–3 (Cambridge: Harvard University Press, 1987).

5. For example, see Anita Allen, *Why Privacy Isn't Everything: Feminist Reflections on Personal Accountability* (Lanham, Md.: Rowman and Littlefield, 2003), and DeCew, *In Pursuit of Privacy*, chap. 5.

6. A classic example of this is W. A. Parent's justification of privacy based on moral respect for persons. See W. A. Parent, "Privacy, Morality, and the Law," *Philosophy and Public Affairs* 12 (1983): 277. A more recent example is Luciano Floridi's claim that privacy is a fundamental

ground theory that is supposed to entail privacy, we are left with little means to adjudicate between different moral claims and interests. My goal in Chapters 2 through 5 is to establish moral claims to privacy without relying on some overarching moral theory or set of principles lurking as hidden assumptions. At appropriate places I will indicate how the theoretical framework provided in the first half of this work applies to an issue being considered in Chapters 6 through 10. If we view privacy not as some mere preference or interest but as a fundamental moral claim, then it will be easier to strike an appropriate balance with other important values such as speech and security.

Chapter 2 begins with several attempts to define privacy. After analyzing several competing conceptions, I offer and defend my own: Privacy may be understood as the right to control access to and use of physical items, like bodies and houses, and information, like medical and financial facts. Physical or locational privacy affords individuals the right to control access to specific bodies, objects, and places. Informational privacy, on the other hand, allows individuals to control access to and uses of personal information no matter how it is codified. Medical information about someone, for example, could be instantiated in a database, recorded on an audio cassette, or carved into stone.

If privacy is defined as a right of control over access to and uses of places and information and if the nature of "places" and "information" forces slightly different forms of justification and legal considerations, then this may undermine any attempt at a unified definition—with privacy over bodies and places being considered one thing, and privacy over information being considered another. Decisional privacy, defined as the right to make certain sorts of fundamental decisions, would then be a third area.[7] Nevertheless, I believe that a "control over access and use" definition is coherent and there is nothing unsettling about distinguishing between and focusing on physical privacy and informational privacy. Similarly, there is nothing incoherent about the notion of "property" as including physical property and intellectual property. Intellectual property and information are, in the typical case, nonrivalrous in a way that tangible property and physical privacy are not. This feature alone would sanction treating these domains

---

and inalienable right because it is the same as personal identity. See Floridi, "The Ontological Interpretation of Informational Privacy," *Ethics and Information Technology* 7 (2005): 195.

7. The rights of adults to make their own decisions about contraceptive use, intimate behavior, whom to marry, and reproductive choice fall under the domain of "control over one's choices." Such decisions seem to include both liberty and privacy dimensions.

separately and lead one to suspect that slightly different arguments will be needed to justify control along both domains. Chapter 2 ends with an analysis of the "right to control access and use" view of privacy in light of several, now classic, cases and illustrations.

My primary purpose in Chapter 3 is to demonstrate the moral value of privacy. Providing an argument or reasons in support of this claim will require several digressions into metaethics. Many theorists simply assume a specific and contentious account of value is correct or that some other principle, like freedom, is valuable, and then explain how privacy is implied by the assumed account or principle. In many instances the entire view rests on intuitions. But against those who doubt the moral value of privacy, this gets us nowhere—alas, all the detractor has to do is challenge the assumption or intuition with a contrary view. My hope is that by offering a plausible and compelling account of moral value and then grounding privacy in this view, I can provide a firm foundation for the value of privacy. Included in the objectivist and relationalist perspective offered is an account of moral bettering and worsening.

Privacy, it is argued, is a core human value—the right to control access to oneself is an essential part of human well-being or flourishing. I explore several historical and cultural understandings of privacy to support this claim. The ability to control access to oneself and to engage in patterns of association and disassociation is a cultural universal. Moreover and more important, individuals who lack this control typically exhibit increased levels of physical and emotional impairment. This claim is also true of numerous nonhuman mammals as well.

Chapter 4 centers on the justification of privacy rights to bodies and locations. Establishing the value of privacy does not, by itself, establish privacy rights. The goal is to derive privacy rights from the relatively uncontroversial moral principle that actions that do no harm are not immoral—a "no harm, no foul" rule. Briefly put, the argument for physical privacy rights runs as follows. In using his own body, capacities, and powers Fred does not morally worsen Ginger relative to how she would have been were Fred absent or had Fred not possessed his own body (whatever this means). When Ginger uses Fred's body, she will almost always interfere with his use and worsen him relative to how he would have been in her absence or had she not possessed the object in question. With numerous qualifications and clarifications, I conclude that Fred's moral claim to control access to his body, capacities, and powers is undefeated and bodily privacy rights emerge.

Since the argument for bodily or locational privacy and informational privacy depends on a version of a "no harm, no foul" principle, some care is taken in establishing the moral weightiness of this rule. Actions that pass this requirement are collectively rational and appropriately respect the moral worth of individuals and their goals and projects. Such a commitment reflects our minimum and, I hope, uncontroversial obligations to one another.

In Chapter 5, "Providing for Informational Privacy Rights," I build on the argument offered in Chapter 4. By possessing and using information about himself, Fred does not necessarily worsen Ginger relative to how she would be in his absence or had Fred not possessed the information in question. Fred's use and possession is thus warranted. Unlike the case where Ginger tries to use Fred's body, when Ginger possesses and uses information about Fred, she does not necessarily worsen him relative to how he would be were she absent or if she did not possess the information in question. After all, information may be nonrivalrously possessed and consumed. Thus further arguments are required to secure informational privacy rights. I present two. I maintain, first, that gathering, possessing, and using information about someone else, especially if that information is sensitive, personal, and easily disseminated, creates risks that are morally relevant. More important, many of these risks are not chosen—they are imposed. A second strand of argument links physical privacy rights with property rights. Through the use of walls, fences, disguises, strong encryption, legitimate deception, trade secrets, and contracts we may be able to justifiably restrict access to information about ourselves.

My primary focus in Chapter 6, "Strengthening Legal Privacy Rights," is to determine the nature and scope of legal protections for informational and locational privacy. If legal systems are to reflect important moral norms, then privacy protections must be codified in the law. In recent times, however, informational privacy protections have not fared well. Privacy-based torts have been undermined through various legal cases and statutes. Moreover, decisional privacy, crudely understood as the right to make private choices in private places,[8] and Fourth Amendment privacy, which protects citizens from unwarranted searches, have been threatened in the name of national security or relegated to fairly narrow areas. I argue that by strengthening the tort of intrusion we may move toward a more robust protection of privacy rights. My goal is to provide a workable model of privacy protection within the legal framework already in place.

8. Two examples of such cases being *Roe v. Wade*, 410 U.S. 153 (1973), and *Griswold v. Connecticut*, 381 U.S. 479 (1965).

In Chapter 7, "Privacy, Speech, and the Law," I examine the tensions between privacy, free speech, and a free press. Judicial hostility toward protecting privacy, especially when free speech issues are present, is widespread. In fact, across hundreds of cases speech nearly always trumps privacy. I argue that privacy concerns should not be so easily sacrificed on the altar of "the public's right to know." The often-noted tension between privacy and speech in the legal realm is due to an expansive but unfounded view of expression. Once the value of privacy is recognized, and once we place ourselves in an unbiased position from which to view these issues, it is argued that "right to know" considerations should be recast in terms of the kinds of information necessary for the continued existence and stability of democratic institutions. Moreover, information that is both invasive and clearly publicly important can almost always be modified so that the invasive properties are diminished or nonexistent. As with other content-based restrictions on expression—such as hate speech or sexual harassment—I will argue for a privacy restriction.

In Chapter 8, "Drug Testing and Privacy in the Workplace," I consider numerous arguments for and against workplace drug testing. If the account of privacy offered in earlier chapters is correct, then there is a fairly strong presumption in favor of individual privacy rights—even in the workplace. Many claim this presumption is overridden by employee consent, public safety arguments, or workplace productivity concerns. I consider each of these arguments and dismiss them as having insufficient merit to undermine individual privacy rights. I give special attention to the consent argument against employee privacy.

On this view, when an employee consents to give up privacy, then there can be no legitimate objections. Employees can waive their rights in exchange for a job and a paycheck. But consent or agreement is only binding if certain conditions have been met. If someone agrees to relinquish privacy while under duress—for example, he or she needs a job and jobs are in short supply—then the agreement seems suspect. If, on the other hand, someone agrees to relinquish privacy in conditions that are fair, it would seem that the agreement would be morally binding. In this chapter I develop a procedure to test the moral bindingness of agreements related to the issues of workplace drug testing and privacy. I argue that in most fields, drug testing is not warranted and unjustifiably invades private domains.

In the most general terms, in Chapter 9 I focus on the tensions between free access and privacy related to digitally stored information. Free access to information, whether stored on networks or in software packages, have long been championed by hackers and, more recently, digital natives. Proponents of this view argue that information should be free because it is a social product, because information is nonrivalrous, and because hacking information provides for better security. Advocates for privacy and intellectual property would disagree with these views. The central question of this chapter is whether or not the free access arguments are strong enough to override a presumption in favor of privacy and intellectual property.

I consider two major strands of argument when establishing a presumption in favor of intellectual property. First, the utilitarian incentives-based view holds that rights to restrict information flow are based on a bargain between content creators and society. Society grants limited rights to control access to intellectual works as an inducement to bring forth new knowledge. The second strand of argument presented is inspired by John Locke and runs parallel to the arguments for privacy offered in earlier chapters. On this view, authors and inventors who produce content and do not worsen their fellows—relative to the appropriate baseline of comparison and measure of value—generate moral claims to their creations. I then present three arguments in favor of free access and find none of them strong enough to override these arguments supporting privacy and intellectual property.

The question of when privacy rights may be justifiably overridden in the name of public security is considered in Chapter 10—"Privacy, Security, and Public Accountability." Balancing privacy and security may require that we trade some of the former for some of the latter. Nevertheless, in many cases security arguments cut the other direction. It is only through the implementation of strong privacy protections, sunlight provisions, and judicial oversight that we obtain an appropriate level of security against government abuse of power, industrial espionage, unwarranted invasions into private domains, and information warfare or terrorism.

In the aftermath of the terrorist attacks of September 11, 2001, there were numerous calls for suppressing civil liberties in the name of national security. A few years after the attacks General Patrick M. Hughes, Department of Homeland Security intelligence chief, noted: "We have to abridge individual rights, change the societal conditions, and act in ways that heretofore were not in accordance with our values and traditions, like giving a police officer or security official the right to search you without a judicial finding of probable cause."[9]

9. General Patrick M. Hughes, quoted in *Congressional Quarterly* (October 27, 2004). See page 32 of http://pirp.harvard.edu/pubs_pdf/hughes/hughes-i03-1.pdf.

Passage and implementation of the USA Patriot Act in October 2001 greatly expanded government surveillance powers. In short, it enables the government, in my opinion, to act without public oversight, to ignore strict probable cause, and to avoid accountability for illegal or unwarranted intrusions into private domains. Policies that create secret courts, allow covert searches and seizures, and suppress information with no public oversight or "sunlight" provisions unjustifiably violate individual privacy rights and have no place in a liberal democracy.

CONCLUSION

John Stuart Mill once said, "It is sometimes both possible and useful to point out the way, though without being . . . prepared to adventure far into it."[10] In this book I will try to do better than merely point the way. Rather than assume several moral principles and derive privacy rights from the top down, I begin with several simple claims about value and a version of a "no harm, no foul" rule. While I argue for both of these starting points at length, my goal is not convince all comers that these claims are beyond dispute, but rather to demonstrate that they are plausible and warranted. From these weak and hopefully widely shared views, I derive a theory of privacy. My hope is to provide a compelling theory of privacy—compelling in the sense of being suitably justified given the subject matter.

It is my belief that technological advances over the next few decades will continue to highlight issues of privacy. Increasing use of video surveillance, facial-recognition technology, data mining, genetic profiling, e-mail surveillance, and the like, along with government-sponsored programs such as Total Information Awareness,[11] indicate that privacy will continue to be threatened. We may indeed have a once-and-for-all choice to travel toward a Watcher society or a Fencer society, and if we are to make this choice between the Watchers and the Fencers, better—far better—the latter.

10. J. S. Mill, *The Logic of the Moral Sciences* (Chicago: Open Court Classics, 1987), 21.

11. Now known as the Information Awareness Office, its mission statement is as follows: "The DARPA Information Awareness Office (IAO) will imagine, develop, apply, integrate, demonstrate and transition information technologies, components and prototype, closed-loop, information systems that will counter asymmetric threats by achieving total information awareness useful for preemption; national security warning; and national security decision making." http://infowar.net/tia/www.darpa.mil/iao/ (accessed December 19, 2008).

2

DEFINING PRIVACY

Privacy is a difficult notion to define in part because rituals of association
and disassociation are culturally relative. For example, opening a door
without knocking might be considered a serious privacy violation in one
culture and yet permitted in another. Definitions of privacy can be couched
in descriptive or normative terms—we can view privacy as a mere condition or as a moral claim on others to refrain from certain activities. Furthermore, some view privacy as a derivative notion that rests upon more basic
rights such as liberty or property.

There is little agreement on how to define privacy, but like other contested concepts—such as liberty or justice—this conceptual difficulty does
not undermine its importance. If only Plato were correct and we could gaze
upon the Forms and determine the necessary and sufficient conditions for
each of these concepts. But we can't, and neither intuitions nor natural
language analysis offer much help. Not doing violence to the language and
cohering with our intuitions may be features of a good account of privacy;
nevertheless, they do not provide adequate grounds for a definition—the
language and the intuitions may be hopelessly muddled.

Moreover, as indicated by the analysis of examples offered throughout
this chapter, there are central cases of privacy and peripheral ones. Aristotle
discussed this idea of central and peripheral cases in talking about "friendship." "[My opponents say] they are not able to do justice to all the phe-

nomena of friendship; since one definition will not suit all, they think there are no other friendships; but the others are friendships."[1] The same may be said of privacy. Some of the core features found in the central cases of privacy may not be present in the outlying cases. One of the ways a conception is illuminated is to trace the similarities and differences between these examples.[2]

Evaluation is a further tool for arriving at a defensible conception of privacy. A perfectly coherent definition of privacy that accords faultlessly with some groups' intuitions may be totally useless. In the most general terms, we are asking, "What is this or that way of classifying privacy good for?" At the most abstract level the evaluation may be moral—we ask, "Does this way of carving up the world promote, hinder, or leave unaffected human well-being or flourishing?" John Finnis echoes this sentiment:

> There is a mutual . . . interdependence between the project of describing human affairs by way of theory and the project of evaluating human options with a view . . . to acting reasonably well. The evaluations are in no way deduced from the descriptions; but one whose knowledge of the facts of the human situation is very limited is unlikely to judge well in discerning the practical implications of the basic values. Equally, the descriptions are not deduced from the evaluations; but without the evaluations one cannot determine what descriptions are really illuminating and significant.[3]

Perhaps the best that can be done is to offer a coherent conception of privacy that highlights why it is distinct and important. In this chapter, after a brief survey of various definitions, I will offer and defend a control over access and use account of privacy. My goal is to provide a normative definition of privacy, although I will sketch a descriptive account as well.[4]

---

1. Aristotle *Eudemian Ethics* 7.2.1236a16–32, in *The Complete Works of Aristotle*, ed. Jonathan Barns, Bollingen Series, 2 vols. (Princeton: Princeton University Press, 1984), 2:1958.

2. The idea of central cases and peripheral cases comes from Finnis, who is citing Aristotle. See John Finnis, *Natural Law and Natural Rights* (Oxford: Clarendon Press, 1980), 11.

3. Ibid., 19.

4. See also Adam D. Moore, "Privacy: Its Meaning and Value," *American Philosophical Quarterly* 40 (Fall 2003): 215–27, and "Defining Privacy," *Journal of Social Philosophy* 39 (Fall 2008): 411–28.

CONCEPTIONS OF PRIVACY

Privacy has been defined in many ways over the last few hundred years.[5] Following Judge Thomas Cooley, Samuel Warren and Louis D. Brandeis called privacy "the right to be let alone."[6] Roscoe Pound and Paul Freund defined it in terms of an extension of personality or personhood.[7] Legal scholar William Prosser separated privacy cases into four distinct but related torts: "*Intrusion*: Intruding (physically or otherwise) upon the solitude of another in a highly offensive manner. *Private facts*: Publicizing highly offensive private information about someone which is not of legitimate concern to the public. *False light*: Publicizing a highly offensive and false impression of another. *Appropriation*: Using another's name or likeness for some advantage without the other's consent."[8]

Alan Westin and others have described privacy in terms of information control.[9] Still others have insisted that privacy consists of a form of autonomy over personal matters.[10] William Parent argues that "privacy is the condition of not having undocumented personal knowledge about one possessed by others,"[11] while Julie Inness defines privacy as "the state of possessing control over a realm of intimate decisions, which include decisions

---

5. For a rigorous analysis of the major accounts of privacy, see DeCew, *In Pursuit of Privacy*, chaps. 1–4. While I do not agree entirely with DeCew's proposed definition of privacy, her analysis is insightful and thought provoking.

6. See Thomas M. Cooley, *A Treatise on the Law of Torts* (Chicago: Callaghan, 1880), and Samuel Warren and Louis D. Brandeis, "The Right to Privacy," *Harvard Law Review* 4 (1890): 193–220.

7. Roscoe Pound, "Interests in Personality," *Harvard Law Review* 28 (1915): 343; Paul A. Freund, "Privacy: One Concept or Many?" in *Privacy: Nomos XIII*, ed. J. Roland Pennock and John W. Chapman (New York: Atherton Press, 1971), 182.

8. Dean William Prosser, "Privacy," *California Law Review* 48 (1960): 383–89; quoted in Ellen Alderman and Caroline Kennedy, *The Right to Privacy* (New York: Alfred A. Knopf, 1995), 155–56.

9. Westin, *Privacy and Freedom*; Adam D. Moore, *Intellectual Property and Information Control: Philosophic Foundations and Contemporary Issues* (New Brunswick, N.J.: Transaction Books, 2001). See also Allen, *Why Privacy Isn't Everything*, and Ruth Gavison, "Information Control: Availability and Control," in *Public and Private in Social Life*, ed. Stanley Benn and G. Gaus (New York: St. Martin's Press, 1983), 113–34.

10. *Eisenstadt v. Baird*, 405 U.S. 438 (1972) at 453. See also Louis Henkin, "Privacy and Autonomy," *Columbia Law Review* 74 (1974): 1410, 1425; Joel Feinberg, "Autonomy, Sovereignty, and Privacy: Moral Ideas in the Constitution?" *Notre Dame Law Review* 58 (1983): 445; Daniel R. Ortiz, "Privacy, Autonomy, and Consent," *Harvard Journal of Law and Public Policy* 12 (1989): 91; and H. Tristram Englehardt Jr., "Privacy and Limited Democracy," *Social Philosophy and Policy* 17 (Summer 2000): 120–40.

11. Parent, "Privacy, Morality, and the Law," 269.

about intimate access, intimate information, and intimate actions."[12] More recently, Judith Wagner DeCew has proposed the "realm of the private to be whatever types of information and activities are not, according to a reasonable person in normal circumstances, the legitimate concern of others."[13] This brief summary indicates the variety and breadth of the definitions that have been offered.

NORMATIVE AND NON-NORMATIVE ACCOUNTS OF PRIVACY

There are two distinctions that have been widely discussed related to defining privacy. The first is the distinction between descriptive and normative conceptions of privacy. A descriptive or non-normative account describes a state or condition where privacy obtains. An example would be Parent's definition, "Privacy is the *condition* of not having undocumented personal knowledge about one possessed by others."[14] A normative account, on the other hand, makes references to moral obligations or claims. For example, when DeCew talks about what is of "legitimate concern of others," she includes ethical considerations.

One way to clarify this distinction is to think of a case in which the term "privacy" is used in a non-normative way: "When I was getting dressed at the doctor's office the other day, I was in a room with nice thick walls and a heavy door—I had some measure of privacy." Here it seems that the meaning is non-normative—the person is reporting that a condition obtained. Had someone breached this zone, the person might have said, "You should not be here. Please respect my privacy!" In this latter case, normative aspects would be stressed.

REDUCTIONIST AND NONREDUCTIONIST ACCOUNTS OF PRIVACY

Reductionists, such as Judith Jarvis Thomson, argue that privacy is derived from other rights such as life, liberty, and property rights—there is no overarching concept of privacy but rather several distinct core notions that have

12. Julie Inness, *Privacy, Intimacy, and Isolation* (New York: Oxford University Press, 1992), 140.

13. DeCew, *In Pursuit of Privacy*, 58, 64. DeCew presents and defends this broad definition, in part, to capture the disparate elements of privacy that have been codified in the law. In any case, I do not think that DeCew's definition is incompatible with my account.

14. Parent, "Privacy, Morality, and the Law," 269.

been lumped together.[15] Viewing privacy in this fashion might mean jettisoning the idea altogether and focusing on more fundamental concepts. For example, Frederick Davis has argued that "if truly fundamental interests are accorded the protection they deserve, no need to champion a right to privacy arises. Invasion of privacy is, in reality, a complex of more fundamental wrongs. Similarly, the individual's interest in privacy itself, however real, is derivative and a state better vouchsafed by protecting more immediate rights."[16] Unlike Thomson and Davis, the nonreductionist views privacy as related to, but distinct from, other rights or moral concepts.

It is my view that the normative and non-normative distinction is important and crucial for conceptual coherence—it is possible and proper to define privacy along normative and descriptive dimensions. Privacy is not special in this regard. For example, liberty is also defined descriptively and normatively. Thomas Hobbes defines liberty as "the absence of external impediment."[17] In this example, as with Hobbes's conception of the state of nature, there no moral "oughts" or "shoulds" present. Alternatively, J. S. Mill defends a normatively loaded account of liberty, opening his classic work *On Liberty* with "The subject of this essay is . . . civil, or social liberty: the nature and limits of the power which can be legitimately exercised by society over the individual."[18] Privacy may also be defined descriptively or normatively.

Second, if we assume a normative definition without considering the justification of the rights involved, it is unclear whether or not privacy is reducible to more "basic" rights or the other way around. This point has been made by Parent and others.[19] Moreover, given the arguments that I offer elsewhere, it is not surprising that there are close connections between privacy, liberty, and self-ownership rights.[20] The very same sort of justifica-

15. Thomson was one of the first to defend a reductionist view of privacy. See Judith Jarvis Thomson, "The Right to Privacy," *Philosophy and Public Affairs* 4 (1975): 295. For an analysis of the reduction versus nonreduction debate, see Amy Peikoff, "No Corn on This Cob: Why Reductionists Should Be All Ears for Pavesich," *Brandeis Law Journal* 42 (2004): 751.

16. Frederick Davis, "What Do We Mean by 'Right to Privacy'?" *South Dakota Law Review* 4 (1959): 20.

17. Thomas Hobbes, *Leviathan*, ed. C. B. Macpherson (New York: Penguin Books, 1985), 189.

18. J. S. Mill, *On Liberty*, ed. E. Rapaport (Indianapolis: Hackett, 1978), 1.

19. See Parent, "Privacy, Morality, and the Law," 279–80; Thomas Scanlon, "Thomson on Privacy," *Philosophy and Public Affairs* 4 (1975): 315–22, cited in DeCew, *In Pursuit of Privacy*, 29; and Jeffrey Reiman, "Privacy, Intimacy, and Personhood," *Philosophy and Public Affairs* 6 (1976): 26–44.

20. See Adam D. Moore, "Justifying Informational Privacy Rights," *San Diego Law Review* 44 (Fall 2007): 808–39; Moore, *Intellectual Property and Information Control*, chap. 8; and Moore,

tion that is offered for privacy rights could be offered for intellectual property rights or perhaps life rights.[21] It is also true that the kind of rights involved will be intimately tied to the form of justification—it would be surprising to find hard-line Kantians and crude consequentialists arriving at the same conception of "rights." However, even if the reductionist is correct, it does not follow that we should do away with the category of privacy rights. The cluster of rights that comprise privacy may find their roots in property or liberty yet still mark out a distinct kind. Finally, if all rights are nothing more than complex sets of obligations, powers, duties, and immunities, it would not automatically follow that we should dispense with talk of rights and frame our moral discourse in these more basic terms.

A CONTROL- AND USE-BASED DEFINITION OF PRIVACY

I favor what has been called a "control-based" definition of privacy.[22] A privacy right is an access control right over oneself and information about oneself. Privacy rights also include a use or control feature—that is, privacy rights allow me exclusive use and control over personal information and specific bodies or locations.

The term "control" may also be given a descriptive or normative treatment. A descriptive account of "control" would likely highlight the power to physically manipulate an object or intangible good. If it is within Smith's power to limit access or use of some object, then we may say that the condition of control obtains. A normative account of "control" would focus on moral claims that should hold independent of the condition. As with the notion of a state or condition of privacy, I think that purely descriptive accounts of control are largely uninteresting—a point I will return to.

"Intangible Property: Privacy, Power, and Information Control," *American Philosophical Quarterly* 35 (October 1998): 365–78.

21. See Moore, *Intellectual Property and Information Control*.

22. This account is similar to Anita Allen and Ruth Gavison's "inaccessibility" view of privacy and Ernest van den Haag and Richard Parker's "control" theory. See Allen, *Why Privacy Isn't Everything;* Gavison, "Information Control"; Charles Fried, *An Anatomy of Values* (Cambridge: Harvard University Press, 1970), chap. 9; Richard Wasserstrom, "Privacy: Some Assumptions and Arguments," in *Philosophical Law*, ed. R. Bronaugh (Westport, Conn.: Greenwood Press, 1979), 148; Hyman Gross, "Privacy and Autonomy," in *Privacy: Nomos XIII*, ed. J. Roland Pennock and John W. Chapman (New York: Atherton Press, 1971), 170; Ernest van den Haag, "On Privacy," ibid., 147; and Richard Parker, "A Definition of Privacy," *Rutgers Law Review* 27 (1974): 280.

One feature of the account that I defend is that it can incorporate many of the features found in the aforementioned definitions. Controlling access to ourselves affords individuals the space to develop themselves as they see fit. Such control yields room to grow *personally* while maintaining *autonomy* over the course and direction of one's life. Moreover, each of Prosser's torts—intrusion, private facts, false light, and appropriation—contains elements of access control and use.[23] While there are interesting connections between privacy and autonomy, I do not think that either is more fundamental than the other or that privacy is valuable simply because it is connected to autonomy. In any case, there are numerous competing theories of autonomy, and it would be uninteresting to simply assume that one of these views is correct and then note that privacy can be derived from it.

William Parent has attacked non-normative control-based definitions of privacy as follows: "Consider the example of a person who voluntarily divulges all sorts of intimate, personal, and undocumented information about [her]self to a friend. She is doubtless exercising control. . . . But we would not and should not say that in doing so she is preserving or protecting her privacy. On the contrary, she is voluntarily relinquishing much of her privacy. People can and do choose to give up privacy for many reasons. An adequate conception of privacy must allow for this fact. Control definitions do not."[24]

Parent maintains that it is implausible to exercise control by giving up control. But why should we say that someone who does this is "preserving or protecting . . . privacy" rather than "giving up" privacy? In this case, by yielding control to others the condition of privacy is diminished or no longer obtains. Similarly, someone may freely limit their own liberty. An exercise of liberty may limit liberty, while an exercise of control may limit control.

Moreover, yielding control over access does not automatically yield control over use. For example, Ginger may allow Fred access to sensitive personal information yet still have the power to stop him from broadcasting this information. Thus, non-normative views of access and use are not undermined by Parent's worries.

Moving to normative accounts, Parent is quick to add in a footnote that those who defend a control definition of privacy might be worried about a *right* to privacy rather than the *condition* of privacy.[25] He charges that if so

23. William Prosser, "Privacy," *California Law Review* 48 (1960): 383–422.
24. Parent, "Privacy, Morality, and the Law," 273.
25. Ibid., 273 n. 11.

they should have made this explicit and in any case are confusing a liberty right with a privacy right.

Parent's argument, however, is anemic. On these grounds we could complain that control definitions of property rights or life rights are similarly confused with liberty rights. Following W. N. Hohfeld and others, the root idea of a "right" can be expressed as follows: "To say someone has a right is to say that there exists a state of affairs in which one person (the right-holder) has a claim on another (the duty-bearer) for an act or forbearance in the sense that, should the claim be in force or exercised, and the act or forbearance not done, it would be moral to use coercive measures to extract the specific performance, or compensation in lieu of it."[26]

This broad characterization holds for both moral rights and legal rights. For example, property is a bundle of rights associated with an owner's relation to a thing, where each right in the bundle is distinct.[27]

Given this, it should be clear that Parent's attack on normative control-based definitions is based on an overly simplistic account of rights. Ginger's property right to a Louisville Slugger yields her a particular sort of control right over the baseball bat in question. It also justifiably limits the liberty of everyone else—they cannot interfere with Ginger's control of the bat

26. Lawrence Becker, *Property Rights, Philosophic Foundations* (London: Routledge and Kegan Paul, 1977), 9. Hohfeld distinguishes four types of rights: claim-rights, liberty-rights, power-rights, and immunity-rights. See W. N. Hohfeld, "Fundamental Legal Conceptions as Applied in Judicial Reasoning," *Yale Law Journal* 23, no. 16 (1916).

27. For a lucid account of full legal ownership or property, see A. M. Honoré, "Ownership," in *Oxford Essays in Jurisprudence*, ed. A. G. Guest (London: Oxford University Press, 1961), 112–28. See also Carl Wellman, *A Theory of Rights: Persons Under Laws, Institutions, and Morals* (Totowa, N.J.: Rowman and Allanheld, 1985). I should note that there are numerous competing conceptions of rights. Robert Nozick views rights as side-constraints on action requiring omissions. The "interest" theory, defended by Bentham, Lyons, MacCormick, Raz, and Waldron, holds that a person has rights insofar as they have a compelling interest that justifies holding others to have the appropriate duty. The "choice" theory of rights, supported by Hart, Montague, and Steiner, holds that a person has a right when others have duties that protect the right-holder's choices. Rainbolt, Feinberg, and Dworkin have also advanced their own conceptions of rights. See Robert Nozick, *Anarchy, State, and Utopia* (New York: Basic Books, 1974); David Lyons, *Rights, Welfare, and Mill's Moral Theory* (Oxford: Oxford University Press, 1994); Neil MacCormick, *Legal Right and Social Democracy: Essays in Legal and Political Philosophy* (New York: Clarendon Press, 1982); Joseph Raz, *The Morality of Freedom* (Oxford: Oxford University Press, 1986); Jeremy Waldron, "Rights in Conflict," *Ethics* 99 (April 1989): 503–19; H. L. A. Hart, *Essays on Bentham* (New York: Clarendon Press, 1982) and *Essays in Jurisprudence and Philosophy* (New York: Clarendon Press, 1983); Phillip Montague, "Two Concepts of Rights," *Philosophy and Public Affairs* 9 (1980): 372–84; Hillel Steiner, *An Essay on Rights* (Oxford: Blackwell, 1994); George Rainbolt, "Rights as Normative Constraints on Others," *Philosophy and Phenomenological Research* 53 (1993): 93–112; Joel Feinberg, *Rights, Justice, and the Bounds of Liberty* (Princeton: Princeton University Press, 1980); and R. M. Dworkin, "Rights as Trumps," in *Theories of Rights*, ed. J. Waldron (New York: Oxford University Press, 1985).

without her consent. A liberty right is not a freedom to do whatever one likes—it is not a license. Liberty rights, like property rights, are limited by the rights of others. Basically, rights, liberty, and control come bundled together. When one gives up control and yields access in an intimate relationship, for example, one is giving up privacy within a limited domain. Parent's attack thus misses the mark—he assumes, without argument, that liberty, property, and control rights are conceptually distinct. As noted earlier, without some account of the justification of these rights, it is fallacious to claim that they must be conceptually distinct.[28]

Parent offers the following definition for privacy. "Privacy is the condition of not having undocumented personal knowledge about one possessed by others."[29] A person's privacy is diminished exactly to the degree that others possess this kind of knowledge about him. Documented information is information that is found in the public record or is publicly available. For example, Parent would consider information found in newspapers, court proceedings, and other official documents open to public inspection publicly available.

There are several problems with this conception of privacy. First, it leaves the notion of privacy dependent upon what a society or culture takes as documentation and what information is available via the public record. Parent acts as if undocumented information is private and documented information is not, and this is the end of the matter. But surely the secret shared between lovers is private in one sense and not in another—this secret is private in the sense of being held in confidence between two individuals and not known by others; it is not private in the sense of being known by a second person. To take another case, consider someone walking in a public park. There is almost no limit to the kinds of information that can be acquired from this public display. One's image, height, weight, eye color, approximate age, and general physical abilities are all readily available. Moreover, biological matter will also be left in the public domain—strands of hair and the like may be left behind. Since this matter, and the information contained within, is publicly available, it would seem that one's genetic profile is public information.

28. DeCew puts the point the following way. "A subset of autonomy cases . . . can plausibly be said to involve privacy interests. . . . They should be viewed as liberty cases in virtue of their concern over decision-making power, whereas privacy is at stake because of the nature of the decision." Judith Wagner DeCew, "The Scope of Privacy in Law and Ethics," *Law and Philosophy* 5 (1986): 165.

29. Parent, "Privacy, Morality, and the Law," 269.

Furthermore, the availability of information is dependent upon technology. Telescopes, listening devices, heat-imaging sensors, and the like open up what most would consider private domains for public consumption. What we are worried about is what *should* be considered a "private affair"—something that is no one else's business. Parent's conception of privacy is not sensitive to these concerns.[30]

Parent could counter, by claiming that he is presenting a definition that is not normatively loaded. For Parent, privacy is the state or condition of not having undocumented personal information about oneself possessed by others. Similarly, liberty might be described as the state or condition of not having restraints on what one may do or think.

Insisting on this way of defining privacy falls prey to what I call the "so what" objection. In general, we are not worried about whether a state of privacy obtains or not—we are concerned about the normative aspects of disassociation or leave taking. When can I justifiably restrict access to myself? When are others morally permitted to cross into private domains? What does it matter if a state or condition of privacy as Parent has defined it exists? What we want to know is whether or not the state or condition in question is morally justified.[31]

Finally, Parent's view of privacy completely ignores what I have called physical or locational privacy. Suppose someone with severe amnesia wanders into your room while you are sleeping and proceeds to pet your head. Independent of documented or undocumented information, many would argue that this is an egregious violation of privacy.[32] Given that no information is involved, it would fall outside Parent's non-normative account. Furthermore, this deficiency along with Parent's failure to include a use dimension—use after access is also important—points to an even deeper

30. Samuel Rickless offers the following counterexample to Parent's view. "Goldberg trains his powerful X-ray device on Rudolf's wall-safe and learns from reading the papers therein that Rudolf was once a member of the Nazi party. As it happens, Goldberg *could* have learned the very same information about Rudolf by reading old issues of *Der Völkischer Beobachter* in the public library, but did not do so." Samuel Rickless, "The Right to Privacy Unveiled," *San Diego Law Review* 44 (2008): 784. Rickless contends that Goldberg violates Rudolf's privacy in this case even though no information that was not already a part of the public record was obtained. If so, possession of undocumented personal information about someone is not a necessary condition for a privacy violation. DeCew also raises this sort of objection. See DeCew, "Scope of Privacy," 152.

31. Judith Wagner DeCew echoes this sentiment. "The general point is that we are not likely to view perpetrating a violation as any less of a violation just because the agent is not the first one to invade the other's privacy." DeCew, *In Pursuit of Privacy*, 30.

32. Thus on Parent's own terms—not doing violence to the language and reflecting our intuitions—his account fails.

failing. Having the capacity and right to regulate access to and uses of bodies, locations, and personal information is essential for human well-being.[33]
In this way, the account of privacy I offer links nicely with value theory and
drives home what I have called the "so what" objection—the distinction
between documented and undocumented personal information does not
usefully capture the relevant value-based concerns.

Like Parent, Judith Jarvis Thomson finds control-based definitions of
privacy puzzling. She argues that a loss of control does not always mean
that we have lost privacy: "If my neighbor invents an X-ray device which
enables him to look through walls, then I should imagine I thereby lose
control over who can look at me: going home and closing the doors no
longer suffices to prevent others from doing so. But my right to privacy is
not violated until my neighbor actually does train the device on the wall of
my house."[34]

First, it is important to note how Thomson slides between non-normative and normative control-based accounts of privacy in this case. At the
start of the case, control is lost but privacy is maintained because the individual who now has control does not exercise it. A control-based *condition*
of privacy no longer obtains, yet a privacy right has not been violated.[35]
Sure enough, this sounds odd—but it is odd because I don't think that
control-based privacy theorists actually intend to support a purely non-
normative conception of privacy. To put the point another way, if we sprin-
kle normativity, so to speak, throughout the definition—privacy is an access
control and use right to places, bodies, or personal information—then
Thomson's attack loses its force. Simply put, a condition of privacy obtains
when others do not have access, while a right to privacy affords control
over access and use.

Thomson continues with a second example. "Suppose a more efficient
bugging device is invented: instead of tapes, it produces neatly typed tran-
scripts (thereby eliminating the middlemen). One who reads those tran-
scripts does not hear you, but your right to privacy is violated just as if he

33. See Chapter 3 and Moore, "Privacy: Its Meaning and Value."

34. Thomson, "The Right to Privacy," 304 n. 1. For a critique of Thomson's view of privacy,
see Scanlon, "Thomson on Privacy."

35. Thomson could reply that her argument goes through by simply replacing "But my
right to privacy is not violated until my neighbor" with "But I do not lose any privacy until my
neighbor" (James Stacey Taylor suggested this reply). While true, this reply does not avoid my
contention that control-based theorists are typically promoting normative conceptions of privacy. Moreover, if correct, Thomson would be attacking a straw man (and would fall victim to
the "so what" objection).

does."[36] But this case fits well with the view of privacy rights as justified control over access to objects and information. Information may take many forms, and thus it may be accessed in many different ways. If an individual has a right to control access to and the use of some bit of information, then it does not matter *how* the information was accessed—what matters is *that* it was accessed. Thomson claims that while "you may violate a man's right to privacy by looking at him or listening to him; there is no such thing as violating a man's right to privacy by simply knowing something about him."[37] This seems true enough. However, by *looking* or *listening* you may be violating his right to control access to information—information that provides the foundation for "knowing."[38] Moreover and more important, you may be violating a use control right. If correct, it would seem that Thomson's critique of control-based definitions of privacy fails.[39]

PRIVACY RIGHTS AND PROPERTY RIGHTS

If property rights and privacy rights are both essentially about control, then maybe privacy rights are simply a special form of property rights.[40] Thomson tends to agree: "The right to privacy is itself a cluster of rights, and it is not a distinct cluster of rights but itself intersects with . . . the cluster of rights which owning property consists in."[41] Thomson is a reductionist about privacy.

It is obvious that property may come in several forms. Intellectual property is generally characterized as nonphysical property where owners' rights surround control of physical manifestations, and this control protects rights to ideas—for example, no matter how a specific poem is instantiated (writ-

36. Thomson, "The Right to Privacy," 304 n. 1.

37. Ibid., 307.

38. One could say that knowing something about someone without justified entitlement may be similar to accepting stolen property. I would like to thank Bill Kline for making this suggestion.

39. For a defense of control-based definitions of privacy against several objections, see Inness, *Privacy, Intimacy, and Isolation*, 47–53.

40. For a lengthier treatment of this issue, see Lawrence Lessig, "Privacy as Property," *Social Research* 69 (2002): 247–69; Eugene Volokh, "Freedom of Speech and Information Privacy: The Troubling Implications of a Right to Stop People from Speaking About You," *Stanford Law Review* 52 (2000): 1049; and Morgan Cloud, "The Fourth Amendment During the *Lochner* Era: Privacy, Property, and Liberty in Constitutional Theory," *Stanford Law Review* 48 (1996): 555.

41. Thomson, "The Right to Privacy," 306. See also Van den Haag, "On Privacy," 147. As I noted earlier, I would add that the rights to life, liberty, and property overlap with one another and with privacy as well.

ten, performed orally, or saved on a Web site) copyright would apply. Rights to control physical goods, on the other hand, allow control over one physical object.

Privacy may be understood as a right to control access to places and ideas independent of instantiation. In terms of location, privacy yields control over access to one's body, capacities, and powers. A privacy right in this sense is a right to control access to a specific object or place. In Prosser's terminology, *intrusions* would violate rights to control access to a specific object. But we may also control access to sensitive personal information about ourselves. In this sense a privacy right affords control over ideas no matter how these ideas are instantiated. For example, when a rape victim suppresses the dissemination of sensitive personal information about herself, she is exercising a right to control a set of ideas no matter what form they take. It matters not if the information in question is written, recorded, spoken, or fixed in some other fashion. More important, even if someone has justifiably accessed sensitive personal information about another, it does not follow that any use of this information is permitted. Again, taking up Prosser's categories, publishing *private facts*, putting someone in a *false light*, or *appropriating* someone's image or style would violate a right to control an entire class of ideas.

While there may be substantial overlap between the notions of property and privacy, it is advantageous to retain the category as we do with intellectual property. If I am correct, privacy claims include claims to control access to places and ideas. This fact alone marks a significant category even if it is a category that falls under the umbrella of property rights.

Consider the following question raised by Thomas Scanlon. "Suppose someone used . . . [an] X-ray device to examine an object in my safe. It seems clear to me that the right which is violated in such a case does not depend on my owning the object examined. Suppose it is your object . . . or someone else's object . . . or someone else's object that I picked up by mistake . . . or there is no object in the safe at all. None of these possibilities removes the wrongfulness of the intrusion."[42] Scanlon concludes that ownership and privacy separate in this case. Scanlon adds: "Suppose, for example, that each person was assigned a plot in the common field to use as a place to bury valuables. Then anyone who . . . [X-rayed] . . . my plot without special authority would violate a right of mine . . . For us, ownership is relevant in determining the boundaries of our zone of privacy, but

---

42. Scanlon, "Thomson on Privacy," 318.

its relevance is determined by norms whose basis lies in our interest in privacy, not in the notion of ownership."[43]

Assuming, however, that privacy rights are rights to control access to and uses of locations and ideas, these examples do not undermine a control-based view of privacy or the view that the concepts of privacy and ownership have significant overlap. If the object or objects were unowned, assuming that the safe and the plot of land are unowned as well, then there would be no privacy invasion. Imagine that the object was a painting of a sunset painted by some long dead artist who gave the work to all of humankind. On the other hand, if we assume that the safe and the plot are owned, then wrongness can be found in interfering with the control conferred by ownership.[44]

Scanlon may reply by arguing that the wrongness is found when someone unjustifiably intrudes and obtains knowledge about someone else—say Crusoe finds out, by using an X-ray device, that Friday is keeping an unowned item in a safe. Such a reply, however, would seem to support a control-based definition of privacy. The wrongness in this case lies in the fact that Friday has a right to control access to certain kinds of information and Crusoe has violated this control—in this case the item examined may not be yours, but the information that it is in your possession may be.

Or consider another case provided by Thomson and discussed by Scanlon. In this case suppose that you steal a publicly owned subway map and put it in your pocket or briefcase. Scanlon contends that if I were to view the map with my X-ray device, I would violate your privacy rights independent of ownership. I am not entitled to look into your pocket or briefcase even if I do not interfere with your property rights to these items.

I would agree with Scanlon if in acquiring the information on the subway map I also acquired, inadvertently or not, personal information about you—for example, the fact that you possessed the map. But if my device were calibrated to only acquire the information found on the publicly owned subway map, then I would not agree that this acquisition includes a privacy violation.

One of the problems with both Scanlon's and Thomson's analyses of

43. Ibid.

44. James Rachels also argues against models that conceive privacy rights as types of property rights: "The right to privacy [is] a distinctive sort of right in virtue of the special kind of interest it protects." James Rachels, "Why Privacy Is Important," *Philosophy and Public Affairs* 4 (1975): 333. As already noted, the fact that privacy protects different sorts of interests does not by itself lead us to the conclusion that privacy and property do not come bundled together.

privacy is that they provide few arguments. They both offer numerous examples that test and sometimes strain our intuitions about privacy. But
perhaps our intuitions about these cases are unclear. Absent an argument
justifying some view or other, little is gained. If privacy is understood as
having accessibility and control over use dimensions, then it is not surprising that there would be overlap with the notion of property.

A FINAL DEFINITION

Richard B. Parker writes: *"Privacy is control over when and by whom the
various parts of us can be sensed by others.* By 'sensed,' is meant simply seen,
heard, touched, smelled, or tasted. By 'parts of us,' is meant the part of our
bodies, our voices, and the products of our bodies. 'Parts of us' also includes objects very closely associated with us. By 'closely associated' is
meant primarily what is spatially associated. The objects which are 'parts of
us' are objects we usually keep with us or locked up in a place accessible
only to us."[45]

A right to privacy can be understood as a right to maintain a certain
level of control over the inner spheres of personal information and access
to one's body and specific locations. It is a right to limit public access to
oneself and to information about oneself. For example, suppose that I wear
a glove because I am ashamed of a scar on my hand. If you were to snatch
the glove away, you would not only be violating my right to property (the
glove is mine to control), you would also be violating my right to privacy—a right to restrict access to information about the scar on my hand.
Similarly, if you were to focus your X-ray camera on my hand, take a picture of the scar through the glove, and then publish the photograph widely,
you would be violating a right to privacy. While your X-ray camera may
diminish my ability to control the information in question, it does not
undermine my right to control access.

Privacy also includes a right over the use of bodies, locations, and personal information. If access is granted accidentally or otherwise, it does not
follow that any subsequent use, manipulation, or sale of the good in question is justified. In this way privacy is both a shield that affords control over

---

45. Parker, "A Definition of Privacy," 281. The account of privacy that I am defending is
similar to the restricted access / limited control view offered by Herman Tavani in a recent article.
See Herman Tavani, "Philosophical Theories of Privacy: Implications for an Adequate Online
Privacy Policy," *Metaphilosophy* 39 (2007): 1–22.

access or inaccessibility and a kind of use and control right that yields justified authority over specific items—like a room or personal information.

As noted in the introduction to this chapter, the normative claims surrounding control over access and use are relative to culture.[46] Judith Wagner DeCew argues that this sort of definition fails because "if a police officer pushes one out of the way of an ambulance, one has lost control of what is done to one, but we would not say that privacy has been invaded. Not just any touching is a privacy intrusion."[47] I think that this sort of attack is too quick. First, whether or not a privacy invasion will have occurred in a case of "touching" will depend on the privacy norms found within the culture in question. A right to control access and use may take many forms. Thus, one cannot refute this definition by finding a single example where a loss of control over bodily access does not include a loss of privacy. Second, the case that DeCew presents may simply be an example of a slight privacy invasion being overridden by other, weightier considerations.

As I have mentioned throughout this chapter, in addition to a *right* to privacy it may also be helpful to define a *condition* of privacy. In defining a condition of privacy we are trying to be descriptive rather than normative. My contention is that a plausible non-normative account of privacy begins with accessibility. That is, the condition of privacy obtains when an individual, place, or personal information is inaccessible. More often than not, individuals voluntarily seek this condition. W. L. Weinstein notes, "If the condition is entered involuntarily, it is isolation when a matter of circumstance and ostracism when a result of the choice of others. Either isolation or ostracism may become loneliness when accompanied by a desire for communication."[48] In many instances privacy is a condition of voluntary seclusion or walling off—individuals seek situations where they are inaccessible. The condition of privacy obtains when an individual freely separates herself from her peers and restricts access. For entities lacking free will, we may talk of separation rather than privacy. When an individual restricts access to himself and to personal information, we may say that a condition of privacy obtains. But there is more to a condition of privacy than voluntary seclusion—for example, one may have a measure of privacy simply by

---

46. See Chapter 3 and Moore, "Privacy: Its Meaning and Value."

47. See DeCew, *In Pursuit of Privacy*, 53.

48. W. L. Weinstein, "The Uses of Privacy in the Good Life," in *Privacy: Nomos XIII*, ed. J. Roland Pennock and John W. Chapman (New York: Atherton Press, 1971), 94.

not being noticed. James Moor and Herman Tavani note that a condition of privacy obtains "in a situation in which one is naturally protected or shielded from intrusion and access by others."[49] I would add that artificial protections and shielding would establish a condition of privacy as well. In any event, if my earlier critique of Parent's non-normative conception of privacy is compelling, then we should not be overly worried about defining a state or condition precisely. We are, and should be, concerned with the normative aspects of privacy.

> Definition: A right to privacy is a right to control access to, and uses of, places, bodies, and personal information.

TEST CASES AND ILLUSTRATIONS

Aside from the examples already mentioned, there are numerous other cases that may be helpful in illustrating and clarifying the account of privacy being defended. These cases will be presented as a series of "on pain of irrationality" arguments. In other words, if you agree with me on this or that case, and there are no relevant dissimilarities in some further case, then on pain of irrationality you should agree with me in the latter case. Notice this would be a powerful way to argue even if in the process we run afoul of some intuition or use of language. The overall goal is to aim at coherence as well as completeness—I take it to be a virtue of the account being offered that it is generally applicable. To begin, consider the following two cases.

> The Loud Fight: suppose that Fred and Ginger are having a fight— shouting at each other with the windows open so that anyone on the street can hear.

> The Quiet Fight: suppose that Fred and Ginger are having a fight— shouting at each other although the windows are closed and they have taken precautions to make sure that others cannot hear them. Suppose someone trains an amplifier on Fred and Ginger's house and listens to them.[50]

49. Tavani, "Philosophical Theories of Privacy," 10. Tavani builds on an account offered in James Moor, "Towards a Theory of Privacy in the Information Age," *Computers and Society* 27 (1997): 27–32.
50. Thomson, "The Right to Privacy," 296.

In the loud fight case it would seem that Fred and Ginger have waived the right to privacy—they have through their actions allowed others who are in a public space to hear the fight. In fact, one might say that Fred and Ginger have imposed their fight on others. In the typical case there is nothing wrong with speaking or being in public—or behaving in such a way that those in public spaces can hear or see us. Light waves and sound waves bounce around, and the typical human is conditioned to perceive and interpret these inputs. Indeed, to condition ourselves otherwise would be dangerous. In these sorts of cases, privacy rights have been waived.

A variation on the loud fight case is where Fred and Ginger use a sound and light encryption device to scramble their words and images. In this example the person on the street can hear and see something but cannot understand these inputs. Here Fred and Ginger are not waiving their privacy rights. If someone were to decrypt the words and images, then there would be a privacy violation. This is similar to the quiet fight case where technology is used to peer into a private zone.

Notice that part of what determines the boundary or scope of a right are the capacities of the individuals involved. For example, consider a case where everyone has super hearing that cannot be turned off. In this instance any utterance will be noticed by others. If we apply the "ought implies can" principle—that is, you can only have a moral obligation to do or refrain from doing something if it is within your capacity to do or refrain from what is required—then we cannot have an obligation not to notice the words of others. Similarly, if humans were inherently clumsy and lost control of their bodies frequently, the boundary or force of property rights would have to be modified. If individuals could not help but to fall onto the property of others, then they could not have an obligation to refrain from doing so. In any case, we should not assume that just because individuals have super hearing notions of privacy simply vanish. Information may take inaudible forms. Moreover, even if access is possible it does not automatically follow that all subsequent uses of the information gained through such access are also permitted.

Developing a full account of when and how rights are waived and the extent or boundary of rights is beyond the scope of this work. Nevertheless, it seems that two tentative points can be offered. First, the boundary or extent of rights is dependent, in part, on the capacities of the agents in question. Second, rights, in part, are waived given general expectations regarding the capacities of individuals and the behavior of the right-holder. Consider a case that helps to illustrate these points.

> The Loud Fight no. 2: Fred and Ginger are having a fight—shouting
> at each other with the windows open. A deaf person is walking nearby
> and turns up his hearing aid and listens to them.[51]

While an individual uses technology in this example to hear what Fred and
Ginger are saying, we should not conclude that privacy has been violated.
As in the loud fight example, Fred and Ginger have certain expectations
related to the sensory inputs of their fellows and knowingly or negligently
engage in behavior that places personal information into a public space.
Thus they have waived their right to privacy in this case. But if Fred and
Ginger were to use a sound and light encryption device and the deaf person
in question were to decrypt the words and images via technology, then we
would have a violation. Consider a different sort of this case.

> The Accidentally Amplified Quiet Fight: A married couple, X and Y,
> are having another quiet fight behind closed doors. But this time an
> unanticipated gust of wind sweeps through the house, knocking down
> the front door, carrying and amplifying the couple's voices so that
> Stuart, who is washing his car in his driveway across the street, hears
> at least some of what X and Y have been saying.[52]

In the accidentally amplified quiet fight case the right to privacy is not
waived, and it also appears not to be violated. A similar case is one where
someone is forcibly picked up by a freak gust of wind and placed in your
convertable. You have not waived your property right and at the same time
it would seem quite odd to maintain that your rights have been violated.[53]
It could be argued that a right has been violated and that there are mitigating factors. But if we also say that rights violations sanction compensation
for losses, then we would have a case where an innocent individual could
be forced to pay damages to a right-holder—supposing that the mere violation of a right causes a loss. I would rather say that the right has not been
violated, it has just been innocently crossed and no compensation is required. To be sure, the person in your car must leave, and your neighbor
who has learned certain facts about you should refrain from broadcasting
this information—as with the super hearing case. That these innocent indi-

51. Ibid., 298.
52. Rickless, "Right to Privacy Unveiled," 786–87.
53. I take this to be similar to a freak gust of wind blowing mud onto a car—perhaps the
owner's property has been damaged, but no one is morally responsible in the typical case.

viduals have come to acquire something of yours does not sanction further use.

The aspect of privacy related to boundary crossings—privacy as control over access—is highlighted in cases where certain zones are penetrated.

> Zone Intrusion: Suppose you look in my safe with your X-ray device to see what it holds—there could be a stolen photo, a borrowed photo, or nothing.[54]

> Mere Zone Intrusion: Just like the first zone intrusion case, although the person looking has no short-term memory and will forget any fact learned immediately.

In the case of zone intrusion a right to control access has been violated even though nothing except a bare fact has been seized. This is further illustrated by the example of mere zone intrusion. In the second case, nothing has been taken—no facts have been learned—all that has happened is that a zone or boundary has been unjustifiably crossed. A variation of the mere zone intrusion case is one where someone with no short-term memory completes a body cavity search of an individual who is temporarily unconscious. While no information is obtained or used, it seems clear that a zone or boundary has been violated—in this last example physical or locational privacy rights have been infringed. Perhaps it is this sort of case where privacy and property begin pull apart—aside from the mere breaching of a boundary, nothing is taken.

Garden variety gossip cases highlight the aspect of trust or implicit agreements to withhold sharing information. Consider the following two examples.

> Gossip Case no. 1: Two friends of yours engage in gossip about you without betraying any confidences.[55]

> Gossip Case no. 2: Smith is recently divorced because he became impotent shortly after the wedding—he shares this information with his closest friend. Jones, also a friend of Smith's, innocently overhears Smith telling his friend and begins to gossip with other friends.[56]

54. Thomson, "The Right to Privacy," 298.
55. Ibid., 311.
56. Rachels, "Why Privacy Is Important," 333.

In the first gossip case, given that you have granted access via the relationship with your friends and no agreement or trust has been broken, there is no concern on the account of privacy being offered. In the second case, however, we have a use violation but not an access violation—Jones innocently overhears Smith. But just because there was no infringement related to access does not mean that Jones can use, manipulate, or broadcast the information in question. Thus the account being defended can offer a plausible answer to the concern being posed in these gossip cases.

Finally, there are several examples that trade on the overlap between solitude, nuisance, coercion, and privacy.

Loud Stinky Neighbors: Your neighbors make a terrible racket all the time—or they cook foul-smelling meals.

Easy Listening Everywhere: Suppose after a vote the city where you live puts up loudspeakers everywhere and plays easy listening music in all public places.

Sensitive Information Assault: Suppose a stranger stops you at a party and begins telling about intimate personal information and problems he is having.[57]

In each of these cases there is an intrusion—a placement of unwanted information, smells, sounds, and images into an area of access control. In these cases of mere access violations it may be granted that there is an aspect of privacy involved. Nevertheless, the typical privacy violation, according to my definition of privacy, contains both access and use violations—and concerns not the placement of unwelcome information, smells, sounds, and images but rather a unjustified taking of information or use of some physical item. Thus there may be other, more important, aspects to these cases than privacy considerations. For example, in cases of sensitive information assault there is a kind of coercion involved—a hijacking of someone's time and consideration. Loud, stinky neighbors and invasive music in public places intrude on individual solitude, and in the worst cases, violate peaceful sanctuaries of contemplation—thus these cases may not primarily focus on privacy interests.

57. These cases are found in Thomson, "The Right to Privacy," 311.

CONCLUSION

I have maintained that privacy should be defined as a right to control access to places, locations, and personal information along with use and control rights to these goods. Nevertheless, it is likely that no definition of privacy will satisfy everyone. It is equally true that how the right is justified will play an important role in refining the definition at issue—thus any attempt to define privacy rights independent of a justifying theory will likely be incomplete.

I have also maintained that being clear about normative and non-normative definitions is crucial for understanding privacy. Many of the so-called counterexamples to various definitions of privacy trade on slippage between descriptive and normative accounts. The numerous cases and examples that help to clarify the conception of privacy under consideration also indicate that the boundary between privacy and other moral concepts—for example, property rights, liberty, and self-ownership—is not always clear and distinct. As noted by Aristotle this is to be expected, for "our discussion will be adequate if it has as much clearness as the subject-matter admits of, for precision is not to be sought for alike in all discussions, any more than in all the products of the crafts."[58]

In closing, I will offer a few remarks to the critic who will complain that no *argument* has been given in favor of the conception of privacy under consideration. I admit that I am somewhat at a loss in trying to counter such an objection. Aside from offering a definition that is conceptually coherent and one that highlights the importance, both practical and moral, of privacy, I think there is little else to be done. How does one argue for a definition independent of these sorts of considerations? As noted in the opening, it is not as if we can determine such definitions by glancing at the stars or gazing at Plato's Forms. In the chapters to come I will argue that the proposed definition is connected in nontrivial ways to human health and well-being—by my lights, little else is needed as justification.

---

58. Aristotle, *Nicomachean Ethics* 1094b 15, trans. W. D. Ross, in *The Complete Works of Aristotle*, ed. Jonathan Barnes, Bollingen Series (Princeton: Princeton University Press, 1984), 2:1730.

3

THE VALUE OF PRIVACY

It is commonly assumed that privacy is morally valuable. As James Whitman notes, "The typical privacy article rests its case precisely on an appeal to its reader's intuitions and anxieties about the evils of privacy violations."[1] Another common strategy is to derive the value of privacy from some other set of moral principles or commitments, such as autonomy or liberal democracy. For example, it is claimed that privacy is necessary for autonomy or liberal democracy; and since these latter ideals have moral value, privacy must as well.

The difficulty with such strategies should be obvious. If someone does not share our anxieties or commitments, then either privacy is not valuable or it is grounded some other way. In the most general terms, my goal in this chapter is to provide a bottom-up account of the value of privacy that does not rely on higher-level principles. After a brief sketch and defense of a few background claims in value theory, I will argue that privacy is a core human value—the right to control access to oneself along with use and control rights to personal information and places is an essential part of human flourishing. There is a near universal need for seclusion or separation at different times for humans as well as nonhuman animals. As we

1. James Whitman, "The Two Western Cultures of Privacy: Dignity Versus Liberty," *Yale Law Journal* 113 (2004): 1155.

shall see, populations that fail to achieve a minimum level of privacy for individual members eventually self-destruct. In this chapter I will provide reasons, evidence, and support for these claims.

VALUES, OBJECTIVITY, AND RELATIONALISM

I believe that the correct account of moral value—an account that avoids charges of arbitrariness, preference manipulation, and species elitism—is both objective and relational. Given that defending these metaethical claims would take us far afield and that I have argued for these claims in depth elsewhere,[2] I will offer only a brief sketch and defense here.

Humans value a wide range of objects, activities, goals, careers, and pursuits. When asked what is valuable, we include things like "a nice day on the golf course," "hanging out with friends," "spicy Indian food," "a fast car," "lots of money," and "privacy." Obviously this list could be continued—there seems no end to what we value. But what makes these things valuable? One common answer is that they are good because they are desired. We desire these things; and so we feel that when we acquire them value has been brought into the world. Such views about value are commonly called subjective preference satisfaction theories or desire fulfillment accounts.

This is an odd view of value.[3] Suppose Fred, who inhabits an island with Ginger, prefers that she not have any privacy. If moral values are couched in terms of subjective preferences or desires, then in seeking to exclude Fred from seeing her or accessing her body, Ginger morally worsens Fred. But this can't be right. Why would Fred's mere arbitrary preferences count morally? The issue here is that since preferences can be arbitrary, and according to this view value is intimately tied to preferences, this arbitrariness will infect value theory.

Another concern for this account of value is preference or desire manip-

2. Adam D. Moore, "Values, Objectivity, and Relationalism," *Journal of Value Inquiry* 38 (Fall 2004): 75–90. In this article, while defending a conception of objectivity and relationalism, I question the notion of "intrinsic" value. For a nice overview of the numerous conceptions of intrinsic value and the problems that accompany each, see Fred Feldman, "Hyperventilating About Intrinsic Value," *Journal of Ethics* 2 (1998): 339–54.

3. For a separate, possibly more damaging, critique of subjectivist accounts of value, see Philippa Foot, *Natural Goodness* (Oxford: Oxford University Press, 2001), 1–24. See also James Griffin, *Well-Being: Its Meaning, Measurement, and Moral Importance* (Oxford: Clarendon Press, 1986). Also, the critique offered against subjective accounts of moral value may not apply to nonmoral legal conceptions of *interests* or *preferences*.

ulation—in this case the desires are not arbitrary, they are contrived. Imagine a situation where a child's preferences are manipulated so that he or she prefers a certain kind of life or detests certain people. Again, it would seem odd to claim that the satisfaction of manipulated desires brings moral value into the world.

In part, these cases attempt to show the implausibility of maintaining the claim that the *sole* standard of value—in fact, that which creates value—is the satisfaction of desires and preferences. This point is echoed nicely by David Ross. "It might be enough (*to eliminate the theory as a plausible contender*) to ask whether anyone finds it even possible to think that goodness could be brought into being by the feeling of some one or other, no matter how vicious or stupid or ignorant he might be."[4]

To more directly attack the subjectivist account of value consider what might be called canonical examples of objective value—pleasure and pain. The subjectivist will agree that pleasure is good and pain bad but insist that this is so because of our attitudes and desires. The objectivist's attack is made nicely by Eric Mack: "But is pleasure good in virtue of the attitude of its subject? Do we perhaps each undergo various pleasures for a while, decide or otherwise come to form a preference for pleasure, and thereupon *make* pleasure a good thing and *give* ourselves reason to pursue it? The case for objectivism rests on the implausibility of affirmative answers to these questions."[5]

The objectivist about value argues that we desire pleasure because it is good independent of our affective states, while the subjectivist holds that it is our preferences that confer value. The former argues that we have reason to pursue pleasure because it is good, while the latter holds that through our desires we give ourselves reasons to pursue pleasure.[6]

If we move from mere desires to lifelong goals and projects, the subjec-

4. David Ross, *The Right and the Good* (London: Oxford University Press, 1930), 83; italics added.

5. Eric Mack, "Moral Individualism: Agent-Relativity and Deontic Restraints," *Social Philosophy and Policy* 7 (1989): 95.

6. Consider a desire creation and satisfaction machine. Once activated, the machine creates in a subject countless easily satisfied desires and preferences—for example, the desire to accumulate small rocks. Upon satisfying such desires the subjectivist appears driven to view that value has been brought into the world—in fact, the more desires satisfied the more value produced. The subjectivist may counter and argue that we each have a second-order desire not to have our desires manipulated in this way. But such a second-order desire would be just as groundless as any other, and there is no reason to think that each of us has such a desire. While this case appeals to moral intuitions, it also highlights how purely subjective accounts of moral value appear to be radically arbitrary. If correct, such arbitrariness would undermine the importance of moral value.

tivist account becomes ever more strained: "One cannot take one's com-mitments to projects as merely psychological quirks for as such they could not command one's reflective loyalties. . . . To value one's projects is to value that at which the projects aim. It is in this way that consideration of rational activity necessarily points beyond itself, to value in the world."[7] Here Loren Lomasky drives home a deep failing in subjectivist accounts of value. The charge is a familiar one. Subjective theories end up making val-ues arbitrary. This runs counter to the notion that to say something is valuable is to endorse it in some fashion. If value is arbitrary, who cares? I am not arguing that individuals do not or cannot subjectively value objects, states of the world, or other individuals. What I am denying is that such valuing is the foundation of moral value.

Fred Feldman appears to endorse a subjective account of value in the case of Stoicus.

> Suppose Stoicus gets exactly what he wants—peace, quiet, no sensory pleasure, and no sensory pain. Suppose that as he receives his daily dose of peace and quiet, Stoicus is pleased. That is, suppose he enjoys the peace and quiet. Suppose he takes attitudinal pleasure in various facts about his life, including the fact that he is not experiencing any sensory pleasure. Suppose Stoicus eventually dies a happy man. He lived 90 years of somewhat boring but on the whole quite enjoyable peace and quiet. Stoicus thinks (right before he dies) that his has been an outstandingly good life.[8]

Feldman argues that while the "sensory hedonist" would have to claim that Stoicus did not have a good life, it is clear that he did. "But if Stoicus was happy with his life, and enjoyed the experiences that came his way, and got precisely what he wanted at every moment, it seems strange to say that there was nothing good about his life."[9] I would agree that it would be odd to claim that there was *nothing* good about Stoicus's life—he did live a life

7. Loren Lomasky, *Persons, Rights, and the Moral Community* (Oxford: Oxford University Press, 1987), 232. Mack makes a similar point. "One does not simply find oneself with long-term projects around which one's life is built in the way that finds oneself with a yen for a kosher dill. The motivational force for such a project does not come from a craving. . . . Rather, it comes in part from a sense that the project is worthy of being undertaken and worthy of accomplishment." Mack, "Moral Individualism," 97.

8. Fred Feldman, "The Good Life: A Defense of Attitudinal Hedonism," *Philosophy and Phenomenological Research* 65 (2002): 610.

9. Ibid.

of his own choosing. Nevertheless, where Feldman claims that such a life is "quite a nice life," I would claim that it is impoverished. Echoing a case discussed later, consider the value or goodness of Stoicus's life if he had formed the "attitudinal pleasure" of experiencing a thousand pinpricks a day. Each day suppose, with an ever increasing severity corresponding to an ever increasing tolerance for sensory pain, Stoicus pricks himself with a needle. After a few years of this, Stoicus thinks to himself as he dies, "I had quite a nice life." Feldman would argue that Stoicus had a good life. I would counter that such accounts of moral value undermine the importance of this area of study. An account of value that can include any content—even contradictory content (suppose Stoicus desires to live a long life and to survive by consuming himself)—is not worthy of much consideration.[10]

While there are other questions that could be considered, I will present only one further objection to desire satisfaction accounts of value—the objection is based on the charge of speciesism.[11] If value is intimately tied to our affections and value is brought into the world only when a desire or preference is satisfied, then those entities that do not have affective states are left out of the moral picture in terms of value. Subjectivist accounts of value would thus be elitist in the sense that only some living entities would be able to produce value by having desires satisfied. The value of everything else in the universe, living or not, would be dependent on the desires or preferences of those beings who happen to have affections. Philippa Foot echoes this charge. These

> theories have the remarkable though seldom mentioned consequence of separating off the evaluation of human action not only from the evaluation of human sight, hearing, and bodily health but also from all evaluation of the characteristics and operations of animals. . . . To be sure, almost everything in the world can be said to be good or bad in a context that sufficiently relates it to some human concern. . . . But features of plants and animals have . . . natural goodness and defect that may have nothing to do with . . . wants.[12]

Likewise, certain features of plants and animals may have goodness and defect independent of *human* affections, desires, preferences, or choice.

10. Consider a further problem for Feldman's account offered in e-mail correspondence by James Stacey Taylor. "What if Stoicus had a single higher-order desire that his desires be frustrated? What would then have to be true for him to be said to have had a good life?"

11. The term "speciesism" comes from Peter Singer's work on the moral status of animals. See Peter Singer, *Practical Ethics* (Cambridge: Cambridge University Press, 1979).

12. Foot, *Natural Goodness*, 25–26.

An objective account of value holds that value exists independent of its apprehension—there are reasons for action, and we have to discover them instead of deriving them from our preexisting desires or preferences.[13] On the account I favor an object or state of the world has value if it sustains, promotes, or furthers the life of the entity in question. Thus, nitrogen in certain amounts would be valuable for plants, protein would be valuable for humans, and oxygenated water would be valuable for fish. In this way value is both *objective* and *relational*.[14] The value of objects or states of the world is not tied to our affections. Moreover, what is objectively valuable for humans will not be the same as what is valuable for plants or other nonhuman animals.

Consider the following case. Suppose that in a few years we are visited by a race of benevolent and rational beings from Alpha Centauri that have free will and an advanced culture. We notice that they are biologically different from humans and other life forms found here on Earth. The Centaurians have acid for blood and consume coal for sustenance. Suppose further that after they figure out our languages we realize the Centaurians are moral beings who act on reflectively endorsed and rationally appraised principle.

We can now ask, "What is of moral value for the Centaurians?" It seems that the nonrelationalist will have to insist that the domain of value for them is the same domain as what is valuable for us. The relationalist, on the other hand, can affirm that they may have different values because of their different natures. Perhaps having control over access to bodies and personal information leads the Centaurians toward an unhealthy life— privacy may not be valuable for them. As noted earlier, there is a kind of elitism that pervades nonrelational accounts of value; as if human beings and their way of perceiving or relating to the world were all that mattered morally. On nonrelational accounts evolved dolphins, Centaurians, not to mention birds, fish, plants, and bacteria are all indirectly related to value. That is, they are only related to value through human contact with, percep-

13. Thomas Nagel, *The View from Nowhere* (Oxford: Oxford University Press, 1986), 139. David Gauthier writes, "To conceive of value as objective is to conceive of it as existing independently of the affections of sentient beings, and as providing a norm or standard to govern their affections." Gauthier, *Morals by Agreement* (Oxford: Oxford University Press, 1987), 47.

14. Fred Feldman, "Some Puzzles About the Evil of Death," *Philosophical Review* 100 (April 1991): 209, and Mack, "Moral Individualism," sketch "agent neutral" or nonrelational accounts of value—although neither author defends this view. Nonrelational accounts of value hold that "a state of affairs S^2 has non-relational value if and only if S^2's presence is a basis for *each agent* to rank the world where S^2 obtains over the world where S^2 does not obtain." Mack, "Moral Individualism," 84.

tions of, or preferences for certain states of the world. When we expand our scope and ask what is valuable for dogs, cats, birds, fish and the like, we are driven away from subjective nonrelational accounts of value—alas, these entities may not have desires or preferences and yet still have values related to them.

One problem for an objective and relational account of value is that such views may leave human life as such outside moral value. Protein is valuable in relation to human life, but what would make human life valuable? If all value is relational, there cannot be any fixed, absolute, or inherent values. Similar points may be made about plant life or nonhuman animal life. If humans, plants, or other living entities have value, it will be in relation to other living entities. Human life considered in and of itself would have no value. Many would view this as a problem.[15]

In reply, the life of an entity, considered apart from any relations it may have, stands outside the domain of value. The life of a solitary human being, who has no relations to other living entities, has no moral value. Likewise, a cup of water existing in a universe with no life and no possibility of life has no value. Fortunately, when we consider the nature of human beings and what is required for our continued existence, beyond mere basic necessities, we see that as social creatures we create and maintain a host of relations that give our lives meaning and value.

Finally, the charges of arbitrariness and preference manipulation do not infect this account, and it is also apparent, on this view, why moral values would be important. In any case, as features of a correct account of value, objectivity and relationalism do not provide much content—they are more like strictures than thick content providers. The task of the remaining two sections of this chapter is to begin to fill in what value is for beings like us.

RATIONAL EUDAIMONISM AND THE GOOD LIFE

In the previous section I argued that an appropriate account of moral value—an account that avoids charges of arbitrariness, preference manipulation, and species elitism—must view value as objective and relational. Objective values are those that exist independent of the affective states of sentient beings. In general, relational values are those that are conditional and come attached to groups or individuals.

15. Thus the account being offered is biocentric or life centered, as opposed to human centered, sentient-being centered, or ecosystem centered.

Following Aristotle, the account of value that I favor is objective in the sense noted above and relational in the sense of being related to groups of living organisms.[16] Thus what is good for plants may not be good for fish, insects, or human beings. That which promotes, sustains, and furthers the life of the entity in question is good for that entity. That which degrades, stagnates, or destroys the life of the entity in question is bad. The content of these goods and bads will be determined by the nature of the entity in question. Philippa Foot echoes this view: "It will surely not be denied that there is something wrong with a free-riding wolf that feeds but does not take part in the hunt, as with a member of the species of dancing bees who finds a source of nectar but whose behavior does not let other bees know of its location. These free-riding individuals of a species whose members work together are just as defective as those who have defective hearing, sight, or powers of locomotion."[17] We may say similar things about competent humans who fail to develop a rational faculty or learn a language.

Eudaimonism is the view that flourishing or well-being is valuable and nonflourishing disvaluable. It is a mistake to interpret eudaimonism as "happiness" because the concept "happiness" contains elements of subjectivity that eudaimonism does not. Happiness as a psychological state of joy is not living well or flourishing but one of its rewards. "The word eudaimonia has a force not at all like 'happiness,' 'comfort,' or 'pleasure,' but more like 'the best possible life.'"[18] As noted in the previous section, what would the notion of happiness—as a state of psychological joy—mean when related to plants, fish, or insects? As an objective yet relational notion, flourishing or well-being stands independent of the affective states of sentient beings.

Following the work of Paul Taylor, we can distinguish among three conceptions of flourishing or well-being. The "self-evaluative" conception of flourishing holds that "to assert that one is happy is to make a value judgment about one's total condition of life. This value judgment consists in

16. For similar views, see John Rawls, *A Theory of Justice* (Cambridge: Harvard University Press, 1971), chap. 7; Aristotle, *Nicomachean Ethics*, bks. 1 and 10; Immanuel Kant, *The Fundamental Principles of The Metaphysics of Morals*, trans. Thomas K. Abbott (Englewood Cliffs, N.J.: Prentice Hall, 1949); Foot, *Natural Goodness*; and Warren Quinn, *Morality and Action* (Cambridge: Cambridge University Press, 1993).

17. Foot, *Natural Goodness*, 16.

18. J. L. Ackrill, "Aristotle on Eudaimonia," in *Essays on Aristotle's Ethics*, ed. A. Rorty (Berkeley and Los Angeles: University of California Press, 1980), 24.

the claim that, with respect to what is really significant in life, one's life is good."[19]

On this view what counts as significant in life is determined subjectively. Individuals may find different things important and thus the standards by which they determine flourishing will be radically subjective. "If the person in question thinks that certain things in life which others think are trivial or shallow are very important, then it is his own values that must be taken into account, not those of others."[20]

This view is similar to the account of value offered in Feldman's Stoicus example and is suspect for the same reasons—it seems to purport the absurd view that an individual flourishes because he says he does.[21] The problems of arbitrary and manipulated desires or preferences loom and need not be rehearsed.

A second and more interesting view is called the "essentialist" conception and identifies flourishing with the type of life that is proper for a human being to live: "According to the essentialist conception . . . a truly happy life is identified with the Good Life for Man. The person who lives such a life is realizing the Human Good, that is, the good for man as man. . . . This is called an 'essentialist' conception because it presupposes that there is such thing as an essential human nature."[22] Likewise, it assumes that plants, insects, birds, and fish all have specific natures that are empirically verifiable. Flourishing is determined in relation to the nature of the entity in question and the environment.

Many have noted that the essentialist conception of flourishing, as it is typically presented, is too rigid. If our essential nature is to continually contemplate ultimate reality through reflection and reason, or serve God, or deprive oneself of pleasure, then few humans could be said to flourish. One could also doubt that there is an essential human nature or essences for any category of things.

19. Paul Taylor, "Happiness and Intrinsic Value," in *Ethical Theory: Classical and Contemporary Readings*, ed. Louis Pojman (Belmont, Calif.: Wadsworth, 1989), 133.

20. Ibid.

21. A critic of my analysis of subjective views of value, bettering and worsening, and harm might argue, "Why can't an individual be flourishing because he judges (not 'says') that he is?" My guess is that this method of avoiding the charge of arbitrariness will succeed only by packing objective criteria into the notion of "judging." For a defense of the view that "getting what one has carefully thought about" is the criterion for leading a good life, see, for example, Richard Brandt, *A Theory of the Good and the Right* (Oxford: Clarendon Press, 1979), 126.

22. Taylor, "Happiness and Intrinsic Value," 129.

Finally, according to the "plan of life" conception, flourishing is attained through the setting, pursuing, and completion of life goals and projects. Taylor places three conditions on what could be correctly labeled a flourishing life given this conception.

> (a) It must be a unified, integrated whole in which a person is carrying out a plan of life. (b) The person himself must be the autonomous creator of that plan. (c) During his life the person must have the opportunity and ability to realize his basic goals according to their ordering in his life plan.[23]

Individuals who freely choose lifelong goals and projects that reflect deep commitments and value judgments are said to flourish on this account. A salient difference between the essentialist and the plan of life conceptions of flourishing is that human nature restricts the kind of ends that it is proper to pursue for the former but not the latter. According to the plan of life view we create ourselves through project pursuit—there is no essential human nature.

Plan of life conceptions open the door, once again, to subjectivity. If any plan or goal were just as good as any other, then it would appear that there may be as many ways of flourishing as there are individuals. Thus both the essentialist view and the plan of life view appear to be deficient. Essentialist conceptions of flourishing seem too rigid—as if there is only one way or a limited number of ways for human beings to lead a good life—while plan of life views appear to be too inclusive.

The correct account of flourishing, I believe, is a balance of these two conceptions. The essentialist view restricts the kinds of life plans that are appropriate for beings like us, while the plan of life view reflects a deep and important characteristic of human nature—we are, if anything else, project pursuers.

IS THERE A HUMAN NATURE?

I maintain that there is a determinant human nature that distinguishes us from other entities and objects—a nature that, while not unchanging, is

---

23. Ibid., 130.

fixed enough to determine flourishing.[24] Who could disagree with the claim that humans need sustenance to continue living while inanimate objects don't? Martha Nussbaum notes: "Highly intelligent people, people deeply committed to the good of women and men in developing countries, people who think of themselves as progressive and feminist and antiracist, are taking up positions that converge . . . with the positions of reaction, oppression, and sexism. Under the banner of their radical and politically correct 'anti-essentialism' march the ancient religious taboos, the luxury of the pampered husband, ill health, ignorance, and death."[25]

Arriving at precise categories and definitions may be difficult, but this does not and should not lead to the rejection of all categories and definitions. Properly functioning adult human beings are composites of body and rational faculty. It is fairly absurd to deny that human beings have both bodies and a mental or rational component—it would seem that the mere voicing of a concern would confirm the view. Nowhere does this account maintain that natures or essences are static or unchanging. For example, via genetic engineering we may be able to rid the necessity of calcium or protein in the human diet.

In the physical realm humans and nonhuman animals have many of the same needs. Food, water, and shelter are immediate needs that each individual must secure within a limited time frame. It is a simple fact of nature that our bodies must take in sustenance in order to continue functioning. Objects or conditions that satisfy these requirements would thus be objectively and relationally valuable. Clothing, shelter, and more generally physical health would also seem required for continued survival. Any object, event, or state of affairs that is necessary for the continued survival and maintenance of our bodies is *de facto* valuable on this account.

As a composite being, though, we also have to consider our mental or rational faculties. Without taking a stand on the metaphysical nature of our minds, I think it is hard to deny that there is two-way interaction between minds and bodies—that is, the mind can affect the body and the body can affect the mind. Extreme hunger can cloud rational judgment, and poor reasoning may lead to bodily sickness or worse. Any object, event, or state of affairs that is necessary for the continued survival and maintenance of

24. For a defense of species-type categorizing, see Michael Thompson, "The Representation of Life," in *Virtues and Reasons,* ed. Rosalind Hursthouse, G. Lawrence, and Warren Quinn (Oxford: Oxford University Press, 1995), and Foot, *Natural Goodness.*

25. Martha Nussbaum, "Human Functioning and Social Justice: In Defense of Aristotelian Essentialism," *Political Theory* 20 (May 1992): 204.

our minds is valuable. As primarily social animals we require communication skills, rationality, and understanding or knowledge.[26]

On this account, a life of both intellectual and physical activity is necessary for human flourishing, and the individual who does not develop her intellectual capacities or engage in an active intellectual life cannot be said to flourish. Similarly, the individual who does not develop her physical capacities or engage in a robust life of physical activity (including material relations) cannot be said to flourish. Notice how this view easily accommodates individual variations. Thus, while human nature may set the boundaries for flourishing, within those boundaries there are many ways to flourish.

Human beings or persons are rational project pursuers, and well-being or flourishing is attained through the setting, pursuing, and completion of life goals and projects. Both of these claims are empirical in nature. Humans just are the sort of beings that set, pursue, and complete life goals and projects. Project pursuit is one of many distinguishing characteristics of humans compared to nonhumans—this is to say that normal adult humans are by nature, rational project pursuers. The second empirical claim is that only through rational project pursuit can humans flourish—in other words, a necessary condition for well-being is rational project pursuit. Certainly this view is plausible. A person who does not set, pursue, or complete any life goals or projects cannot be said to flourish in the sense of leading a good life—in much the same way that plants are said not to flourish when they are unhealthy or when they do not get enough sunlight or nourishment.

Following John Rawls, we may say that a person's life plan is rational if it is consistent with the principles of rational choice.[27] These principles are "effective means," "inclusiveness," and "the greater likelihood." The principle of effective means holds that "given the objective, one is to achieve it with the least expenditure of means or given the means one is to fulfill the objective to the fullest possible extent."[28] The principle of inclusiveness holds that "one plan is to be preferred to another if its execution would achieve all the desired aims of the other plan or one or

26. Aristotle divides human goods into three groups—external goods, goods of the soul, and goods of the body. "Of these three classes goods of the soul are considered goods in the strictest and truest sense." *Nicomachean Ethics*, 1098b10–20. I see no reason to advocate the primacy of goods of the soul. As composite beings we would cease to be human beings without each of these realms.

27. Rawls, *A Theory of Justice*, 407–33.

28. Ibid., 410.

more further aims in addition."[29] The principle of greater likelihood holds that if two plans, call them X and Y, have roughly the same ends and plan Y has a greater chance of being realized, then it would be rational to pursue Y instead of X.

Moreover, to say that a life plan or project is rational is to say that it accommodates both general and specific facts about human nature. A general fact about human nature is that humans are project pursuers or that humans covet things. Specific facts are facts about specific individuals, such as Crusoe cannot jump more than three inches and is under six feet tall. If Crusoe's life plan is to become a starting center in the NBA, his project is irrational. As things stand, and assuming that he has no other special capacities, Crusoe will not achieve his goals and is therefore not aiming at the good.

My position concerning rationality is clearly anti-Humean. A distinguishing feature of Humean and neo-Humean accounts of rationality is the view that ends, goals, and lifelong projects are not the proper subjects of rational appraisal. On this view, individuals just have ends, goals, or desires, and rationality is merely a kind of means-to-ends efficiency. The rational person is one who takes the most efficient steps to satisfy her desires, even if the desires are questionable in certain respects. If your end is to eat chocolate ice cream until a gustatory rejection occurs, then there will be one way, or a number of equally good ways, to satisfy this desire. Proceeding, straightaway, to the ice cream store and beginning the binge may be the most efficient means to this end. If so, then on the Humean account we would call this person "rational."

In one way I think that Hume was correct. Whatever your ends, there are more efficient and less efficient ways of achieving them. I part company with Hume when I argue that ends, goals, and desires can be rationally appraised. This is just to say that means-to-ends rationality is not the whole of rationality. To call an action or a plan of action rational is also to reflectively endorse the end or goal. For example, suppose you wanted to see how long you could survive by consuming nothing but your own body parts. If you were to carry out this project in an efficient manner, then the Humean would have to call you rational. On my view, while we may call you efficient, given your end, the end and your pursuit of it would be considered manifestly irrational—certainly not something that can be re-

29. Ibid.

flectively endorsed.[30] Bernard Gert put the point the following way: "Most philosophers who put forward the 'maximum satisfaction of desires view' of rationality overlook the fact that because of mental disorder, or madness, some people have irrational desires. . . . If the account of rationality allows someone with a mental disorder to have coherent and considered preferences for death, pain, and so on, it seems as if someone who held that account would be forced to regard a person who wanted to kill himself in the most painful way possible way as acting rationally."[31] The traditional Humean "maximum satisfaction of desires view" of rationality is so entrenched that some theorists are willing to swallow this *reductio ad absurdum* unflinchingly.

Rationality, the ability to reason correctly, is a kind of master virtue. It is both a part of human nature and a means by which we select life plans that are suitable for beings like us. Warren Quinn and Philippa Foot remind us that there is an uneasy fit between Humean conceptions of rationality and the notion that it is a good thing to be rational—*for what would be so important about practical rationality if it could aim at anything?*[32] "Rational choice should be seen as an aspect of human goodness, standing at the heart of the virtues rather than out there on its own."[33]

On the account that I am defending, a plan of life conception of flourishing must accommodate specific and general facts about human nature. As rational beings our selection of life plans will be restricted by the principles of rational choice. Put another way, individuals who pursue life plans that run afoul of rationality cannot be said to flourish. Moreover, life plans that fail to recognize other important features of human nature—for example, that we are social animals, or that we covet things—will fall short of human well-being or flourishing.

Gert seems to endorse the view that rationality, in a sense, is constrained by value as well. "People act irrationally when they act in ways that they know . . . or should know, will significantly increase the probability that

30. For a defense of a view similar to the one I offer, see Quinn's *Morality and Action*, especially chap. 11, "Rationality and the Human Good." See also David Schmidtz, *Rational Choice and Moral Agency* (Princeton: Princeton University Press, 1995). Korsgaard writes, "To say that there is a practical reason for something is to say that the thing is good, and vice versa." Christine Korsgaard, "The Reasons We Can Share: An Attack on the Distinction Between Agent-Relative and Agent-Neural Values," in *Altruism*, ed. Ellen Frankel Paul, Fred Miller Jr., and Jeffrey Paul (Cambridge: Cambridge University Press, 1993), 25.

31. Bernard Gert, "Rationality, Human Nature, and Lists," *Ethics* 100 (January 1990): 289.

32. Foot, *Natural Goodness*, 62.

33. Ibid., 81.

they . . . will suffer any of the items on the following list: death, pain . . . disability, loss of freedom, or loss of pleasure, and they do not have an adequate reason for so acting."[34] Gert goes on to define rational acts in a similar fashion and concludes that "the lists that are used to define rationality provide our most basic values, so that they clarify how morality is grounded in human nature and rationality."[35] In defending the items on the list as providing the foundation for rationality Gert denies the possibility of providing arguments—they are basic.[36] In any case the relationship between rationality, values, and privacy is an important part of the argument in support of privacy rights that will be taken up in subsequent chapters. In the crudest form, collective rational oughts constrained by various basic values, in part determined by human nature, will justify a version of a "no harm, no foul" principle that will in turn ground locational and informational privacy rights. But this is getting ahead of ourselves—the current task is to establish the value of privacy.

THE VALUE OF PRIVACY

While privacy rights may entail obligations and claims against others— obligations and claims that are beyond the capacities of most nonhuman animals—a case can still be made that separation is valuable for animals. Although privacy may be linked to free will, the need for separation provides an evolutionary first step. It is this capacity of free will that changes mere separation into privacy. Alan Westin in *Privacy and Freedom* notes: "One basic finding of animal studies is that virtually all animals seek periods of individual seclusion or small-group intimacy. This is usually described as the tendency toward territoriality, in which an organism lays private claim to an area of land, water, or air and defends it against intrusion by members of its own species."[37] More important for our purposes are the ecological studies demonstrating that overcrowding threatens survival. In such conditions animals may kill each other, or engage in suicidal reductions of the population, or suffer what might be called a "biochemical die-off." John Christian's study of a herd of Sika deer illustrates the point:

---

34. Gert, "Rationality, Human Nature, and Lists," 280.
35. Ibid., 300.
36. Gert does acknowledge that evolution provides an obvious explanation for why most of us desire to avoid pain, death, and the like.
37. Westin, *Privacy and Freedom*, 8.

"Mortality evidently resulted from shock following severe metabolic distur-
bance, probably as a result of prolonged adrenocortical hyperactivity, judging from the historical material. There was no evidence of infection,
starvation, or other obvious cause to explain the mass mortality."[38] In this
case the inability to separate from other members of the same species apparently caused a die-off so that herd numbers could accommodate separation.

John Calhoun notes that experiments with rats and spacing in cages
show that a certain level of separation is necessary for the species. The lack
of separation leads to the disruption of social relationships and increases of
disease, high blood pressure, and heart failure. Calhoun allowed Norway
rats, which were amply fed, to breed freely in a quarter-acre pen. Their
number stabilized at 150 and never exceeded 200.[39] With a population of
150, fighting became so disruptive to normal maternal care that only a few
of the young survived. If placed in privacy-enhanced pens, the same area
could support 5,000 rats.[40] Moreover, these results hold across a wide range
of species, supporting the contention that having the ability to separate, like
food and water, is a necessity of life.[41]

If it is plausible to maintain that humans evolved from nonhuman animals, then it is also plausible that we may retain many of the same traits.
For example, Lewis Mumford notes similarities between rat overcrowding
and human overcrowding. "No small part of this ugly urban barbarization
has been due to sheer physical congestion: a diagnosis now partly con-
firmed by scientific experiments with rats—for when they are placed in
equally congested quarters, they exhibit the same symptoms of stress, alien-

38. John Christian, "Phenomena Associated with Population Density," *Proceedings of the
National Academy of Science* 47 (1961): 428–49.

39. Paraphrased from Edward Hall, "Proxemics," *Current Anthropology* 9 (1968): 86. See
also John Calhoun, "The Study of Wild Animals Under Controlled Conditions," *Annals of the
New York Academy of Sciences* 51 (1950): 113–22.

40. Alan F. Westin, *Privacy and Freedom* (New York: Atheneum, 1968), 10. See also H. E.
Howard, *Territory in Bird Life* (London: J. Murray, 1920); W. C. Allee, *The Social Life of Animals*
(Boston: Beacon Press, 1958); Edward Hall, *The Hidden Dimension* (New York: Doubleday, 1966);
Robert Ardrey, *The Territorial Imperative* (New York: Atheneum, 1966); and John Calhoun, "A
Behavioral Sink," in *Roots of Behavior,* ed. E. L. Bliss (New York: Hafner, 1962), and "Population
Density and Social Pathology," *Scientific American* 206 (1962), 139–46.

41. See, for example, Allee, *Social Life of Animals*; Edward Deevey, "The Hare and the
Haruspex," *Yale Review* 49 (December 1960): 161–79; Thomas Gilliard, "On the Breeding Behav-
ior of the Cock-of-the-Rock," *Bulletin of the American Museum of Natural History* 124 (1963):
31–68; Robert Snyder, "Evolution and Integration of Mechanisms That Regulate Population
Growth," *National Academy of Sciences* 47 (1961): 449–55; and Vero Wynne-Edwards, *Animal
Dispersion in Relation to Social Behavior* (Edinburgh: Oliver and Boyd, 1962).

ation, hostility, sexual perversion, parental incompetence, and rabid violence that we now find in Megapolis."[42] In any case, I will now turn to the question of whether this necessity for well-being is found in human cultures. If so, like other basic requirements for living, we may plausibly conclude that privacy is valuable.

THE CULTURAL ROOTS OF PRIVACY

One could argue that privacy is a cultural phenomenon and its form or content depends on customs and social practices.[43] Independent of society, when we are by ourselves, there is no need for privacy. Thus there is nothing inherent in human nature that makes privacy valuable for all humans. This view is quickly modified as soon as it is admitted that we are, by nature, social animals. We need companionship and intellectual stimulation as much as food and shelter. Quoting Westin, "The work of leading scientists such as Darling, Fisher, and Wynne-Edwards shows that it is not security per se that brings animals of the same species together, but a desire for stimulation of their fellows."[44]

It may be possible via environmental and genetic manipulation to change human nature in radical ways that will undermine my contention that privacy is valuable for humans. For those future relatives of ours, privacy may not be important. But surely this would not undermine my current claim that privacy is valuable for beings like us, nor would it undermine the view that human beings have a determinant nature at a specific time and place.

To continue, of the thousands of cultures studied there are a rare few that appear to contain no privacy. The Tikopia of Polynesia, the Tlingit Indians of North America, and the Java of Indonesia as well as a few others

---

42. Lewis Mumford, *The City in History* (New York: Harcourt Brace, 1961), 210; cited in Theodore D. Fuller et al., "Chronic Stress and Psychological Well-Being: Evidence from Thailand on Household Crowding," *Social Science Medicine* 42 (1996): 267. This view is echoed by Desmond Morris, who writes, "Each kind of animal has evolved to exist in a certain amount of living space. In both the animal zoo and the human zoo [when] this space is severely curtailed . . . the consequences can be serious." Desmond Morris, *The Human Zoo* (New York: McGraw Hill, 1969), 39.

43. See Philippe Ariès and Georges Duby et al., eds., *A History of Private Life*, trans. Arthur Goldhammer, 5 vols. (Cambridge: Belknap Press of Harvard University Press, 1987–91).

44. Westin, *Privacy and Freedom*, 10. See also F. Fraser Darling, "Social Behavior and Survival," *Auk* 69 (1952): 183–91; James Fisher, "Evolution and Bird Sociality," in Julian Huxley et al., *Evolution as a Process* (London: Allen & Unwin, 1954); and Wynne-Edwards, *Animal Dispersion*.

have cultural systems that appear to leave everything open for public consumption. These are important cases because individuals in such societies may flourish in the absence of privacy—if true, we will have found a telling counterexample to my claim that privacy is necessary for human flourishing.

Before more closely examining these cases, I would like to note that one avenue of response would be to further relativize the central claim about privacy. Rather than maintain that privacy is a necessary condition for human well-being full stop, the claim could be weakened to include only advanced cultures or societies that have moved beyond hunter gatherer or purely agricultural models.[45] Such a restriction is not necessary, however, because while privacy may take many forms, it appears everywhere. Consider the following cases.

> *Tikopia of Polynesia* . . . the Tikopia help the self to be continuous with its society. . . . They find it good to sleep side by side crowding each other, next to their children or their parents or their brothers and sisters, mixing sexes and generations; and if a widow finds herself alone in her one-room house she may adopt a child or a brother to allay her intolerable privacy. . . .
>
> Work among the Tikopia is also socially conceived and structured; and if a man has to work alone, he will probably try to take a little child along.[46]

> *Tlingit Indians of North America*. There are no skeletons tucked away in native families, for the acts of one are familiar to all of the others. Privacy is hardly known among them. It cannot be maintained very well under their system of living, with families bunched together. . . . The Tlingit's bump of curiosity is well developed and anything out of the ordinary, as an accident, a birth, a death or a quarrel, never fails to draw a crowd. . . . They walk in and out of one another's homes without knocking on the door. A woman may be in the very act of changing her garments when [someone] steps in unannounced to

---

45. Fuller et al. note, "A shift in requirements for privacy is, in fact, one aspect of the 'civilizing process' discussed by Elias." Norbert Elias, *The Civilizing Process* (New York: Urizen Books, 1978); cited in Fuller et al., "Chronic Stress," n. 15. J. S. Mill made a similar move in excluding "backward states of society" from applications of his liberty principle. Mill, *On Liberty*, chap. 1.

46. Dorothy Lee, *Freedom and Culture* (Englewood Cliffs, N.J.: Waveland Press, 1959), 31.

visit her husband. This does not embarrass her in the least. She proceeds as if no one had called.[47]

Java of Indonesia. In Java people live in small, bamboo-walled houses . . . there are no fences around them . . . and no doors. Within the house people wander freely just about any place any time, and even outsiders wander in fairly freely almost any time during the day and early evening. In brief, privacy in our terms is about as close to nonexistent as it can get. . . . Except for the bathing enclosure (where people change their clothes) no place is really private.[48]

Westin notes that these cases and others like them do not "prove that there are no universal needs for privacy and no universal processes for adjusting the values of privacy, disclosure, and surveillance within each society."[49] In many cases it appears that isolation, rather than privacy, is being avoided. Nevertheless, the Java still have bathing enclosures, while the Tlingits and Tikopia hide behind psychological walls to ensure private domains.[50] They hide nothing that can be seen and reveal nothing that cannot. Moreover, in each of these cultures there are time restrictions on access—for example, visiting someone in the middle of the night or staying too long would be generally prohibited.

Cultural universals have been found in every society that has been systematically studied.[51] Westin argues that there are aspects of privacy found in every society—privacy *is* a cultural universal. This view is supported by John Roberts and Thomas Gregor, "Societies stemming from quite different cultural traditions such as the Mehinacu and the Zuni do not lack rules and barriers restricting the flow of information within the community, but the management and the functions of privacy may be quite different."[52]

47. Livingston Jones, *A Study of the Thlingets of Alaska* (New York: H. Revell, 1914), 58; quoted in Westin, *Privacy and Freedom,* 12.

48. Clifford Geertz, unpublished paper; quoted in Westin, *Privacy and Freedom,* 16.

49. Westin, *Privacy and Freedom,* 12.

50. For a nice example of this sort of behavior, see Masahiko Mizutani, James Dorsey, and James H. Moor, "The Internet and Japanese Conception of Privacy," *Ethics and Information Technology* 6 (2004): 121–28.

51. See George Murdock, "The Universals of Culture," in *Readings in Anthropology,* ed. E. A. Hoebel, J. D. Jennings, and E. R. Smith (New York: McGraw-Hill, 1955).

52. John Roberts and Thomas Gregor, "Privacy: A Cultural View," in *Privacy: Nomos XIII,* ed. J. Roland Pennock and John W. Chapman (New York: Atherton Press, 1971), 199–225. The public/private distinction was also well understood in China during the Warring States period— 403 B.C. to 221 B.C. Like Aristotle, Confucius (551–479 B.C.) distinguished between the public activity of government and the private affairs of family life. Confucius also contends that "a

Barry Schwartz, in an important article dealing with the social psychology of privacy, provides interesting clues as to why privacy is universal.[53] According to Schwartz privacy is group preserving, maintains status divisions, allows for deviation, and sustains social establishments. As such, privacy may be woven into the fabric of human evolution.

Privacy preserves groups by providing rules of engagement and disassociation. "If the distraction and relief of privacy were not available . . . the relationship would have to be terminated."[54] Without privacy or what may be called a dissociation ritual, there could be no stable social relation. As social animals we seek the company of our fellows but at some point interaction becomes irritating and there is a mutual agreement to separate. Thus having "good fences" would be necessary for having "good neighbors." James Rachels echoes this view:

> We now have an explanation of the value of privacy in ordinary situations in which we have nothing to hide. The explanation is that, even in the most common and unremarkable circumstances, we regulate our behavior according to the kinds of relationships we have with the people around us. If we cannot control who has access to us, sometimes including and sometimes excluding various people, then we cannot control the patterns of behavior we need to adopt (this is one reason why privacy is an aspect of liberty) or the kinds of relations with other people that we will have.[55]

Schwartz also notes that privacy helps maintain status divisions within groups. A mark of status is a heightened level of access control. For example, enlisted men in the armed services have less privacy than commissioned officers. Line-level employees work without doors or secretaries, while

---

private obligation of a son to care for his father overrides the public obligation to obey the law against theft" and that "a timid man who is pretending to be fierce is like a man who is so 'dishonest as to sneak into places where one has no right to be, by boring a hole or climbing through a gap.'" Confucius, *Analects*, trans. Arthur Waley (London, 1938), 2:21; cited in B. Moore, *Privacy*, 223.

53. Barry Schwartz, "The Social Psychology of Privacy," *American Journal of Sociology* 73 (1968): 741–52.

54. Ibid., 741.

55. Rachels, "Why Privacy Is Important," 331. It seems that Parent would agree: "If others manage to obtain sensitive personal knowledge about us they will by that very fact acquire power over us. . . . [A]s long as we live in a society where individuals are generally intolerant of life styles, habits, and ways of thinking that differ significantly from their own . . . our desire for privacy will continue unabated." Parent, "Privacy, Morality, and the Law," 276.

managers and CEOs employ numerous privacy-enhancing devices. Phyllis McGinley writes: "The poor might have to huddle together in cities for need's sake, and the frontiersman cling to his neighbor for the sake of protection. But in each civilization, as it advanced, those who could afford it chose the luxury of a withdrawing place. Egyptians planned vine-hung gardens, the Greeks had their porticos and seaside villas, the Romans put enclosures around their patios. . . . Privacy was considered as worth striving for as hallmarked silver or linen sheets for one's bed."[56]

By protecting status divisions and determining association and disassociation rules, privacy has a stabilizing effect on groups and social orders. Privacy also protects and leaves room for deviation within groups, for it is through experiments in living that new ideas are introduced into groups and, if good, are adopted.[57]

Privacy is built into the very fabric of social establishments. Doors, hallways, fences, window blinds, walls, as well as psychological withdrawal mechanisms each serve to separate individuals at appropriate times from their peers. Moreover, the placement and maintenance of such barriers play an important part of one's self-identity. "The very act of placing a barrier between oneself and others is self-defining, for withdrawal entails separation from a role and, tacitly, from an identity imposed upon oneself via that role."[58] Along a scale sliding from public to private we each take on different roles, in part, defined by the barriers that we place on access.

Growing up can be understood as the building of a series of walls—the walls of privacy.[59] Infants are without privacy. As infants grow into toddlers

---

56. Phyllis McGinley, "A Lost Privilege," in *Province of the Heart* (New York: Viking Press, 1959), 56.

57. A classic treatment enumerating the benefits of free thought and experiments in living is John Stuart Mill's *On Liberty*. Plato, on the other hand, advocated the elimination of private spheres of activity. "The first and highest form of the state and of the government and of the law is that in which there prevails most widely the ancient saying, that 'Friends have all things in common.' Whether there is anywhere now, or will ever be, this communion of women and children and of property, in which the private and individual is altogether banished from life, and things which are by nature private, such as eyes and ears and hands, have become common, and in some way see and hear and act in common, and all men express praise and blame and feel joy and sorrow on the same occasions, and whatever laws there are unite the city to the utmost—whether all this is possible or not, I say that no man, acting upon any other principle, will ever constitute a state which will be truer or better or more exalted in virtue." Plato, *The Laws* 5.738d–e, in *The Collected Works of Plato*, trans. Benjamin Jowett (New York: Greystone Press, 1930). Plato views privacy as something that is of little inherent value in relation to the perfect state. Moreover, he recognizes no psychological, sociological, or political needs for individuals to be able to control patterns of association and disassociation with their fellows.

58. Schwartz, "Social Psychology of Privacy," 747.

59. See Rene Spitz, "The Derailment of Dialogue," *Journal of the American Psychoanalytic Association* 12 (1964): 752–75. "Both animals and humans require, at critical stages of life, specific

and begin to communicate with language, they express wishes for separation at times. Schwartz notes that as this process continues the "door of privacy" closes "halfway as a recognition of self development during childhood, it shuts but is left ajar at pre-puberty, and closes entirely—and perhaps even locks—at the pubertal and adolescent stages when meditation, grooming, and body examination become imperative."[60] Toddlers and small children begin requesting privacy as they start the process of self-initiated development. More robust patterns of disassociation continue as children enter puberty. Finally as young adults emerge, the walls of privacy have hardened, and access points are maintained vigorously.

Could we imagine, however, a culture that prospers without individuals attaining any measure of privacy—like the Watcher society mentioned in the first chapter? Alexander Rosenberg writes: "For all their desirability, could a just society get along without intimacy, friendship, and love? We can perfectly well imagine a desert island society and a scenario of impeccable justice and moral probity in which the inhabitants have no interest in the sort of social relations that moral social psychologists extol. . . . Alternatively, we can imagine a society replete with friendship, intimacy, and love, but without privacy."[61] We can indeed imagine some of these things, as we can imagine evolved humans who do not need protein or water to survive. Such entities would have different requirements for flourishing. I do not believe, given our current capacities and tendencies, that we can imagine a society where friendship, intimacy, and love obtain but where privacy is nonexistent. The very relation of association and disassociation that comprises friendship, intimacy, and love is central to the notion of privacy. It would seem impossible to have an "intimate" relationship absent control over access.[62] Robert Gerstein agrees and argues that intimacy requires control over observation. He writes, "We cannot continue to be immersed in the experience of intimacy if we begin to observe ourselves or other things around us. . . . We cannot at the same time be lost in an experience and be

amounts of space in order to act out the dialogues that lead to the consummation of most of the important acts of life." Spitz, 753.

60. Schwartz, "Social Psychology of Privacy," 749. See also Erik Erikson, *Childhood and Society* (New York: W. W. Norton, 1950), 219–31, and Jane Kessler, *Psychopathology of Childhood* (Englewood Cliffs, N.J.: Prentice Hall, 1966).

61. Alexander Rosenberg, "Privacy as a Matter of Taste and Right," *Social Philosophy and Policy* 17 (2000): 71.

62. Rachels notes, "Thus a man may be playful and affectionate with his children (although sometimes firm), businesslike with his employees, and respectful and polite with his mother-in-law. And to his close friends he may show a side of his personality that others never see—perhaps he is secretly a poet, and rather shy about it, and shows his verse only to his best friends." Rachels, "Why Privacy Is Important," 326.

observers of it. . . . There is a great difference between the way we experience our own action when we intend them to be observed by others and
the way we relate to them when we are immersed in intimacy."[63] Observation by a third party undermines the grounds for intimacy by imposing a
role on the parties involved. We begin thinking about how our actions or
behavior will be interpreted by those observing.

CONCLUSION

While privacy may be a cultural universal necessary for the proper functioning of human beings, its form—the actual rules of association and dis-
engagement—is culturally determined.[64] The kinds of privacy rules found
in different cultures depend on a host of variables, including climate, religion, technological advances, and political arrangements. As with the necessities of food, shelter, and education we should not jump to the conclusion
that because the forms of privacy are culturally dependent that privacy is
subjective "all the way down"—relationalism does not entail subjectivity.[65]

In 1969 Edward Hall noted a link between a lack of privacy and psychological and physical disorders in humans and nonhuman animals: "The
disorders of Calhoun's overcrowded rats bear a striking resemblance to . . .
Americans who live in densely packed urban conditions. . . . Chombart de
Lauwe has gathered data on French workers' families and has demonstrated
a statistical relationship between crowded living conditions and physical
and social pathology. In the United States a health survey of Manhattan
(Srole et al. 1962) showed that only 18% of a representative sample were
free of emotional disorders while 23% were seriously disturbed or incapacitated."[66]

These results are supported by numerous more recent studies.[67] Overcrowding in prisons has been linked to violence, depression, suicide, psy-

---

63. Robert S. Gerstein, "Intimacy and Privacy," *Ethics* 89 (October 1978): 77–78.

64. See Herbert Spiro, "Privacy in Comparative Perspective," in *Privacy: Nomos XIII*, ed. J.
Roland Pennock and John W. Chapman (New York: Atherton Press, 1971), 121–48.

65. It is surprising how many privacy scholars make this mistake. Amitai Etzioni agrees with
Fred Cate when the latter writes, "Privacy is . . . contextual and subjective. It is neither inherently
beneficial nor harmful." Fred Cate, *Privacy in the Information Age* (Washington, D.C.: Brookings
Institution Press, 1997), 31. See also Amitai Etzioni, *The Limits of Privacy* (New York: Basic Books,
1999), 199.

66. Hall, "Proxemics," 86.

67. See, for example, Andrew Baum and Stuart Koman, "Differential Response to Antici-
pated Crowding: Psychological Effects of Social and Spatial Density," *Journal of Personality and
Social Psychology* 34 (1976): 526–36; Jes Clauson-Kaas et al., "Urban Health: Human Settlement
Indicators of Crowding," *Third World Planning Review* 18 (1996): 349–63; J. N. Edwards and Alan
Both, "Crowding and Human Sexual Behavior," *Social Forces* 55 (1977): 791–808; Fuller et al.,

chological disorders, and recidivism. There is even evidence suggesting that the response to stress caused by overcrowding is culturally relative.[68]

Moreover, Theodore Fuller and his colleagues have convincingly established that household crowding has "strong and consistent detrimental effects on psychological well-being."[69] Fuller and his colleagues studied crowding in Thailand, but the conclusions fit nicely with results from an earlier study on crowding in Chicago.[70] These findings, coupled with the substantial body of research documenting the causal relationship between psychological well-being and health leads to a seemingly unavoidable conclusion.[71] The inability to control access has detrimental effects on well-being that may apply across a wide range of cultures and practices.

Given all of this I believe that one can, with great confidence, claim that privacy is valuable for beings like us.[72] Having the ability and moral authority to regulate access to and uses of locations and personal information is an essential part of human flourishing and well-being. The forms of privacy may be culturally relative, but the need for privacy is not.

"Chronic Stress"; Griscom Morgan, "Mental and Social Health and Population Density," *Journal of Human Relations* 20 (1972): 196–204; David Farrington and Christopher Nuttal, "Prison Size, Overcrowding, Prison Violence and Recidivism," *Journal of Criminal Justice* 8 (1980): 221–31; Paul Paulus, Verne Cox, and Garvin McCain, "Death Rates, Psychiatric Commitments, Blood Pressure and Perceived Crowding as a Function of Institutional Crowding," *Environmental Psychology and Nonverbal Behavior* 3 (1978): 107–16; and Barry Ruback and Timothy Carr, "Crowding in a Women's Prison," *Journal of Applied Social Psychology* 14 (1984): 57–68.

68. E. I. Megargee, "The Association of Population Density, Reduced Space, and Uncomfortable Temperatures with Misconduct in a Prison Community," *American Journal of Community Psychology* 5 (1977): 289–98; Frank Porporino and Kimberley Dudley, *An Analysis of the Effects of Overcrowding in Canadian Penitentiaries* (Ottawa: Research Division, Programs Branch, Solicitor General of Canada, 1984); Verne Cox, Paul Paulus, and Garvin McCain, "Prison Crowding Research: The Relevance of Prison Housing Standards and a General Approach Regarding Crowding Phenomena," *American Psychologist* 39 (1984): 1148–60; Garvin McCain, Verne Cox, and Paul Paulus, "The Effect of Prison Crowding on Inmate Behavior" (Washington, D.C.: U.S. Department of Justice, 1980); Paulus, Cox, and McCain, "Death Rates," 107–16; Farrington and Nuttal, "Prison Size," 221–31.

69. Fuller et al., "Chronic Stress," 278.

70. S. V. Kasl, "Stress and Health," in *Annual Review of Public Health*, ed. L. Breslow, J. Fielding, and L. Lave, 1984, 319, and Alan Booth and John Cowell, "Crowding and Health," *Journal of Health and Social Behavior* 17 (1976): 204; cited in Fuller et al. "Chronic Stress," 279.

71. W. R. Grove and Michael Hughes, *Overcrowding in the Household* (New York: Academic Press, 1983).

72. Given this and the arguments of the next two chapters, I contend that privacy is a universal right (contra Bill Talbott's omission). See William J. Talbott, *Which Rights Should Be Universal?* (Oxford: Oxford University Press, 2005), 163. Talbott has recently changed his mind regarding privacy. See William J. Talbott, *Human Rights and Human Well-Being* (Oxford: Oxford University Press, 2010), chap. 13.

4

JUSTIFYING PRIVACY RIGHTS TO BODIES AND LOCATIONS

One of our most cherished rights, a right enshrined in law and notions of common morality, is the right of individuals to control access to bodies, places, and locations. Violations of this basic right are seen as some of the most serious of injustices. If the results of Chapter 3 are compelling, then we can say with some certainty that privacy rights are valuable for beings like us. Many will not find this result troubling or in need of much justification. Nevertheless, establishing the claim that the condition of privacy is valuable or that privacy rights are valuable still does not *establish* or *justify* privacy *rights*—moral claims against others to do or refrain from doing certain things.[1]

As I noted in Chapter 2, privacy may be understood as a right to control access to and uses of specific places and information. In terms of places or locations, privacy yields control over access to one's body and home. A privacy right in this sense is a right to control access to a specific object—I will use the term "physical" or "locational" privacy when considering this aspect of privacy rights. But we may also control access to sensitive personal information about ourselves—or what may be called "informational" pri-

---

1. R. G. Frey puts the point the following way. "To say that our lives would go better if certain things about ourselves were not known does not show that we enjoy an entitlement concerning such information; it does not even establish a presumption of privacy." R. G. Frey, "Privacy, Control, and Talk of Rights," *Social Philosophy and Policy* 17 (2000): 47.

vacy. For example, when an average citizen suppresses the dissemination of sensitive personal information about herself, she is exercising a right to control a set of ideas no matter what form they take. In this chapter I will offer an argument that justifies physical or locational privacy rights based on a kind of "no harm, no foul" rule. In the next I will take up the task of justifying informational privacy rights.

DERIVING PHYSICAL PRIVACY RIGHTS

David Gauthier provides a promising starting point for deriving rights to control access to one's body, capacities, and powers.[2] Gauthier uses a version of the Lockean "enough and as good" proviso on acquisition as a general constraint on action to ensure that the initial bargaining position—where we agree about the benefits and burdens of social interaction—is fair.[3] The proviso, as Gauthier argues, provides a fair bargaining position because it provides for basic rights and thus eliminates prior acts of predation and parasitism from undermining the moral force of the agreement.[4] If an agreement is made under duress of some sort, suppose a gun is pointed at someone or a forceful threat has been made, then it can hardly be claimed that the obligations generated from the agreement are binding. Independent of Gauthier's contractarian aims, however, the proviso functions to provide access control and use rights to one's body, capacities, and powers.

Gauthier interprets the Lockean proviso so that it prohibits worsening the situation of another, through interaction with that person, except to avoid worsening one's own position.[5] The base point for determining bettering and worsening is how those affected would be in your absence, and the terms of being worsened are determined by preference satisfaction. "We may treat 'better' and 'worse' as unproblematic; one situation is better for some person than another, if and only if it affords him greater expected

---

2. Also see Moore, *Intellectual Property and Information Control,* chaps. 4 and 5.

3. See John Locke, *The Second Treatise of Government,* ed. C. B. Macpherson (Indianapolis: Hackett, 1980), chap. 5, sec. 27. It is important to note that for Gauthier, the proviso does not have independent moral weight outside his contractarian argument. Gauthier, *Morals by Agreement.*

4. See Don Hubin and Mark Lambeth, "Providing for Rights," *Dialogue* 27 (1988): 489–502, for a more detailed discussion of the issues presented in this section.

5. Gauthier, *Morals by Agreement,* 203.

utility."[6] Expected utility, for Gauthier, is couched in terms of subjective preference satisfaction. Consider the following proviso: "If no one's position is worsened in terms of subjective preference satisfaction by another's action compared to how they would be were the action-taker absent, then the action is permitted."[7]

Gauthier uses this proviso to assign basic rights in the following way. Each individual, in the absence of others, may expect to use his own powers but not theirs. How one would be in the *absence* of others provides the basis for comparison. Continued use of one's own body and capacities in the presence of others may fail to better their situation, but it does not, in itself, worsen their situation compared to how they would be were the action-taker absent. Finally, using the body and powers of another, in interfering with their own use, does worsen their situation and is therefore prohibited. Gauthier writes: "Thus the proviso, in prohibiting each from bettering his situation by worsening that of others, but otherwise leaving each free to do as he pleases, not only confirms each in the use of his own powers, but in denying to others the use of those powers, affords to each the exclusive use of his own."[8] He concludes that each individual's rights to their body and powers are thus justified. A right to control one's own body, capacities, and powers would include access and use rights; and if correct, we will have established physical privacy rights.

PROBLEMS FOR GAUTHIER

While providing a useful starting point, Gauthier's derivation of basic rights is not without problems. Below, five seemingly decisive objections to Gauthier's view will be considered.

---

6. Ibid.

7. It is important to note that compensation is typically built into the proviso and the overall account of bettering and worsening. Suppose that controlling access to her body, capacities, and powers allows Ginger to develop certain talents that positively impact Fred so much that Fred's lost liberties to use Ginger's body for his ends are overbalanced by other benefits. Gauthier echoes this point in the following case. "In acquiring a plot of land, even the best land on the island, Eve may initiate the possibility of more diversified activities in the community as a whole, and more specialized activities for particular individuals with ever-increasing benefits to all." Gauthier, *Morals by Agreement*, 280. Moreover, compensation can occur at both the level of the act and the level of the practice. Maybe individual acts of worsening will be compensated by the increased opportunities and the like conferred on each individual within the system of property relations.

8. Gauthier, *Morals by Agreement*, 209.

The first objection is that subjective preference standards of moral value are misconceived. For example, suppose Fred prefers that Ginger not control her body, capacities, or powers.[9] In fact, suppose this preference consumes him and generally centers his world. If bettering and worsening are couched in terms of subjective preference, then Ginger worsens Fred's situation by controlling her body, capacities, and powers. Put aside for a moment the baseline—how Fred would be were Ginger absent. The question at hand is why would Fred's arbitrary and perhaps silly preference matter in any way when determining value and bettering or worsening?[10]

When Gauthier considers an argument for property rights in a later section, he not only switches the baseline—from how A would be in B's *absence* to how A would be if B had left the object in question for *common use*—but he also seems to affirm an objective account of value. "Planned intensive cultivation made possible by her security of tenure may well make it possible for her to live better on a part of the island sufficiently small that the others would be better off . . . she may produce sufficient food to meet the needs of several families . . . her appropriation may enable everyone to improve [their] situation."[11] Notice that subjective preferences never enter this account and would be morally irrelevant if they did.

The second objection concerns the base point for determining bettering and worsening—how Ginger would be were Fred absent.[12] Suppose that while eating dinner Ginger begins to choke and Fred rushes to her aid.[13] As he pounds her on the back in an attempt to dislodge the food, he also stabs her in the leg. While her life is saved, Ginger's leg is severely damaged. The

9. One could object to this case on the grounds that it depends on individuals taking an interest in one another's interests—this is to say that they have "tuistic" desires. Gauthier assumes that the proviso is intended to apply to interaction under the assumptions of individual utility maximization and mutual unconcern or disinterestedness. For problems with Gauthier's assumption, see Don Hubin, "Non-Tuism," *Canadian Journal of Philosophy* 21 (1991): 441–68.

10. The objection usually voiced at this point is that the argument depends on an "odd" preference. If we rule out such preferences, there is no problem. While initially plausible, I have yet to come across any generally accepted procedure that tells us which preferences count that don't also introduce an "objectifying" element into the account. See Chapter 3 and Moore, "Values, Objectivity, and Relationalism."

11. Gauthier, *Morals by Agreement*, 216.

12. There is a vast body of philosophical literature on notions of "coercion," "threats," and "offers," much of which centers on what has been called "empirical" or "value-free" conceptions of coercion as opposed to "moralized" theories of coercion. Despite the overlap between the view I defend and many of the cases and issues discussed in the literature on coercion, I will only engage this material in connection with particular cases. For a rigorous analysis of and introduction to the literature on coercion, see Alan Wertheimer, *Coercion* (Princeton: Princeton University Press, 1987).

13. Adapted from Kagan, *Limits of Morality*, 97.

problem should be obvious. If Fred had been absent, then Ginger would have died. So by simultaneously saving her and stabbing her Fred does not worsen Ginger. Yet there is something wrong about saying that Fred bettered, or at least did not worsen, Ginger in this case.

Furthermore, how long of an *absence* are we to imagine? If "absence" is characterized as "never existed," "then parents would have to harm their children very badly before it would count as worsening the situation of their children."[14] The parent who consistently invaded her child's private space will not typically worsen that child relative to the base point—assuming of course that if the parent had never existed, the child would not have existed.

A third objection is captured in the following case provided by Don Hubin and Mark Lambeth: "Dr. Demento . . . has discovered a drug that will put people into a trance for eight hours and rejuvenate their bodies so that they need no sleep. The fiendish doctor realizes that he has a way to use the bodies of others without making them any worse-off than they would have been in his absence. . . . In addition to making his temporary zombies work in his lab at night, he engages in vile and disgusting sex acts with them which he videotapes . . . and sells at great profit in foreign countries."[15] As Hubin and Lambeth note, Gauthier's derivation of body rights depends on the assumption that Demento's use of your body, capacities, and powers necessarily interferes with your use of them. The Demento case shows that this assumption is not always true.

A fourth objection builds on the Demento case and compensation for actions that worsen others. Given Gauthier's view that worsenings may be overbalanced or compensated for by other considerations, we may call into doubt the very robustness of the body rights generated.[16] Suppose that Demento uses your body, capacities, and powers, yet adequately compensates you for the loss—after being compensated, your level of well-being is higher after his use of your body than before. In such cases you may be at liberty to use your own body, capacities, and powers, and Demento may be able to use them as well, provided that appropriate compensation is offered.

Finally, we may ask what justifies the use of the proviso—why think that a kind of "no harm, no foul" rule is a sufficient foundation for privacy

14. Hubin and Lambeth, "Providing for Rights," 492 n. 4.

15. Ibid., 495.

16. This argument draws directly from Eric Mack, "Gauthier on Rights and Economic Rent," *Social Philosophy and Policy* 9 (1992): 171–200.

rights or any rights for that matter? Here we are wondering about the moral weightiness of the proviso and its ability to deliver the cluster of moral oughts that make up rights.

While each of these objections point to deep problems with Gauthier's justification of body rights, I believe that his account can be saved. After presenting a sketch of an account of moral bettering and worsening, built on the results of Chapter 3, and providing an argument for the appropriate base point of comparison, I will return to these objections and indicate how they may be answered.

A PARETO-BASED PROVISO

The proviso permits individuals to better themselves so long as no one is worsened. The base-level intuition of a Pareto-improvement is what lies behind the notion of the proviso: One state of the world, S_1, is Pareto-superior to another, S_2, if and only if no one is worse off in S_1 than in S_2, and at least one person is better off in S_1 than in S_2.[17] If no one is harmed by an action and one person is bettered, then the action ought to be permitted. In fact, it is precisely because no one is harmed that it seems unreasonable to object to a Pareto-superior move. Thus, the proviso can be understood as a version of a "no harm, no foul" principle.

In implementing a Pareto-based proviso we must consider and answer two questions. First, how do we measure bettering and worsening? Do we measure pleasure and pain, subjective states of joy and preference satisfaction, or do we use some other criterion? Fundamentally this is a question of moral value. Second, after deciding on a measure, what states or conditions do we compare? We could compare and measure value now versus some other time or the value present two weeks from now compared to some other state. To determine bettering and worsening we must compare and measure the relative values in two states—this is known as the baseline problem. I'll take each of these questions up in turn.

17. S_1 is *strongly* Pareto-superior to S_2 if everyone is better off in S_1 than in S_2, and *weakly* Pareto-superior if at least one person is better off and no one is worse off. State S_1 is Pareto-optimal if no state is Pareto-superior to S_1. A *super-weak* Pareto principle would require that no one be harmed full stop. Adapted from G. A. Cohen, "The Pareto Argument for Inequality," *Social Philosophy and Policy* 12 (1995): 160. Unless indicated, I will use Pareto-superiority to stand for *weak* Pareto-superiority. The "Pareto" condition is named after Vilfredo Pareto (1848–1923), an Italian economist and sociologist.

MORAL BETTERING AND WORSENING

As I have noted, Gauthier's derivation of access rights to one's body, capacities, and powers depends on an unsatisfactory account of value. Building on the arguments offered in Chapter 3, I believe that the correct account of moral value is objective and relational—objective in the sense of not being tied to affective states and relational in terms of being related to groups of living organisms. Given that we are physical beings who pursue projects in the world of objects, it will be these objects and our relations to these objects that provide the basic material for value claims. Consider friendship, for example, as a part of having and maintaining deep personal relationships. Minimally, to create or maintain a friendship one must be able to communicate. Short of telepathy, this will require manipulating a host of physical things such as one's body, cell phones, cars, and the like—likewise with accomplishment, autonomy, understanding, rational project pursuit, and other candidates of moral value.

In general, it is not how you fare vis-à-vis some particular object that determines your level of material well-being. Imagine someone protesting your acquisition of a grain of sand from an endless beach, claiming that she can now no longer use *that* grain of sand and has thereby been worsened. What is needed is an "all-things-considered view" of material well-being or wealth, income, and opportunities to acquire wealth. A better interpretation of "worsening" and "bettering" is that we are concerned with keeping others at the same *level* of material well-being. To be able to achieve or sustain a certain *level* of material well-being is important because it determines the range of individual physical activity that directly affects project pursuit. A particular object is not important as long as there is an ample supply of other substitutable items that can be used or acquired freely. What difference does it make whether or not you can use some particular object in conditions of abundance? Locke claims, and rightly so, that an acquisition "can be of prejudice to no man" when there is enough and as good left over. It does not count as worsening when someone has been deprived of using or acquiring a particular object, provided relative abundance—that is to say, her *level* of material well-being—might be unchanged. In fact, it would be unreasonable to complain about such supposed worsening.

Bodies, capacities, and powers—unlike rocks, cars, land, or other physical items—appear not to be fungible. One rock may be just as good as any other, but this is not the case concerning one's body. How you fare vis-à-vis your body, capacities, and powers is significant in a way that how you fare vis-à-vis some external object is not. While fungibility is an important component in any correct account of moral bettering and worsening, there may be some items that are not fungible.[18]

At a specific time each individual has a certain set of things she can freely use and other things she owns, but she also has certain opportunities to use and appropriate things. This complex set of opportunities along with what she can now freely use or has rights over constitutes her position materially—this set constitutes her level of well-being and provides the measure for determining moral bettering and worsening.

THE BASELINE PROBLEM

There is a sort of artificiality inherent in talking about individuals acquiring rights to control their own bodies, capacities, and powers. It is not as if at one point in time we lack these rights and then, "*presto!*" we obtain them. As we grow into adulthood, we gradually obtain these rights, and they may fade away at the end of life—it is very much a process of coming to be and passing away.

To clarify the issues that surround setting the base point of comparison, let us consider the following example. Two thousand years from now Roy, an adult human clone, awakes from hypersleep. He is alone in the universe except for Leon, another clone, who remains asleep. Assume that after some time of self-initiated development Roy acquires physical privacy rights—he has rights to control access to and use of his body, capacities, and powers. Leon awakes and begins the process of self-initiated development. But we may wonder whether Leon worsens Roy by seeking exclusive control over

18. Opportunities are also valuable. Suppose it is the case that before Crusoe's appropriation of some object, Friday's level of material well-being is Z, and it remains Z after Crusoe's appropriation. Crusoe's appropriation would then be justified on grounds of Friday's current level of well-being. But there are also Friday's future opportunities to achieve a certain level of material well-being to consider. It is only when Crusoe's appropriation leaves Friday no worse off in both of these senses, or Crusoe pays compensation, that an appropriation is justified. If Friday gathered five bushels of apples a day to eat before Crusoe's appropriation of a plot of land and Friday's situation remains the same after the appropriation (Friday still gathers five bushels of apples a day in the same amount of time) and gathering five bushels of apples a day exhausts Friday's opportunities to improve his situation, then Crusoe has not made Friday worse off and the proviso is satisfied. This would amount to a "no loss" requirement in terms of Friday's level of well-being. For a more detailed discussion of opportunities and value, see Moore, *Intellectual Property and Information Control*, chap. 4.

his body, capacities, and powers. More to the point, which two situations should Roy and Leon consider in determining whether or not Leon's actions worsen anyone? We could compare the case where Leon obtains exclusive body rights to the case where Roy was still in hypersleep and not yet a self-owner. Or we could compare the case where Leon acquires exclusive body rights to the case where Roy has already acquired body rights—or to some other state.

Assuming that Roy legitimately acquired rights to control his own body, capacities, and powers in the first place, his level of material well-being will have changed—loosely speaking, Roy now holds exclusive title to an object. If bettering and worsening are to be evaluated in terms of an individual's level of material well-being and this measure changes over time, then the baseline of comparison must also change. This is to affirm a dynamic, rather than static, comparison point. The problem with static base points is that they fail to include morally relevant changes in well-being—changes that may occur as time passes.

At this point I would like to clear up a common confusion surrounding the baseline of comparison. Just as an example, what if a perverse inventor creates a genetic enhancement technique that will save lives but decides to keep the technique secret or charge an excessive price for the treatment? Those individuals who had, before the creation, no chance to survive now have a chance and are worsened because of the perverse inventor's refusal to let others use the machine.

The baseline this case implies cannot be correct. On this view, to determine bettering and worsening we are to compare how individuals are before the creation of some value, in this case the genetic enhancement technique, to how they would be if they possessed or consumed that value. But we are all worsened in this respect by any value that is created and held exclusively. I am worsened by your exclusive possession of your car because I would be better off if I exclusively controlled the car—even if I already owned hundreds of cars. Any individual, especially those who have faulty hearts, would be better off if they held title to my heart compared to anyone else's holding the title. I am also worsened when you create a new philosophical theory and claim authorship—assuming it is a valuable theory, I would have been better off if I had authored the theory, so you have worsened me. Clearly this account of the baseline makes the notions of bettering and worsening too broad.[19]

19. See Colin Farrelly, "Genes and Social Justice: A Reply to Moore," *Bioethics* 16 (2002): 75.

THE PROBLEMS RECONSIDERED

I hope it is clear how the proposed view of bettering and worsening avoids the problem of arbitrary, silly, or manipulated preferences that infects Gauthier's view—the proposed account is objective not subjective. If Fred were to prefer that Ginger not control her own body, capacities, and powers, such a preference would be irrelevant to determining moral bettering and worsening. An individual's level of material well-being—grounded in human nature or Aristotelian necessities—determines bettering and worsening independently of desires, preferences, and affections. Properly constituted individuals will have the appropriate desires and preferences, but these affective states and their realization do not generate value.

The second difficulty presented for Gauthier's account concerned the base point of comparison—what would have happened had the action-taker been absent. Presumably, if the action-taker had been absent, the action in question would not have happened. If some other agent had attempted the action in question, then her base point would have been the same and so on and so forth. When Ginger exercises control over her body, capacities, and powers in the presence of Fred, he is not worsened—not compared to the case where Ginger is absent. But when Fred simultaneously saves her and stabs her, she cannot claim to have been worsened because it is assumed that if Fred were absent, then Ginger would have died. Clearly something has gone awry in this case.

Such examples trade on a difficulty in describing acts. We could describe the action in this case numerous ways: Fred saved Ginger's life by pounding her on the back and dislodging the food; Fred stabbed Ginger in the leg; Fred exhaled, jumped three feet across the room, dropped his napkin and hit Ginger in the back while imagining how his actions would cause others to worship him as a hero; and so on. I hope it is clear that simply because there is practically an infinite number of ways to describe an action it does not follow that each description is equally good.[20]

On Gauthier's behalf we may insist that there are at least two—and possibly many more—distinct actions present in this case. Taken by itself the

20. Eric D'Arcy and David Lyons independently arrived at roughly the same answer to the problem of act description. In general they distinguish among acts, circumstances, and consequences. The solution that both seem to advocate is that we use moral norms to determine the relevant description of a particular act. Since utilitarians are concerned with the goodness of consequences, we should describe an act in such a way that all the relevant consequences are included. See Eric D'Arcy, *Human Acts* (Oxford: Clarendon Press, 1963), 1–61, and David Lyons, *Forms and Limits of Utilitarianism* (Oxford: Clarendon Press, 1965), chap. 2.

first action, dislodging the food that Ginger was choking on, would pass the proviso, while the second, stabbing Ginger in the leg, would not. It is not as if these two actions must come together—as if a necessary part of the act of saving included the act of stabbing. If it did, then there would be no problem. These replies apply equally to a "moment before," or "had the action not occurred" base point for determining bettering and worsening. Moreover, there is no question of how long an absence we are to consider.

Consider the case where Fred says to Ginger, "I will save your life, but only if you become my house servant." Independent of whether this is a coercive threat or offer we may ask at least two important questions. First, assuming that Ginger does not indicate agreement with the offer, does Fred's inaction—and Ginger's subsequent death—worsen her? Second, would Ginger's agreement under duress and subsequent failure to comply with Fred's terms constitute a harm to Fred? *Assuming that there are no other moral obligations in force,* Fred's inaction and Ginger's death would not constitute a morally relevant harm. If it did, then any inaction—where some action could prevent a harm—would violate the proviso and constitute a morally relevant worsening.[21]

Taking up the second question—I would argue that Ginger's agreement under duress and subsequent failure to comply with Fred's terms do not constitute a harm to Fred. Fred's baseline does not include all the benefits he could secure through "forced" contracts any more than Ginger's baseline includes all the benefits she could obtain if others gave her things. To put the point another way, Ginger has a legitimate rational complaint against Fred's insistence that she has agreed to, and therefore should, become his servant. Moreover, those of us who fail to aid others or prevent harm to others have a legitimate complaint as well. Why should our lives be subject to the demands of others without conditions? Suppose I could easily reach out, take an apple, and eat it—thus providing myself sustenance—but fail to do so. It seems quite implausible to say that in this case those who fail to act and provide the apple have harmed me. Many of these issues are taken up later in the section on the moral weightiness of the proviso.

Consider the following version of a "no harm, no foul" rule: "If no one's position is worsened (in terms of her level of material well-being including opportunity costs) by another's action compared to how they were the

---

21. I hasten to note that I do not deny the possibility of positive obligations existing between two individuals—where failure to live up to an obligation would constitute a morally relevant worsening. What I deny is that such positive obligations exist between any two individuals or groups of individuals regardless of history, circumstance, or agreement.

moment before the action occurred, then the action is permitted."[22] Given that concurrent use of one's body, capacities, and powers is unlikely, Roy would worsen Leon by using Leon's body. How, we may ask, could Leon engage in rational lifelong project pursuit if he did not have exclusive control of his own body? As noted before, unlike other objects in the world, bodily control does not appear to be fungible. That is, I can use this or that piece of wood for a walking stick in a way that I cannot use this or that body for running.

When Roy uses his body, capacities, and powers in the presence of Leon, Roy does not necessarily worsen Leon relative to how Leon would have been compared to the moment before Roy acted. When Leon uses Roy's body, capacities, and powers, Roy is worsened relative to how he would have been compared to the moment before Leon's action. The first case establishes permission to use, while the second establishes exclusivity. Together they provide the foundation for rights claims.

But what of the Dr. Demento case, which challenges the assumption that using someone else's body necessarily interferes with their use of it? First, one could merely agree that in such cases no worsening has occurred and such actions are justified. In providing the foundation for physical privacy rights, the proviso need not be exceptionless.

It is also true that the world will not likely mirror the assumptions in the Demento case anytime soon—while not always the case, the assumption that using someone else's body necessarily interferes with their use of it is highly likely. Also, consider how fanciful the case gets when we imagine the possibility of being awoken at night, or receiving a phone call, being startled awake in time to jot down the outline of a dream you were having that will become the basis of a novel, and so on. Demento would have to control all of this to not interfere and thereby worsen. Here it seems as if notions of bodily control, actions, and autonomy are bundled together.

It is also true that as we pursue goals and projects, new capacities, talents, and abilities may be created. Our choices may change us. These self-created aspects of ourselves didn't exist prior to creation; thus it would be difficult to maintain that others are worsened by our exclusive dominion over these capacities relative to the appropriate base point.

22. If opportunities are valuable, as I think they are (see note 18), then we have the beginnings of an answer to the Epicurean argument against death being a harm to the person who dies. We compare how a person is prior to the act of killing—which presumably includes a future of values and opportunities—to the case where that future does not exist. For a similar answer to this Epicurean worry, see Feldman, "Some Puzzles."

Consider the following reply, however: "Suppose Fred acquires and develops forensic skills. As a side effect of learning this valuable trade Fred is now also able to kill far more efficiently, given his knowledge of things that can harm the human body. The only thing that keeps Fred from using this knowledge is his will, and that could well change as he pursues other projects. If Fred's will changes, Ginger is definitely worse off compared to how she was prior to the creation of Fred's new skills and talents. Even before Fred's will changes one could make the argument that Ginger is less safe."[23] But, as with the problem of act description mentioned earlier, we can distinguish a capacity or talent for forensics from the development of a will able to kill others. Moreover, these can be distinguished from the act of killing—Fred may have the will and the capacity but never actually kill. Thus developing a capacity, even the capacity to kill effectively, by itself does not necessarily worsen others. Even developing an insensitive will would not worsen others if attached to someone physically inept. But when attached to an able body, developing an insensitive or evil will may impose risks on others that justify interference. The physically and mentally robust assassin in training may be justifiably restrained or monitored.

In the second version of the Demento case, the worsening caused by interference with someone else's body, capacities, and powers is overbalanced by other values offered as compensation. There are two, by my lights, compelling answers to this question. First, one could bite a softened bullet so to speak. Compensation for such interference would be exceedingly high. Losing control over one's body and capacities to others, even momentarily, undermines autonomy and project pursuit in deep ways. To engage the world as physical beings requires sustained and not haphazard control of our bodies—control that may be snatched away at any moment. Given that lifelong project pursuit requires sustained control over one's body, capacities, and powers, the compensation required for seizing the body and capacities of another will be exceptionally high.

In an interesting discussion of boundary-crossing acts, Robert Nozick offers several further considerations that support this claim.[24] Fear of bodily invasion or seizure of one's body may impose costs that must be considered when determining compensation. Typically, it is not as if Fred can use Ginger's body, capacities, and powers via some kind of telepathic mind control—Fred must physically impose himself to attain such control. The

---

23. I am indebted to Bill Kline for suggesting this concern.
24. Nozick, *Anarchy, State, and Utopia,* 63–87.

possibility of such seizures will affect Ginger in important ways; for instance, she may take preventive measures.

Assuming risk is another cost that befalls Ginger when Fred seeks to control her body, capacities, and powers. Ginger may become ill, infirm, or incapacitated while under Fred's control. It is one thing to bear these risks oneself as a part of growth and autonomous project pursuit. It is quite another to have such risks imposed by another with their own agenda. For that matter, knowing of the existence of sociopaths and the like, Ginger has little assurance that Fred will ever relinquish control once he has it. And further still, Ginger may never be in a position to know if Fred actually has the means to fully compensate. While not ruling out the possibility of compensation for using the body, capacities, and powers of another, such considerations indicate that actual compensation for this worsening is unlikely.[25]

The other strategy for answering this problem is to deny that compensation is possible for such interfering. On this view, having sustained control over one's body, capacities, and powers is so vital to human flourishing that compensation is impossible. Consider the too common occurrence of someone unjustly imprisoned for a lengthy period of time.[26] What compensation, we may ask, would be sufficient for such a loss? Money, opportunities, land, social recognition, and the like all seem insufficient in whatever amounts imagined to cover the loss of liberty and autonomy suffered.[27] Lost time, moreover, is not something that can be recovered. For these reasons, I believe that compensation for the worsening that occurs in using the body, capacities, and powers of others would be exceedingly high or practically impossible.

25. Suppose, however, rather than imagine a case where someone's body is seized, we imagine a more mundane case—say one where someone's hair is touched. When Fred touches Ginger's hair, he may worsen her through interference and yet easily compensate her for the loss. Individual acts of interference, like the hair-touching example, may be permitted on the account being offered. Like a million pinpricks, though, numerous instances of interfering, even in seemingly mundane ways, will have a devastating effect. Thus we may have good reasons to prohibit such practices.

26. The Georgia Innocence Project, http://www.ga-innocenceproject.org/articles.html (accessed August 14, 2007), claims that over two hundred prisoners have been exonerated via genetic testing.

27. Suppose I offered you $100 million for one day's imprisonment—wouldn't most of us accept such an offer? But first, notice how the example has been subtly changed—a deal is offered not imposed. Second, this case considers a relatively short time of imprisonment. Finally, most of us assume that if freedom is not granted after twenty-four hours that someone will come to our aid. What if we have no such guarantee—no assurances that freedom will be restored, or the $100 million paid, or that the jailor will not take other liberties?

But suppose for the sake of argument that compensation could somehow be offered in these cases. By ruling out the option of using other people's bodies provided adequate compensation, a liberty to use will have been lost but something else gained—one is now assured of exclusive control of one's own body, capacities, and powers. Giving up a liberty to use others is surely worth an exclusive right to control oneself. Thus, if we glance upward from the level of acts toward a system of social engagement, we may find that worsenings at one level may be overbalanced by benefits provided at another.

THE MORAL WEIGHTINESS OF THE PROVISO

While Gauthier uses the proviso to provide for basic rights, which in turn provide for a fair bargaining situation to determine the distribution of the benefits and burdens of social interaction, we may inquire whether or not a Pareto-based proviso has moral weight outside social contract arguments. I believe that it does.

First, to adopt a less-than-weak Pareto principle would permit individuals, in bettering themselves, to worsen others. Such provisos are troubling because they may open the door to predatory activity. Part of the force of a Pareto-based proviso is that it provides little or no grounds for rational complaint—it appears to be a discussion stopper. Moreover, if we can justify privacy rights with a more stringent principle, a principle that is harder to satisfy, then we have done something more robust, and more difficult to attack, when we reach the desired result.

To require individuals to better others while bettering themselves is to require them to give others free rides. In the absence of social interaction, what reason can be given for forcing one person, if she is to benefit herself, to benefit others? If, absent social interaction, no benefit is required, then why is such benefit required within society?[28] Moreover, those who are required to give free rides can rationally complain about being forced to do so, while those who are left (all things considered) unaffected have no room for rational complaint. The crucial distinction that underlies this position is between worsening someone's situation and failing to better it, and I take this intuition to be central to a kind of deep moral individualism.[29]

---

28. I have in mind Nozick's Robinson Crusoe case in *Anarchy, State, and Utopia*, 185.

29. The distinction between worsening someone's position and failing to better it is a hotly contested moral issue. See Gauthier, *Morals by Agreement*, and the sources cited in note 2. Shelly

As a kind of "no harm, no foul" rule a Pareto-based proviso reflects our separate existences and how we flourish through the setting and pursuing of lifelong goals and projects. If we were always at the call of maximizing utility or serving the projects of others, there would be scant room for the kinds of self-creation via project pursuit that ground moral agency. In its favor, the proviso prohibits predation and freeloading while leaving room for autonomous experiments in living.[30]

While speculative and an area of future work, I believe a Pareto-based proviso is rationally endorsed. Consider the following argument, which builds on the account of rationality sketched in the previous chapter. Rationality as a type of "master virtue" is a capacity that we develop and is both a part of human flourishing and instrumental in project pursuit.[31] Rational oughts are hypothetical in the sense that if you have some end, then you ought rationally to do this or that to achieve that end.[32] Moral oughts, on the other hand, are categorical—they prescribe actions independent of one's chosen goals or subjective preferences. But if I am correct about the connection between rationality and flourishing for beings like us, we will each share certain ends—these ends, while pluralistic, are determined by

Kagan, *The Limits of Morality* (Oxford: Oxford University Press, 1989), chap. 3; John Harris, "The Marxist Conception of Violence," *Philosophy and Public Affairs* 3 (1973–74): 192–220; John Kleinig, "Good Samaritanism," *Philosophy and Public Affairs* 5 (1975–76): 382–407; and Eric Mack, "Bad Samaritanism and the Causation of Harm," *Philosophy and Public Affairs* 9 (1979–80): 230–59, and "Causing and Failing to Prevent Harm," *Southwestern Journal of Philosophy* 7 (1976): 83–90.

30. I acknowledge that my use of the proviso urges a very different conception of what we owe each other than is typically assumed by welfare liberals such as John Rawls or Cecile Fabre. Since engaging the vast literature in support of welfare liberalism is well beyond the scope of this work, I will only make one brief comment. By my lights these theorists, in presenting their accounts of justice or what we owe each other, employ rather thick moral principles or assumptions that push the debate in a way they would like. For example, Rawls's assumptions that constrain the choice situation in the original position appear to rule out certain conceptions of justice without argument. Cecile Fabre, on the other hand, advances a "sufficiency condition" where individuals have a positive right to the material resources necessary for a decent life. If I am correct, the proviso represents a less controversial starting point—how can someone legitimately complain about an action if it leaves others better off or unaffected? Moreover, it is arguably the case that a Pareto-based proviso would be picked by Rawlsian contractors behind the veil of ignorance. See Rawls, *A Theory of Justice,* and Cecile Fabre, "Justice, Fairness, and World Ownership," *Law and Philosophy* 21 (May 2002): 249–73.

31. Korsgaard writes, "To say that there is a practical reason for something is to say that the thing is good, and vice versa." Korsgaard, "Reasons We Can Share," 25. While I agree that if X is good there exists a compelling reason to do or obtain X, it does not automatically follow from my view that if there is a reason for X, then X is good. Alas, I may have reason to satisfy some trivial want, and it would not follow that satisfying that desire would be good.

32. This is sometimes called "instrumental rationality." See David Hume, *A Treatise on Human Nature,* bk. 2, secs. 3 and 4. For a defense of an anti-instrumentalist view of rationality, see Quinn, *Morality and Action,* esp. chap. 11, "Rationality and the Human Good." See also Schmidtz, *Rational Choice and Moral Agency.*

our nature. Value theory thus shapes and restricts the theory of rationality. All collectively rational acts that aim at the good are moral, and all collectively irrational acts that aim at disvalue are immoral.[33] Collective rational oughts that aim at the good are categorical. Moreover, one benefit of grounding moral normativity in rational normativity is that no special properties are posited and no special ways of apprehending these norms are necessary.

Actions that do not violate the proviso and aim at the good are collectively rational and thus moral. In any case, such actions are morally permitted. Alternatively, actions that are both collectively irrational and aim at harm are prohibited by the proviso and immoral.[34] More minimally, such actions are inconsistent with moral requirements and prohibited.

Acts permitted by a Pareto-based proviso while aiming at human values are collectively rational; such acts promote, maintain, or further human flourishing, and given this, we each have compelling reasons to perform such acts or to stand out of the way while others perform them. Minimally, no compelling reasons can be given to prohibit such acts.

Acts that are prohibited by the proviso are collectively irrational in negative non-zero-sum cases. In a zero-sum game the gains of the winning players equal the losses of the losing players. In a non-zero-sum case it is possible for the gains and losses to add up, so to speak, to either positive or negative numbers. Suppose Fred and Ginger both receive a plus one or a minus one—the former would represent a *positive* non-zero-sum outcome, the latter a *negative* non-zero-sum outcome. In negative non-zero-sum cases someone is harmed and no good comes of it. Suppose that by using Fred's body Ginger worsens Fred and receives no benefit from the use. This would be an example of a Pareto-inferior move—a move where no one is bettered and at least one person is harmed. In such cases we each would have compelling reasons not to perform such acts.

In zero-sum cases Fred's loss would be canceled out by Ginger's gain. While such actions may violate a Pareto-based proviso, they are not collectively irrational. Take for example the case where Ginger must stand on Fred to keep her head above water (thus killing him) and vice versa. Collective rationality might have nothing to say in such cases.

Christine Korsgaard writes, "Ask yourself, what is a reason? It is not just

33. It may be possible to have collectively rational acts and collectively irrational acts that do not include a value component.

34. See Christine Korsgaard, "Skepticism About Practical Reason," in *Moral Discourse and Practice*, ed. S. Darwall, A. Gibbard, and P. Railton (Oxford: Oxford University Press, 1997), 373–87, and in the same volume, Korsgaard, "The Sources of Normativity," 389–406.

a consideration on which you in fact act, but one on which you are supposed to act; it is not just a motive, but rather a normative claim, exerting
authority over other people and yourself at other times. To say that you
have a reason is to say something relational, something which implies the
existence of another. . . . It announces that you have a claim on that other,
or acknowledges her claim on you."[35] My contention is that the proviso, in
picking out which actions are collectively rational, provides the kind of
categorical normativity of which Korsgaard speaks. David Schmidtz also
seems to echo this view: "My endorsement begins to look like characteristi-
cally moral endorsement when grounded in the thought not that *I* have
reason for endorsement but that *we* have reason for endorsement. While
endorsement as rational need not go beyond the first-person singular, endorsement as moral at a minimum goes beyond the first-person singular to
the first-person plural."[36]

The upshot of this discussion is that one may plausibly maintain that the
proviso illuminates significant relations between moral agents who pursue
projects and flourish in a physical world. Actions permitted by the proviso
are collectively rational and perhaps moral. Non-zero-sum actions prohibited by the proviso are collectively irrational and perhaps immoral.
Whether we have discovered a fact about morality (morality is equivalent
to collectively rational acts with value content) or provided one source of
moral normativity (morality is dependent on rational oughts with value
content), we will have established the weightiness or importance of the
proviso.

The structure of this now lengthy, two-part argument justifying bodily
privacy rights can be stated as follows.

Argument 1: Justifying Use and Possession Claims

P1. If the use or possession of some object does not worsen anyone,
then such actions are permitted.

---

35. Korsgaard, "Reasons We Can Share," 51.
36. Schmidtz, *Rational Choice and Moral Agency*, 143. In considering the plausibility of this
view, Schmidtz reminds us of a salient example of acting morally in a prisoner's dilemma situation. Paraphrasing Schmidtz, in such a situation each agent must make a choice independent of
her fellows, yet receive a payoff that is dependent on everyone's choices. The players act in a way
that is individually rational but results in an outcome that is collectively irrational. Each individual acting to maximize her own gain affords each a suboptimal result—if both could cooperate,
the result would be better for both. If we view the dilemma from what Smith calls the singular
perspective, reason instructs us to defect. From the plural perspective, "we find something horribly irrational about individual rationality." Schmidtz, 143.

P2. In using his own body, capacities, and powers, Fred does not (typically) worsen anyone relative to the appropriate baseline of comparison.

C3. So, Fred's use and possession of his body, capacities, and powers are permitted (in the typical case).

Argument 2: Turning Use and Possession Claims into Rights

P1. If the use or possession of some object worsens someone, then such use is prohibited.

P2. Ginger's use of Fred's body will (typically) worsen Fred compared to the appropriate base point.

C3. Ginger's use or possession of Fred's body, capacities, and powers is prohibited (in the typical case).

When Fred is free to use something or not and others are prohibited from interfering with Fred's actions, then we say that Fred has a right.[37] In this case Fred is at liberty to use his own body, capacities, and powers. Ginger and everyone else are prohibited from interfering with Fred's use and possession. If we couple this case with the notion of collective rationality and a correct account of moral value, we arrive at moral normativity.

The linchpin of both arguments is the first premise, hence the digression into justifying the moral weightiness of the proviso. If actions permitted by the proviso are collectively rational, and collective rational oughts are moral oughts, then the first argument will produce use and possession rights. If actions prohibited by the proviso are collectively irrational and collective irrational oughts are immoral, then Fred will be left with exclusive control over his body, capacities, and powers.

One difficulty is that actions prohibited by the proviso are not all *collectively* irrational, as has already been noted—Ginger may have to stand on Fred's head to avoid drowning and vice versa. But let us consider a rule covering a class of acts rather than individual acts. The rule would be something like "I use or possess the body, capacities, or powers of other individ-

---

37. For a defense of this view of rights, see Rainbolt, "Rights as Normative Constraints on Others." There are numerous competing conceptions of rights that are compatible with this argument as well. See Nozick, *Anarchy, State, and Utopia;* Lyons, *Rights, Welfare, and Mill's Moral Theory;* MacCormick, *Legal Right and Social Democracy;* Raz, *Morality of Freedom;* Waldron, "Rights in Conflict"; Hart, *Essays on Bentham* and *Essays in Jurisprudence and Philosophy;* Montague, "Two Concepts of Rights"; Steiner, *An Essay on Rights;* Rainbolt, "Rights as Normative Constraints on Others"; Feinberg, *Rights, Justice, and the Bounds of Liberty;* and Dworkin, "Rights as Trumps."

uals." Following such rules would typically yield strongly Pareto-inferior results—everyone would be worsened and no one bettered. In such cases no rational project pursuit or other candidates for flourishing such as friendship, autonomy, or understanding could take place. Conversely, following the rule "I use and possess my own body, capacities, and powers" would be strongly Pareto-superior—such use and possession typically benefits everyone and harms no one. The oughts and ought nots produced by collective rationality could thus provide for moral oughts and, in this case, physical privacy rights. Since rights are rules that cover classes of actions, such a strategy is plausible. Moreover, the possibility that rights may be overridden in specific cases is left open.

A critic of this view might argue as follows. While Fred might be permitted to stand on his head while waiting for the bus because the action is harmless, this does not count as a *justification*. Absent some special reason, it is silly to engage in such behavior. And if someone were to ask Fred why he was standing on this head, it would do no good to reply, "Because it is permitted."[38] Being permitted to do something is not a justification.

But in reply, we are not considering arbitrary or silly behavior in the formal arguments just stated—this sort of critique has missed the point of Chapter 3 and the earlier remarks about actions that are collectively rational. Having control over access to and uses of places and information is a fundamental human value. As such it is something we can each rationally endorse. Obviously this is not the case for standing on one's head while waiting for the bus. The problem with this critique is that it applies to a general form of the argument without consideration of how the argument has been narrowed.

Moreover, this critique appears to fail in the general case as well. Suppose that Fred has rights to control his body, capacities, and powers—he is at liberty to do what he wills short of violating the rights or moral claims of others. Given that he is not harming anyone else by standing on his head and he is acting within his rights, it would seem his behavior is both permitted and *justified*. It is not even clear that Fred is acting irrationally. It is only if we apply a "thicker" notion of moral justification—one that is likely to be dependent upon a particular view of ethical theory that has been assumed and not argued for—that we can deny these considerations.

---

38. An anonymous reviewer suggested this concern.

A SECOND DERIVATION OF BODILY PRIVACY RIGHTS

A second, yet related justification is possible if we treat the proviso as a mechanism that determines when use rights are overridden. Undefeated claims of this sort may be properly called rights.[39] The difference is that in the first argument the proviso itself generated the oughts in question while in the argument to come it merely strengthens moral oughts already in place. Consider the following argument:

P1. Possession, laboring on, and self-creation yield weak presumptive claims to use one's own body, capacities, and powers.[40]

P2. If no one is worsened by such use, then the weak presumptive claims generated by possession and labor are undefeated.

P3. It is the case that others are not (necessarily) worsened by some individual's use of his own body, capacities, and powers.

C4. Thus, the weak presumptive claims to use one's body, capacities, and powers, generated by possession, use, and labor, remain undefeated and rights emerge.

Justification for the view that labor or possession may generate prima facie claims against others could proceed along several lines. First, labor, intellectual effort, and creation are generally voluntary activities that can be unpleasant, exhilarating, or anything in between. That we voluntarily do these things as sovereign moral agents may be enough to warrant noninterference claims against others.[41] A second, and possibly related, justification is based on desert. Sometimes individuals who voluntarily do or fail to do certain things deserve some outcome or other. Thus, students may deserve high grades, and criminals may deserve punishment. When notions of desert are evoked, claims and obligations are made against others—these nonabsolute claims and obligations are generated by what individuals do or fail to do. Thus, in fairly uncontroversial cases of desert we are willing to acknowledge

39. See Clark Wolf, "Contemporary Property Rights, Lockean Provisos, and the Interests of Future Generations," *Ethics* 105 (1995): 791–818.

40. For a feminist defense of bodily property rights (self-ownership), see Donna Dickenson, *Property in the Body: Feminist Perspectives* (Cambridge: Cambridge University Press, 2007).

41. See Becker, *Property Rights,* 121 n. 2, and Karl Marx, *Capital* (New York: International Publishers, 1967), vol. 1, pt. 8, chap. 25.

that weak claims are generated, and if desert can properly attach to labor or creation, then claims may be generated in these cases as well.[42]

Mere possession, labor through self-creation, and minimal respect for the moral agency of others may justify the weak presumptive claims mentioned in the first premise. Simple respect for individuals would prohibit wresting from their hands an unowned object that they acquired or produced. If no one is harmed by such use or possession, what legitimate claim could counter the claims already in place? Here a Pareto-based proviso indicates when others may have legitimate claims against an established weak presumptive right of use and possession. If by possessing and using your own body, capacities, and powers you worsen no one relative to the appropriate base point, then they could have no compelling claim that would override the weak presumptive claims provided by possession and labor.

Fred's use and possession of his own body, capacities, and powers does not worsen Ginger compared to how she would be were Fred absent or had the action not occurred. Were Fred absent, Ginger would not have had any opportunities to use Fred's body. If Fred's use had not occurred, Fred would not exist—alas, we come attached to our bodies in this way. The moment before Fred's use would be the moment before Fred's existence, so to speak. In any case Ginger would not have been worsened.

Ginger's use of Fred's body does worsen Fred relative to his situation were Ginger absent, had the act not occurred, or the moment before the action. Fred's rights over his body, capacities, and powers emerge from prior use and possession claims—bodily privacy rights have been established.

Expanding simple bodily privacy rights to more general locational privacy rights could proceed several ways. Joining together informational privacy and property rights may yield a more expansive view of physical privacy. Personal information is often codified in tangible items—goods that we own or control. In many cases we erect different sorts of barriers to control access to locations because these spaces contain information about us. Through the use of property rights and contracts we may expand

42. Another justification for the view that labor or possession may generate prima facie claims against others could be grounded in respect for individual autonomy and sovereignty. As sovereign and autonomous agents, especially within the liberal tradition, we are afforded the moral and legal space to order our lives as we see fit. As long as respect for others is maintained, we are each free to set the course and direction of our own lives, to choose between various lifelong goals and projects, and to develop our capacities and talents accordingly. I hasten to add that at this point we are trying to justify weak noninterference claims.

our privacy rights. Keys, doors, fences, encryption, and other barriers serve to wall off specific places from public access. In this way, the expansion of bodily privacy rights to locational privacy rights would be dependent on property rights and informational privacy.

CONCLUSION

Understood as a right to control access to places and information and use rights as well, a right to privacy is connected to notions of self-ownership. Privacy rights are broader in that they would include rights to control personal information, whereas self-ownership does not appear to afford such control. Nevertheless, there is significant overlap between bodily privacy rights and self-ownership rights. Hence, arguments in support of self-ownership may be of some service here.

In general, there are three strategies that have been used to justify self-ownership. The first is the straightforward claim that self-ownership is intuitive and foundational. The second is an argument to the best explanation holding that self-ownership is a unifying moral principle that explains the wrongfulness of slavery, unprovoked killing, and body part redistribution.[43] The final strategy is to ground self-ownership on some more basic moral principle, such as a Pareto-based proviso.

I have employed these same strategies in justifying physical privacy rights. Those who feel the same theoretical pull I do may need nothing more than the first two strategies. Nevertheless, both of these strategies rest on our moral intuitions and are thereby subject to the following sort of critique. Those who do not have these intuitions will find them groundless—intuitions, alas, are not justifications. Simply asserting contrary intuitions would halt the dialogue, hence the digression into the complexities surrounding the proviso and the argument in support of the proviso. If correct, we will have some compelling support for our moral intuitions.

While I have used the proviso as a vehicle to establish locational privacy rights, and indicated why the actions it permits and prohibits are rationally and perhaps morally important, we may wonder how the proviso fares as a general constraint on action—as a foundational moral principle. While somewhat speculative, I believe that a Pareto-based proviso may be such a

---

43. Eric Mack uses this strategy in "Self-Ownership, Marxism, and Egalitarianism," *Politics, Philosophy, and Economics* 1 (2002): 237–76.

principle. Justifying this claim would take us well beyond the scope of our concern and will not be considered further at present.

If I am correct, controlling access to one's body, capacities, and powers is permitted by the proviso. In most cases, interfering with someone's body rights will be non-zero-sum and prohibited by the proviso. Bodily or locational privacy rights will have thus been established. The last four chapters of this work will focus on when and how this right may be justifiably overridden.

Bodily privacy rights are Aristotelian necessities, and as such it is not surprising that we consider them ends and collectively rational. Moreover, I think it is plausible to maintain that collectively rational oughts are moral oughts. Collectively rational oughts are categorical, prescribe action, and aid in conflict resolution. Thus, the theory of the good, coupled with an account of collective rational oughts, may determine part of the theory of the right.

5

PROVIDING FOR INFORMATIONAL PRIVACY RIGHTS

The introduction and advancement of what has become known as "information technologies" has dramatically changed our abilities to control personal information. Bits of information stored in analog form in various locations have now been digitized and, in many cases, linked to ever-expanding information networks. Individual profiles related to purchasing preferences and habits assembled through data mining are bought and sold like any other commodity. The ease with which highly personal information is retrieved, compiled, disseminated, and stored represents an important change from our analog past. While it is true that most, if not all, of the privacy invasions mentioned in the chapters to follow could have happened prior to the "digital age," the difference is not just a matter of degree—there is a difference in kind.

Genetic profiling, facial recognition technology, video surveillance, computer spyware, cell phone records, and financial information databases are each implicated in the ever-expanding threat to informational privacy. As these technologies become linked and searchable, they will offer up private lives for consumption by those with access.[1]

Many do not find any of this troubling in the least. "What do you have

---

1. Many of these threats to privacy are examined in Robert O'Harrow's *No Place to Hide* (New York: Free Press, 2006).

to hide?" they might ask. Moreover, since most of the information found via the sources mentioned is "publicly" available, it is not your information to control. When an individual steps onto a public street and others take note, this bit of information has entered the commons and is beyond the control of any individual. There is no privacy in public places.

I think that this view of information access, control, and use is false—there is privacy in public. Building on the account offered in Chapter 4, I will offer an argument that justifies individuals owning or having claims to their own personal information. If individuals have informational privacy rights, and we couple this together with rights to control access to places or locations, a general right to privacy will have been established. I hasten to note that if correct, the account offered will not produce absolute or unbreachable walls of privacy: the question of when, how, and where privacy rights may be overridden will be considered in the chapters that follow.

JUSTIFYING INFORMATIONAL PRIVACY RIGHTS

Before offering an argument in support of informational privacy rights, I would like to discuss two important differences between what I have called locational or physical privacy and informational privacy—differences that parallel in many ways the differences between intangible property and physical property. Information, including sensitive personal information, is "nonrivalrous," which means that it can be possessed, consumed, or considered by many individuals concurrently. Unlike physical bodies, bicycles, and cellular phones, which can only be used by one person at a time, the set of facts that describe your last vacation can be possessed and used by many individuals simultaneously.[2]

One way to clarify the nonrivalrous nature of information possession or ownership is to compare it with the ownership of physical or tangible property. Physical property rights restrict what can be done with one's property. For example, you cannot justifiably run your car through my house. Tangible property rights also limit intangible property rights in that you cannot justifiably instantiate your intangible property in my physical property—you can't build your new motor out of my nuts and bolts without consent.

---

2. It may be objected that some intangible works are rivalrous, for example, the *Mona Lisa* or Michelangelo's *David*. What is rivalrous about these works is not the ideas that are embodied in the canvas or stone, but the physical works themselves. We can all hang *copies* of the *Mona Lisa* in our living rooms—we just can't have the original embodiment.

As with tangible property rights, intangible property rights restrict what individuals can do with their physical property. You cannot copy my intangible property and instantiate it in your physical property. The way in which intangible property is different from tangible property is that rights to intangible property do not necessarily limit other intangible property rights. My right to control the set of facts that describes the events of your last camping trip does not necessarily limit your right to control the same facts. Assuming that we both have legitimate title, our rights are nonrivalrous in this respect.

Basically, goods can be created or discovered, and are rivalrous or nonrivalrous.[3] Loosely speaking, created objects are those that are brought into existence by the autonomous actions of some agent, whereas discovered objects are those which exist independent of autonomous action. For example, the stick that you come upon while walking would be discovered. If you were to modify the stick—maybe you shorten it, carve a handle, and the like—those new parts would be created, not discovered. Or again, if you decide to go to the park this afternoon, the facts that capture the event are created, whereas your age or height would be, in the typical case, discovered.

Furthermore, while personal information is both discovered and created, either type can be copied. The fact that Fred has cancer may be considered by many individuals at the same time yet be genetically determined. Information about Fred's capacity to play guitar would be created, in a sense, by Fred himself. Had Fred not acted, there would be no capacity and hence no information about Fred's musical virtuosity.

Some may argue, however, that a distinction between created and discovered personal information, marked by what is autonomously chosen or not, is somewhat murky. Consider Fred's inability to play golf. Surely this inability is something he could have overcome. Given his choice, perhaps it is correct to say that his inability was chosen and thus created rather than discovered. While it is possible that some inabilities are created and thus chosen, for example, my listening to loud rock music causes me to lose the ability to hear, most are not. Human beings come into the world with few capacities and abilities and a practically infinite number of inabilities and incapacities. Finite life spans and other facts of human nature limit the

---

3. See Patrick Croskery, "The Intellectual Property Literature: A Structured Approach," in *Owning Scientific and Technical Information*, ed. Vivian Weil and John Snapper (New Brunswick: Rutgers University Press, 1989), 270.

number of abilities and talents we may develop. Inabilities that are impossible for beings like us, such as flying unaided to the moon, are not and cannot be chosen. These facts about us are discovered, not created. Inabilities that are within our power to change but have not been overcome through autonomous action are also discovered. We don't create these inabilities—they exist prior to or come into being along with our agency.

The same is true about facts. The fact that Ginger is thirty-six-years old or that she was born on Earth rather than the moon exists independent of her choices. Facts that are within our power to change but have not been created through autonomous action are also discovered. As with inabilities we don't create these facts. Another class of facts are those that are created but not through autonomous action. For example, when a flea jumps in the air or when a small child cries, the facts generated are created but not freely chosen.

THE ORIGINAL ACQUISITION OF INFORMATION

As already noted, while privacy, broadly defined as a right to control bodies and information, is morally valuable, it has not been established that individuals have moral claims to control personal information. One way to begin is by asking how claims to control intangible objects, like facts about someone, are generated. In the argument that follows I will employ a version of John Locke's proviso on acquisition. "For this labor being the unquestionable property of the laborer, no man but he can have a right to what that is once joined to, at least where there is *enough and as good left for others.*"[4] Locke claims that so long as the proviso that enough and as good is satisfied, an acquisition does not prejudice anyone. Viewed as a kind of "no harm, no foul" rule, actions that pass this standard leave little room for rational complaint—I have called this a Pareto-based proviso. As with the derivation of physical privacy rights, the strategy will be to use a version of the proviso to generate informational privacy claims and rights. If using and controlling one's own personal information does not worsen others relative to the appropriate base point, then use claims will have been

4. John Locke, *The Second Treatise of Government*, ed. C. B. Macpherson (Indianapolis: Hackett, 1980), chap. 5, sec. 27; italics mine.

generated.[5] Consider a modified version of the final argument offered in support of physical privacy in the previous chapter.

P1. The value of privacy related to human well-being grounds a weak presumptive claim to use and control personal information.

P2. Respect for persons, possession, self-creation, and project pursuit grounds a weak presumptive claim to use and control personal information.

P3. If no one is worsened by such use, then the weak presumptive claims generated by the value of privacy and respect for persons are undefeated—actions that pass a Pareto-based proviso are permitted (no harm, no foul).

P4. It is typically the case that others are not worsened by some individual's use and possession of their own personal information.

C5. Thus, the weak presumptive claims to use and control such information are, in many cases, undefeated, and moral claims (perhaps rights) emerge.

The importance of privacy for human flourishing, along with a concession that the promotion of certain fundamental values is a moral requirement, may provide adequate support for the first premise. Only a pure deontologist would deny that good and bad consequences, especially related to basic needs, generate weak presumptive claims.

Support for the second and third premises was offered in Chapter 4 and need not be rehearsed. The truth of the fourth premise seems fairly obvious in light of my characterization of a Pareto-based proviso. When individuals use and control their own personal information, it will be the case that others are not necessarily worsened. Consider some health-related fact that Crusoe comes to know about himself. To consider whether or not Friday has been worsened, we compare how he is prior to Crusoe's coming to know the fact in question to Friday's situation after Crusoe's discovery. In either case Friday is unaware and is thereby not worsened by Crusoe's use and control. On the other hand, suppose that Crusoe knows that he is a

---

5. I would like to note that those who claim collective ownership of information also face the problem of original acquisition. Why is it the case that just because someone enters a public space that society automatically obtains moral claims to control the information in question? Simply claiming that the information was found in a public place does not count as justification for collective control—there is no argument here, just an assertion. This sort of concern was originally raised by Nozick. See *Anarchy, State, and Utopia,* 178.

violent sleep-walker and Friday is planning to sleep nearby. In this case, it seems that Friday has been (or will be) worsened by Crusoe's nondisclosure.

If the argument so far has been compelling, then it will be conceded that individuals have moral claims to use and control access to their own personal information. But since information is nonrivalrous, it is not clear that using and controlling personal information about others worsens them. To simplify matters, imagine a state-of-nature situation where Fred exists in isolation. Over the years, Fred may acquire a host of information about himself—say for example, he likes spicy food. In fact each of Fred's actions, his life story so to speak, may be captured as information. Suppose that when Ginger comes along she is not worsened by Fred's possession and use of the aforementioned information. Fred's use and possession claims would then be undefeated, and rights may emerge. In any case, Fred's right to control information about himself does not exclude the possibility of others owning such information. As already noted, an important feature of intangible objects, like information, is that they may be nonrivalrously consumed.

It is also the case that Ginger does not *necessarily* worsen Fred by seeking to use and possess information about him. Suppose that upon seeing Fred, Gingers notes that he has green eyes. Surely Ginger's mere possession of such information does not worsen Fred relative to how he would be in her absence or compared to the moment before the acquisition. But when Ginger offers information about Fred up for public consumption—suppose that she shares this information with a much wider audience than Fred could have ever reached in the course of his daily public activity—she does worsen him in terms of increased risk, commercial exploitation, and the like. This is, in essence, the first argument that I will offer for exclusive informational privacy rights. The second argument will link together the weak presumptive claims that labor, respect for others, and desert may offer, with physical property rights, to secure informational privacy.

Underlying the arguments justifying informational privacy rights that I will consider is the distinction between public and private. As was noted in earlier chapters, we may characterize the condition of privacy, as opposed to a privacy right, as a state of voluntary separation where an individual retreats from contact with her fellows employing the use of walls, both physical and mental, clothes, locked doors, and the like. Through these mechanisms distance and separation are achieved—a condition that is essential for human flourishing if the conclusion of Chapter 2 is correct. Private space is typically guaranteed by property rights, although not always.

But as social animals our need for disassociation is counterbalanced by our need for contact with others. In our public lives we step from behind walls and diminish distance. We reach out and associate with our fellows, offering some of ourselves up for public consumption while holding other aspects of ourselves undisclosed. The distinctions between acquaintances, friends, family, and lovers can be understood in terms of differing levels of access.[6] Somewhere on the continuum between one's innermost thoughts that are never shared and what one offers up for anyone's consideration we switch from the private to the public. I am not overly concerned with the exact point where the switch occurs, although my guess is that it is in large part culturally determined.

Jeff Weintraub delineates four broad conceptions of the public/private distinction that play important roles in several distinct discourses.

1. The liberal-economistic model, dominant in most "public policy" analysis . . . which sees the public/private distinction primarily in terms of the distinction between state administration and the market economy. 2. The republican-virtue approach, which sees the "public" realm in terms of political community and citizenship, analytically distinct from *both* the market and the administrative state. 3. The approach . . . which sees the "public" realm as a sphere of fluid and polymorphous sociability, and seeks to analyze the cultural and dramatic conventions that make it possible. 4. . . . . to conceive of the distinction . . . in terms of the distinction between the family and the larger economic and political order.[7]

While admittedly imprecise, the conception that I favor contains elements of 1, 3, and 4. When facts about someone are made public "in terms of the distinction between the family and the larger economic and political order," risks are created. Moreover, these imposed risks are morally relevant when determining harm.

6. See Rachels, "Why Privacy Is Important," 323–33.
7. Jeffrey Weintraub, "The Theory and Politics of the Public/Private Distinction," in *Public and Private in Thought and Practice*, ed. J. Weintraub and K. Kumar (Chicago: University of Chicago Press, 1997), 7. See also Benn and Gaus, *Public and Private in Social Life.*

THE RISK ARGUMENT

Central to the risk argument is the claim that in connected societies where information trading is both efficient and nearly without cost, disclosure of personal information opens individuals up to certain risks—such as being controlled by entities with their own agendas.[8] Typically, such control comes in two flavors. First, governments use such information to retain domination and expand power. The following quotation from a Chinese military newspaper applies a number of these issues to information war.

> After the Gulf War, when everyone was looking forward to eternal peace, a new military revolution emerged. This revolution is essentially a transformation from the mechanized warfare of the industrial age to the information warfare of the information age. Information warfare is a war of decisions and control, a war of knowledge, and a war of intellect. The aim of information warfare will be gradually changed from "preserving oneself and wiping out the enemy" to "preserving oneself and controlling the opponent." Information warfare includes electronic warfare, tactical deception, strategic deterrence, propaganda warfare, psychological warfare, network warfare, and structural sabotage.[9]

Two further examples should suffice in establishing the plausibility of this claim. Keeping records of citizens has been, and continues to be, a way for governments to maintain control over their populations. Nicholas Kristof writes:

> Behind a locked door on the second floor of the Beijing Engineering Design Institute is a small room stacked with files from floor to ceiling.
> There is a file here on each of the institute's 600 employees, and although they are never allowed to peek inside, they live their lives with their files looming over them.
> As part of China's complex system of social control and surveillance, the authorities keep a *dangan,* or file, on virtually everyone

8. For a nice discussion of risk and harm, see Kagan, *Limits of Morality,* 87–91. Kagan's presentation seemingly runs parallel to or provides support for the view offered here.

9. *Jiefangjun Bao,* Chinese army newspaper; cited in John Carlin, "A Farewell to Arms," *Wired,* May 1997.

except peasants. Indeed, most Chinese have two *dangan:* one at their workplace and another in their local police station. . . . A file is opened on each urban citizen as he or she enters elementary school, and it shadows the person through school to college and employment.[10]

Particularly for officials, students, professors, and Communist Party members, the *dangan* contain political evaluations that affect career prospects and permission to leave the country.

A different case, but one that is equally alarming, is what happened in Orchemenos, a small village in Greece. In that village, there are many individuals who have a gene that causes sickle-shaped red blood cells. The problem is that when two parents both carry the gene their offspring may develop sickle-cell anemia. In an effort to prevent this disease government researchers tested everyone in the village so that marriages between gene carriers could be avoided: "A group of researchers tested the villagers at Orchemenos, assuming that carriers would behave rationally and would pair with noncarriers in order to mix the genes safely and protect the community's children. The noncarriers, however, refused to cooperate. Even though the gene is harmless on its own, carriers became stigmatized and noncarriers refused to marry them. In the end, the carriers became a shunned subclass who were forced to marry among themselves, making the situation even worse than before."[11]

While the researchers' goals were noble, they obviously failed to foresee the ramifications of disclosing this kind of personal information.[12]

Second, corporations may use personal information to overwhelm individuals in a sea of solicitations and promotional advertisements. A classic example is when Equifax produced Lotus Marketplace, a database full of

10. Nicholas D. Kristof, "For Chinese, Lives in Files, Perpetually Open and Overhead," *International Herald Tribune,* March 19, 1992, 5; quoted in Anne Wells Branscomb, *Who Owns Information?* (New York: Basic Books, 1994), 16.

11. Charles Platt, "Evolution Revolution," *Wired,* January 1997, 200.

12. Current American practice allows companies and individuals to gather, sell, and buy almost any kind of information, including sensitive personal information. Moreover, access to personal information stored on databases held by companies and other citizens is purely voluntary—companies do not have to show you the information that they have gathered about you. And in any case, you have very little control over what can be done with this information. If a company or the government wants to sell this information, there is little that you can do about it. For example, the U.S. Postal Service sells your change of address to marketing companies, who then send you mountains of junk mail. The USPS gets paid by the junk mailers for the change of address and the junk mail. See Branscomb, *Who Owns Information?* 9.

personal information, with the intent of selling it to small businesses, which could then focus on likely customers. Corporations also use personal information to control employees. For example, medical information, drug habits, marital status, and results from psychological tests may follow an employee like capitalist *dangan*.

In the most extreme cases, sharing personal information about someone else with a third party, say a home address and religious affiliation, may have serious consequences. German Jews in the 1930s, and more recently Muslims in the United States, know this all too well. In these instances an individual acting without an agenda may cause great harm by providing information to a government or corporation.

There used to be domains of person's life that were totally inaccessible. A person's home and bedroom, notebook and hard drive, were all sanctuaries against the prying eyes and ears of others. It is alarming that digital technology is sweeping these domains away. Deborah Johnson accurately captures this sentiment: "We have the technological capacity for the kind of massive, continuous surveillance of individuals that was envisioned in such frightening early twentieth-century science fiction works as George Orwell's *1984* and Zamyatin's *We*. The only differences between what is now possible and what was envisioned then are that much of the surveillance of individuals that is now done is by private institutions (marketing firms, insurance companies, credit agencies), and much of the surveillance now is via electronic records instead of by direct human observation or through cameras."[13]

In the typical case, without video, audio, and other kinds of robust surveillance, when Fred steps onto a public street, he both creates certain facts about himself and relinquishes exclusive control of this information to those who share the public domain. The information captured by others is held in nonpermanent mediums like memory and is acquired by a relatively small number of people. In such cases Fred incurs few risks and the sharing of such information by second and third parties poses little threat. Please note that Fred could disguise himself or go out at night to further limit public access to personal information. Hinting at the property rights argument to come, Fred could use his property to justifiably limit access to personal information.

But when information is captured digitally via video and audio surveillance or with some other more permanent medium, Fred is subjected to

---

13. Deborah Johnson, *Computer Ethics* (Upper Saddle River, N.J.: Prentice Hall, 1994), 84.

increased risks. Such information may lie unused for decades and then be resurrected by those in power or with commercial agendas. Societies where personal information trading or data mining is facilitated through the use of technology, like digital environments, the use and control of personal information opens individuals up to risks and losses. If so, the disclosure of such information will worsen Fred relative to the base point of absence or prior to disclosure, and a step toward informational privacy rights will have been established.

A serious objection to the risk argument is the possibility that the risks imposed on individuals through the manipulation of personal information are counterbalanced by other values such as increased opportunities or security. Data-mining companies that gather information about Ginger's purchasing habits may be able to more narrowly pitch products and services. If Ginger likes cowboy boots, data-mining companies could provide her with information about the most up-to-date styles. Alternatively, Ginger's government could provide enhanced security for her and others by using data-mining techniques to search for criminal behavior.

To use an admittedly imperfect analogy, consider the risks foisted on someone else when they are included in a game of Russian roulette without consenting. The typical game consists of a gun with six chambers, one bullet, and somebody's head. The bullet is loaded, the chamber is spun, the gun is pointed at someone, and the trigger is pulled. Surely the risks involved in such a game worsen the victim relative to the appropriate base point. But one could argue that having digitally stored personal information available for others to exploit is not like playing a game where the gun has only six chambers—it is more like a game where the gun has a thousand chambers and some of the chambers yield benefits not burdens. True enough, but then again we are not playing a one-round game either. Imagine playing an iterated game with hundreds, if not thousands, of rounds played over a lifetime. Moreover, as one plays the game the risks of certain payoffs may increase with the changing times. And in the typical case, the burdens and benefits will be imposed, not freely chosen.

Two further considerations, suggested by Helen Nissenbaum, deserve mention at this point. Nissenbaum notes that data shifting, defined as using information gathered for one purpose in some new way, violates what she calls "contextual integrity." "In the public surveillance currently practiced, information is routinely shifted from one sphere to another, as when, for example, information about your supermarket purchases is sold to a list service for magazine subscriptions."[14] An admittedly extreme case of data shifting occurred when a stalker of actress Rebecca Shaefer secured her home address from state licensing records and murdered her.

These considerations provide a compelling answer to what might be called the consent argument *against* informational privacy. On this view individuals have no privacy rights because they have, by stepping into the public domain or by sharing information, agreed that others may own and control this information. But even if consent, however thin it might be, is given for the initial disclosure of disparate bits of information, it does not follow that consent has also been given for data shifting and the aggregation of this information.[15]

Furthermore, the notion of consent implied in this argument against informational privacy may be challenged. Appearing in public is a necessity for most of us. Thus, the argument that individuals have no privacy rights in public because they "freely" choose to relinquish personal information is suspect—consent of this sort is clearly not the sort of "discussion stopper" that some think. Or consider the case where a "Watcher" videotapes someone else's every public move and uploads this information to the Web. It would be difficult to maintain that by entering the public domain one has consented to such monitoring.

This is not to say that privacy should never be overridden for the sake of increased security or market opportunities, but rather that, given the risks and benefits of such disclosure, the rule, both moral and legal, should be against allowing such activity.

BODILY ACCESS AND PROPERTY RIGHTS ARGUMENT

Suppose that Fred creates and wears an antidisclosure suit that shields him in public spaces entirely. All that his fellows know is that someone is present—they do not know if Fred is old or young, male or female, tall or short. In simply wearing his antidisclosure suit Fred does nothing wrong—he does not necessarily worsen anyone. In this example to discover much about Fred would require violating his property rights or liberty rights. The

14. Helen Nissenbaum, "Protecting Privacy in an Information Age: The Problem of Privacy in Public," *Law and Philosophy* 17 (1998): 585.

15. See Chapter 8 for an analysis of consent-based arguments for relinquishing privacy rights. See also Adam D. Moore, "Employee Monitoring and Computer Technology: Evaluative Surveillance v. Privacy," *Business Ethics Quarterly* 10 (2000): 697–709.

suit and what it shields are his to control. While odd and probably perverse, if Fred were to reveal nothing about himself to anyone at any time it would be perfectly appropriate.[16] Another way to put the point is that Fred's rights to control access to his body, capacities, and powers—what I have called physical *privacy* rights—coupled with physical *property* rights, will afford him near complete control over the information that he creates through daily activity.

As noted earlier, the information that Fred chooses to reveal about himself may be owned by Ginger and others. A part of reaching out and developing social relationships with others will be the voluntary disclosure of personal information. Nevertheless, whatever kind of information we are considering there is a gathering point that individuals have control over. For example, in purchasing a new car and filling out the loan application, few would deny we each have the right to demand that such information not be sold to other companies. I would argue that this is true for any disclosed personal information, whether it be patient questionnaire information, video rental records, voting information, or credit applications. In agreeing with this view, one first has to agree that individuals have the right to control their own personal information. Binding agreements about controlling information presuppose that one of the parties has the right to control this information.

As a direct consequence of the proliferation of computer environments, information-gathering points will become the battleground over the control of personal information. Individuals who wish to maintain control over this kind of information will insist on confidential disclosure agreements before yielding any personal information. The American Express Card case is a nice example of individuals controlling how personal information is gathered and sold. In May 1992 American Express, under pressure from various sources, agreed to allow cardholders to opt out of the credit company's policy of gathering and selling the purchasing habits of its members. For the young and the yet unborn, information-gathering points will be very important. Those who wish to maintain privacy will have to be very careful with personal information. For the rest of us, who already are on at least a hundred mailing lists and fifteen databases, these points are important as well.[17] Old and outdated information is relatively worthless, and so as time passes we can, in a sense, distance ourselves from old personal data.

16. Assuming of course that Fred is not shielding immoral *and* criminal activity.
17. Branscomb, *Who Owns Information?* 9.

Aside from controlling information-gathering points though the use of contracts or the manipulation of physical property, there is at least one other way in which individuals can protect themselves from invasions of privacy by digital monitoring.[18] This idea was first suggested by J. P. Barlow of the Electronic Frontier Foundation. It may be possible to detach one's physical self from one's virtual self through the use of encryption—the online equivalent of an antidisclosure suit. The proposal is to encrypt all information that links data about you to your name, address, or social security number—leaving no unencrypted links between your physical self and your electronic identity. Individuals would then just become numbers that are identified with specific data packets. Barlow writes, "From the standpoint of credit assurance, there is no difference between the information that John Perry Barlow always pays his bills on time or that Account #345 8849 23433 (to whomever that may belong) is equally punctilious."[19] And better still, different kinds of personal information could be encrypted with different codes, resulting in better protection. I may wish my doctor to have access to my physical self and to my medical records—suppose the tests that she just administered show a need for surgery—but there is no need for her to know my voting record or that I prefer to watch "spaghetti" westerns rather than Friday night situation comedies.

While there may be a number of problems with maintaining an encrypted identity over long periods of time, it should be clear how technology can work on behalf of individuals maintaining control over their own personal information. The growth of computer technology may have played a leading role in laying open personal information for public consumption, but it can also provide part of the answer. Through the use of encryption technology, coupled with the control of information-gathering points, individuals will be able to secure personal information and privacy.

18. Gary Marx proposes the following. "1. Don't give out any more information than is necessary. 2. Don't say things over a cellular or cordless phone that you would mind having overheard by strangers. 3. Ask your bank to sign an agreement that it will not release information about your accounts to anyone lacking legal authorization and that in event of legal authorization, it will contact you within two days. 4. Obtain copies of your credit, health, and other records and check for accuracy and currency. 5. If you are refused credit, a job, a loan, or an apartment, ask why. 6. Remember that when you respond to telephone or door-to-door surveys, the information will go into a databank. 7. Realize that when you purchase a product or service and file a warranty card or participate in a rebate program, your name may well be sold to a mailing-list company." Marx, "Privacy and Technology," *Whole Earth Review,* Winter 1991, 91–95; quoted in Johnson, *Computer Ethics,* 100.

19. John Perry Barlow, "Private Life in Cyberspace," *Communications of the ACM* 34 (1991): 23–25.

To summarize the bodily control and property rights argument in support of informational privacy, we begin with four plausible claims. First, individuals have use and possession claims concerning information about themselves. Second, individuals have access control rights over their bodies, capacities, and powers. Third, individuals may acquire physical and intellectual property that will aid in restricting access to personal information. And finally, a general right to make contracts will afford individuals further control over personal information. Taken together, these rights, claims, and liberties provide the foundation for informational privacy.

One problem for the second argument in support of informational privacy is that given disparities in holdings and the subsequent ability to fence oneself off from the outside world, some individuals will have more privacy than others. The rich will be able to hide behind walls, fences, lawyers, and butlers, while the not so fortunate will be left exposed to public consumption. Consider the following case.

> On the night of October 30, 1979 . . . an NBC television camera crew entered the apartment of Dave and Brownie Miller in Los Angeles, without their consent, to film the activities of Los Angeles Fire Department paramedics called to the Miller home to administer life-saving techniques to Dave Miller, who had suffered a heart attack in his bedroom. The NBC television camera crew not only filmed the paramedics' attempts to assist Miller, but NBC used the film on its nightly news without obtaining anyone's consent. In addition, after it had received complaints from both Brownie Miller and her daughter, Marlene Miller Belloni, NBC later used portions of the film in a commercial advertising an NBC "mini-documentary" about the paramedics' work.[20]

One would suspect that if the Millers had employed guards, security fences, and perhaps "high-priced" lawyers, they would have been successful in protecting their privacy.

While true, I believe that this objection is fairly anemic. Individuals will still be able to keep sensitive personal information secret by manipulating what property they do hold. It is not as if disguises or paying cash will cease to work. Individuals with little in terms of property holdings will still be able to restrict information leakage through second and third parties via

---

20. *Brownie Miller et al. v. National Broadcasting Co. et al.*, 187 Cal. App. 3d 1463 (1986).

contracts and agreements. And finally, if moral norms are to be reflected in the law, legal privacy guarantees codified in state and federal statutes will cover everyone. Even the Millers had a door to control access to private spaces—that the door was open is meaningless when determining trespass and intrusion.

Moreover, that a moral right to informational privacy, built up out of bodily access rights, information use claims, physical and intellectual property, and a general right to make contracts, is held in differing degrees is hardly surprising or alarming. Finally, if such disparities open certain individuals up to more risk, then we could fall back on the risk argument to secure informational privacy.

PEEPING TOMS AND INFORMATIONAL PRIVACY

Having said all of this, I would like to test the model of informational privacy that has been offered with a very tricky case dealing with personal information control. A salient example of a privacy violation is the all too familiar garden-variety Peeping Tom. Suppose Tom, after sneaking through the bushes and pulling aside a blind, licentiously watches Ginger, who is about her house. Maybe Tom watches Ginger take a shower or dress for bed. We can all agree that what Tom does is immoral given that Ginger does not know Tom is there and has not consented to being watched. But why? The answer typically given is that Tom violated Ginger's right to privacy.

In a two-person world it might be difficult to see how Ginger is worsened by Tom's peeping. Putting aside property rights violations—Tom is standing on Ginger's land and has interfered with Ginger's control of the window blind—it would seem that Ginger is not worsened in terms of her level of material well-being. Tom's actions do not open Ginger up to third-party risks of control or manipulation because there are no third parties. Moreover, suppose that he is not recording the encounter so any information obtained will fade with his memory.

It does no good to say that Ginger is worsened by Tom's peeping because she has a general wish or desire not to be watched in this way. Desires and wishes are not the foundations of value claims. If they were, then Tom's preference to view Ginger would have moral weight as well.[21] One could

21. See Chapter 3 and Moore, "Values, Objectivity, and Relationalism."

claim that Ginger's interests have been violated. But the "interest" view of harm is equally subjective. For example, Joel Feinberg seems to equate violating someone's interests with morally harming them. "We must include in the category of 'hurts' not only physical pains but also forms of mental distress. . . . Some forms of mental distress (e.g., "hurt feelings") can be ruled out simply on the ground that they are too minor or trivial to warrant interference. Others are so severe that they can lead to mental breakdowns."[22] First, one wonders who it is that gets to decide which interests are trivial or minor. Second, it is not at all clear that extreme mental distress counts either—for example, a grandmother I know is severely distressed and depressed by the existence of those who do not share her religious views. The very existence of atheists causes her extreme emotional pain. It would seem that those who defend an interest account of harm would have to acknowledge this sort of emotional distress as a moral harm—perhaps sanctioning coercion. Finally, the interest view (as with the preference or desire fulfillment account) may be modified by some mechanism that indicates which interests count—the typical candidates usually smuggle in an objectifying component like strictures of rationality or a basic needs account of value.

Continuing with the Peeping Tom case, in a two-person world we may have to say that Tom does nothing wrong in watching Ginger. In this way the Peeping Tom case would mirror the Demento case discussed in Chapter 4. In the real world, however, Tom's acquisition of information about Ginger does create risks that are morally relevant to Ginger's well-being. Maybe Tom innocently mentions Ginger's open window to James the burglar. Maybe impulses to "just look" will lead to infatuation and desires for possession. Moreover, Ginger's knowledge of Tom's act is irrelevant to questions of bettering and worsening. She might never know of the risks foisted on her by Tom yet still be worsened.

As we move upward from the two-person case to institutions, legal systems, and cultural norms that affect relations across numerous individuals, and if we keep in mind that voluntary separation is necessary for human well-being, then we will have provided adequate grounds for forbidding Tom's behavior. His act by itself may not worsen, but allowing such a practice would. Allowing a practice of "secret" watching would expose targets

22. Joel Feinberg, "Grounds for Coercion: Hard Cases for the Harm Principle," in *Applied Social and Political Philosophy*, ed. Elizabeth Smith and Gene Blocker (Englewood Cliffs, N.J.: Prentice Hall, 1994), 270.

to risks to which they have not consented and likely cause preventive measures to be taken. In the most general terms, such a practice would allow the Toms to obtain power over their targets and foist upon them risks not unlike the secret spying programs used by the government.

One virtue of this account of informational privacy is that the "no harm, no foul" rule applies to individual acts of information control and to practices or institutions of information management. For example, the game of capitalism does not need to include the practice of buying and selling "sucker" phone lists by telemarketers. We have all heard of the horror stories where some telemarketer calls a lonely elderly person and proceeds to sell junk at exorbitant prices. Selling genetic information about policyholders to insurance companies would also violate the harm standard—in the absence of these practices, the individuals in question would be better off.

Moreover, this account provides justification for sex offender notification laws. Convicted pedophiles and rapists have given up rights to control information related to their crimes by violating the physical body rights of their victims. And given the high rates of recidivism connected to some of these crimes, risks are foisted on communities where these predators reside.

If I am correct, individuals have justified use and possession claims over personal information so long as the nonworsening proviso is satisfied. Since information is nonrivalrous, however, this argument does not justify informational privacy—personal information may be possessed and used by others without harm. But the digitization, manipulation, and dissemination of personal information may unjustifiably harm by imposing risks. And independent of risks, physical privacy and property rights may secure informational privacy—perhaps mandating an "opt in" policy with respect to personal information trading and sharing.

As noted in the opening, none of this should be construed as supporting unbreachable walls of privacy. It is not as if we should visit serious legal or moral punishment on someone for documenting a private fact about someone else. Nevertheless, if the account offered in the last few chapters is correct, then documenting or sharing private facts does have a moral component that should be recognized. Unlike one individual capturing information about another on a home movie or family picture, the digitization, dissemination, and broadcasting of private facts have clear moral importance.

STRENGTHENING LEGAL PRIVACY RIGHTS

It has been argued that individuals have locational privacy rights as well as rights to control personal information. These rights or moral claims, however, are not absolute. A theory that generated exceptionless moral rights that could never be justifiably overridden is as absurd as the view that such rights should be tossed aside for mere incremental gains in social utility. In the chapters to come the "weightiness" of privacy claims will be considered in the areas of freedom of speech, drug testing, free access arguments, and public accountability or security. If employers have overriding rights to monitor employees, digital natives and hackers strong arguments in support of free access, or law enforcement agents compelling claims of security, then the presumption in favor of privacy, already established, will have been counterbalanced by competing claims.

The task at hand, however, is to determine the nature and scope of legal protections for privacy. If legal systems are to reflect important moral norms, then privacy protections must be codified in the law. In recent times privacy protections have not fared well—as we shall see. The first part of this chapter will offer an overview of the legal protections of privacy in the United States. Privacy protections are typically broken into three general categories—common law privacy torts, constitutional provisions, and statutory regulations. The second part will focus on numerous cases that indicate the weakness of these privacy protections. In the third part, I will argue that by strengthening the tort of intrusion we may move toward a more robust protection of this basic moral right—the chapters to come will consider how legal privacy might be strengthened in other areas.

LEGAL PROTECTIONS OF PRIVACY IN THE UNITED STATES

As I have noted, legal privacy protections within the United States can be broken down into three categories. Common law torts protect privacy by allowing individuals to sue others in civil court. Constitutional privacy protects U.S. citizens from unjustified governmental intrusions into private domains. Finally, various statutory regulations at the local, state, and federal levels protect privacy. We will take them up in turn.

Privacy Torts

While privacy protections were implicated in the common law doctrines of nuisance, trespass, and restrictions on eavesdropping, one of the first discussions of privacy occurred in Judge Thomas Cooley's treatise on torts in 1880.[1] In *De May v. Roberts* (1881) the Michigan Supreme Court echoed Cooley's view acknowledging an individual's right to be let alone. "The plaintiff had a legal right to the privacy of her apartment . . . and the law secures to her this right by requiring others to observe it, and to abstain from its violation."[2]

In 1890, Samuel D. Warren and Louis D. Brandeis issued a call to arms in their article "The Right to Privacy." Hinting at times to come, Warren and Brandeis noted: "Recent inventions and business methods call attention to the next step which must be taken for the protection of the person, and for securing to the individual what Judge Cooley calls the right 'to be let alone.' Instantaneous photographs and newspaper enterprise have invaded the sacred precincts of private and domestic life; and numerous mechanical devices threaten to make good the prediction that 'what is whispered in the closet shall be proclaimed from the house-tops.'"[3]

1. Thomas Cooley, *A Treatise on the Law of Torts* (Chicago: Callaghan, 1880). See also *Commonwealth v. Lovett*, 4 Clark 5 (Pa. 1831); *State v. Williams*, 2 Overt. 108 (Tenn. 1808); *State v. Pennington*, 3 Head 299 (Tenn. 1859); *Corps v. Robinson*, 2 Wash. C.C. 388 (1809); and Westin, *Privacy and Freedom*, 330–38.

2. *De May v. Roberts*, 9 N.W. (Mich. 1881) at 149; cited in Richard Turkington and Anita Allen, *Privacy Law: Cases and Materials*, 2nd ed. (St. Paul, Minn.: West Group, 2002), 23.

3. Warren and Brandeis, "Right to Privacy," 194.

The remedy for such invasions was to create a new tort. Torts are, in general, a negligent or intentional civil wrong that injures someone and for which the injured person may sue for damages. In 1960, in an effort to clarify matters, legal scholar Dean William Prosser separated privacy cases into four distinct but related torts—*intrusion, appropriation, private facts,* and *false light*—which I mentioned in Chapter 2.

Following Warren and Brandeis, Prosser offered a common law foundation for these privacy torts. The first Restatement of Torts in 1939 recognized this common law right,[4] and Prosser's four torts were incorporated into the second Restatement of Torts in 1977.[5]

Andrew McClurg notes, "Courts in at least twenty states have explicitly or implicitly accepted each of the four torts . . . several other states have adopted the . . . torts of intrusion, public disclosure of private facts, and appropriation . . . virtually all states have recognized a tort cause for invasion of privacy in some form."[6] Thus by the mid-1970s common law protections of privacy were widespread within the American legal landscape. Nevertheless, as we shall see later in this chapter, each of these protections has been either eliminated or severely restricted.

Constitutional Privacy

Constitutional protections of privacy may be broken into three areas— decisional privacy, First Amendment privacy, and Fourth Amendment privacy. Privacy related to the Third and Fifth Amendments will not be considered.[7] Because of issues related to constitutional interpretation, this area of privacy is fairly complex and controversial. Many scholars deny that the Constitution protects privacy except in a very narrow range of cases— for example, the Fourth Amendment's prohibition against "unreasonable searches and seizures" of "houses, papers, and effects."[8] In any case, my goal in this section is to indicate the current state of privacy protections in

4. Prosser, "Privacy," 386.

5. Restatement (Second) of Torts 652B–652E (1977).

6. Andrew McClurg, "Bringing Privacy Law Out of the Closet: A Tort Theory of Liability for Intrusions in Public Places," *North Carolina Law Review* 73 (1995): 989.

7. Both the Third Amendment, which prohibits the quartering of soldiers in private homes without consent, and the Fifth Amendment, which prohibits self-incriminating testimony, protect privacy interests. See, for example, *Engblom v. Carey*, 677 F.2d 957 (2d Cir. 1982); *Boyd v. United States*, 116 U.S. 616 (1886); and *Schmerber v. California*, 384 U.S. 757, 765 (1966).

8. See, for example, Robert Bork, *The Tempting of America: The Political Seduction of the Law* (New York: Simon and Schuster, 1990).

U.S. law. In the last section of this chapter and the chapters to come changes and recommendations will be proposed.

Decisional Privacy

In *Griswold v. Connecticut* (1965), a statute prohibiting the dissemination of contraceptive devices and information, even to married couples, was struck down because it would, in part, allow the police to violate the "the sacred precincts of marital bedrooms."[9] Justice Douglas, writing the majority opinion in *Griswold*, claimed that a legal right to privacy could be found in the shadows or penumbras of the First, Third, Fourth, and Fifth Amendments to the Constitution.

Douglas argued that by protecting the rights of parents to send their children to private schools and for associations to assemble and restrict access to membership lists, the First Amendment implies a legal protection for privacy. Combined with the Third and Fourth Amendments, which protect against invasions into one's home, and the Fifth Amendment, which affords individuals the right not to disclose information about themselves, Douglas thought the sum was a legal right to privacy.

Also in *Griswold*, Justice Goldberg invoked the Ninth and Fourteenth Amendments in support of privacy. Goldberg claimed that privacy was one of the rights retained by the people and that the "due process" clause of the Fourteenth Amendment protects privacy as a value "implicit in the concept of ordered liberty."[10]

A number of judicial decisions solidified the Douglas and Goldberg line of argumentation. In *Loving v. Virginia, Stanley v. Georgia, Eisenstadt v. Baird,* and *Carey v. Population Services* the Court struck down laws that prohibited interracial marriage, possession of pornographic materials in one's own home, and distribution of contraceptives to unmarried persons.[11]

One of the most important and controversial applications of this line of reasoning came in 1973 with *Roe v. Wade.* Justice Blackmun argued, "The right to privacy, whether it be founded in the Fourteenth Amendment's concept of personal liberty and restrictions upon the state action, as we feel it is, or, as the District Court determined, in the Ninth Amendment's reservation of rights to the people, is broad enough to encompass a woman's decision whether or not to terminate her pregnancy."[12] Thus, in gen-

9. Douglas, *Griswold v. Connecticut,* 381 U.S. 479 (1965) at 383.
10. *Griswold,* 381 U.S. 479 (1965) at 383.
11. *Loving v. Virginia,* 388 U.S. 1 (1967); *Stanley v. Georgia,* 394 U.S. 577 (1969); *Eisenstadt v. Baird,* 405 U.S. 438 (1972); *Carey v. Population Services,* 431 U.S. 678 (1977).
12. *Roe v. Wade,* 410 U.S. 153 (1973), at 164–65.

eral terms, the court recognized that individuals have privacy rights to be free from governmental interference related to certain sorts of decisions.

First Amendment Privacy

Privacy is also protected by securing the rights of anonymous communication and confidentiality of one's associations.[13] Sometimes the ability to speak freely relies heavily upon anonymity. For example, the Supreme Court of New Jersey has held that an anonymous online speaker has a First Amendment right to remain unidentified.[14]

> Anonymous pamphlets, leaflets, brochures and even books have played an important role in the progress of mankind. [citing *Talley v. California*] Great works of literature have frequently been produced by authors writing under assumed names. Despite readers' curiosity and the public's interest in identifying the creator of a work of art, an author generally is free to decide whether or not to disclose his or her true identity. The decision in favor of anonymity may be motivated by fear of economic or official retaliation, by concern about social ostracism, or merely by a desire to preserve as much of one's privacy as possible. Whatever the motivation may be, at least in the field of literary endeavor, the interest in having anonymous works enter the marketplace of ideas unquestionably outweighs any public interest in requiring disclosure as a condition of entry. Accordingly, an author's decision to remain anonymous, like other decisions concerning omissions or additions to the content of a publication, is an aspect of the freedom of speech protected by the First Amendment.[15]

Many individuals would not speak their minds, engage in whistle blowing, challenge popular views, or denounce those in power without the ability to remain anonymous. Much of the discourse in online environments would not occur without anonymity and encryption. Just as an example, consider

13. See, for example, Nadine Strossen, "Protecting Privacy and Free Speech in Cyberspace," *Georgetown Law Journal* 89 (2001): 2107, and Susan Brenner, "The Privacy Privilege: Law Enforcement, Technology, and the Constitution," *Journal of Technology Law and Policy* 7 (December 2002): 123–94.

14. *Dendrite Int'l v. Doe No. 3*, 342 N.J. Super. 134 (App. Div. 2001). See also *Buckley v. American Constitutional Law Found*, 525 U.S. 182, 197–90 (1999); *ACLU v. Miller*, 977 F. Supp. 1228 (N.D. Ga. 1997); *Bates v. City of Little Rock*, 361 U.S. 516 (1960); *NAACP v. Alabama ex rel. Patterson*, 357 U.S. 449 (1958); and *McIntyre v. Ohio Elections Comm'n*, 514 U.S. 334 (1995).

15. *Dendrite Int'l v. Doe No. 3*, 342 N.J. Super. 134 (App. Div. 2001) at 149. See also *Talley v. California*, 362 U.S. 60 (1960), and *Bates v. Little Rock*, 361 U.S. 516 (1960).

the numerous anonymous philosophical works, or works published under a pseudonym, that have challenged the religious orthodoxy. People have been killed for what they have said; anonymity thus plays a key role in preserving human life, while allowing new ideas to emerge.

As noted by Douglas in *Griswold*, the First Amendment also protects the privacy of associations and groups to peaceably assemble. In *NAACP v. Alabama* (1958) the state of Alabama required the National Association for the Advancement of Colored People to submit the names and address of all members within the state. The U.S. Supreme Court held that compelled disclosure of the NAACP membership lists would have the effect of undermining the association. The "petitioner has made an uncontroverted showing that on past occasions revelation of the identity of its rank-and-file members has exposed these members to economic reprisal, loss of employment, threat of physical coercion, and other manifestations of public hostility."[16] Edward Bloustein has proposed an explicit link between individual privacy and the right of association: "The right to be let alone protects the integrity and dignity of the individual. The right to associate with others in confidence—the right of privacy in one's associations—assures the success and integrity of the group purpose."[17]

Privacy has a role in protecting information access as well. For example, suppose someone, living prior to the Civil War in the American South, wanted to explore the idea that blacks and women were the moral equals of white men. Having private access to theories and views related to this matter would be important. In *Urofsky v. Gilmore* (1999) six professors employed by several public universities in Virginia challenged "the constitutionality of a Virginia law restricting state employees from accessing sexually explicit material on computers that are owned or leased by the state."[18] Denial of access and requiring permission, they argued, would have the effect of suppressing research. Thus, in some instances, anonymous access and authorship are necessary for freedom of thought and expression.

Fourth Amendment Privacy

In a long series of cases and judicial decisions, this area of law has protected citizens from unreasonable searches and seizures. The Fourth Amendment

16. *NAACP v. Alabama*, 357 U.S. 449 (1958) at 463.

17. Edward Bloustein, "Group Privacy: The Right to Huddle," in *Individual and Group Privacy*, ed. Edward J. Bloustein, 123–86 (New Brunswick: Transaction Books, 1978). See also *Boy Scouts of America v. Dale* (99–699) 530 U.S. 640 (2000).

18. *Urofsky v. Gilmore*, 995 F. Supp. 634, 634 (E.D. Va. 1998), rev'd en banc, 216 F.3d 401 (4th Cir. 2000), *cert. denied*, 121 S. Ct. 759 (2001).

states: "The right of the people to be secure in their persons, houses, papers, and effects, against unreasonable searches and seizures, shall not be violated, and no Warrants shall issue, but upon probable cause, supported by Oath or affirmation, and particularly describing the place to be searched, and the persons or things to be seized." This amendment grew out of opposition to "Writs of Assistance," which were general warrants utilized by the English crown to authorize government agents to enter any house or other establishment and seize contraband. Writs of this sort, often used against political or business rivals, were generally detested by American colonists as "fishing expeditions." In 1760 James Otis attacked such writs, citing the long English tradition of "a man's house is his castle."[19] Addressing the English Parliament William Pitt wrote, "The poorest man may in his cottage bid defiance to all the force of the crown. It may be frail—its roof may shake—the wind may blow through it—the storm may enter, the rain may enter—but the King of England cannot enter—all his force dares not cross the threshold of the ruined tenement."[20]

While there were numerous cases and developments in Fourth Amendment jurisprudence during the 1800s and early 1900s, our modern view begins to take shape with *Olmstead v. United States* (1928).[21] In *Olmstead* the court ruled that the Fourth Amendment against unreasonable searches and seizures applied to physical things like houses, notebooks, and receipts, but not to electronic communications. To violate the prohibition against unwarranted searches and seizures an officer would have to physically trespass on the property of the defendant. Since electronic eavesdropping did not constitute trespass, such surveillance did not violate the Fourth Amendment. Thirty-nine years later the Supreme Court, in *Katz v. United States*,[22]

19. James Otis, "In Opposition to Writs of Assistance," delivered before the Superior Court, Boston (February 1761), http://www.zprc.org/histdocs/OppositiontoWrits.html. See *Entick v. Carrington*, 19 Howell's State Trials 1029, 95 Eng. 807 (1705).

20. William Pitt the elder, Earl of Chatham, speech in the House of Lords, 1763, http://www.thinkexist.com/quotes/William_Pitt_the_elder/. Henry Peter Brougham, *Historical Sketches of Statesmen Who Flourished in the Time of George III*, vol. 1 (Glasgow: R. Griffin, 1839), 52. See also Thomas M. Cooley, *A Treatise on the Constitutional Limitations Which Rest upon the Legislative Power of the States of the American Union* (Boston: Little, Brown, 1903). Cooley wrote, "The maxim that 'every man's house is his castle' is made a part of our constitutional law in the clauses prohibiting unreasonable searches and seizures, and has always been looked upon as of high value to the citizen" (425).

21. *Olmstead v. United States*, 227 U.S. 438 (1928). For earlier cases, see *Boyd v. United States*, 116 U.S. 616 (1886); *Gouled v. United States*, 255 U.S. 298 (1921); *Weeks v. United States*, 232 U.S. 383, 392 (1914); *Carroll v. United States*, 267 U.S. 132, 158 (1925); and *Agnello v. United States*, 269 U.S. 20, 30 (1925).

22. *Katz v. United States*, 389 U.S. 347 (1967).

overturned the *Olmstead* decision, affirming that privacy interests may be found in personal communications as well as "persons, houses, papers, and effects." In *Katz* the physical "trespass" doctrine of *Olmstead* was repudiated, and it was generally acknowledged that a "search" could include both physical and electronic or technological invasion.

In place of the physical trespass doctrine of earlier times the *Katz* court offered a "reasonable expectation of privacy" test.[23] If an individual has a reasonable expectation of privacy, then a warrant must be obtained. Justice Harlan, in his concurring opinion, offered two requirements in determining if a search has occurred. "These requirements were, first, that a person have exhibited an actual (subjective) expectation of privacy and, second, that the expectation be one that society is prepared to recognize as 'reasonable.'"[24]

Also in 1967, the Supreme Court struck down specific sections of a New York eavesdropping statute in *Berger v. New York*.[25] Anita Allen and Richard Turkington note: "The New York statute authorized the issuance of an eavesdrop order if there was 'reasonable ground to believe' that evidence of a crime 'may be obtained.' The (Supreme) Court held that the probable cause requirement of the Fourth Amendment applied to the electronic surveillance in the case but did not decide whether the 'reasonable ground' language was constitutionally sufficient because the statute was found to violate the constitution on other grounds—the 'particularization' requirement of the Fourth Amendment."[26]

Thus, in *Berger* and *Katz* the Supreme Court sought to extend Fourth Amendment protections to electronic communications. Physical trespass was not necessary, probable cause applied, and the "particularization" requirement—detailing the communications to be seized and the allowable duration of the surveillance—applied as well. These changes in Fourth

---

23. Many privacy scholars view this change as an advance over the old trespass doctrine. I disagree for two reasons. First, with the change from a trespass or property model to an "expectation" model, privacy is given a weaker foundation and is more easily traded away for other, more fundamental values. Second, the notions of "reasonableness" and "expectations" are troubling and ambiguous. For example, an individual's expectation for privacy may be manipulated in obvious ways.

24. Turkington and Allen, *Privacy Law*, 95. See also *Rakas v. Illinois*, 439 U.S. 128 (1978); *United States v. White*, 401 U.S. 745, 786 (1971); *Smith v. Maryland*, 442 U.S. 735, 740 (1979); *Alderman v. United States*, 394 U.S. 165 (1969); *Mincey v. Arizona*, 437 U.S. 385 (1978); *Payton v. New York*, 445 U.S. 573 (1980); *Rawlings v. Kentucky*, 448 U.S. 98 (1980); and *Terry v. Ohio*, 392 U.S. 1, 19 (1968).

25. *Berger v. New York*, 388 U.S. 41 (1967).

26. Turkington and Allen, *Privacy Law*, 89.

Amendment jurisprudence affected several statutes, including the Omnibus Crime Control and Safe Street Act of 1968.[27]

The "plain view" doctrine established in *Coolidge v. New Hampshire*[28] permitted police observations conducted during a warranted intrusion. Thus a police officer who has a warrant to search for documents and who inadvertently notices, for example, a marijuana plant growing in a planter would be allowed to use this evidence even though the warrant did not specify a drug search.

The "open view" doctrine, on the other hand, allowed for observations made when no search was being conducted. If a police officer, while walking down the street, noticed a marijuana plant growing in a backyard, the officer could use this information without a warrant because no "search" was conducted. The open view doctrine has been extended to cover aerial observations. Tom Bush writes, "According to this approach 'the sky, like a road, is a highway over which those licensed to do so may pass . . .' aerial views, like views from the road, do not implicate fourth amendment interests."[29] Unaided observations from a nonintrusive altitude do not violate Fourth Amendment protection. What is observed is also important in that the courts have drawn a distinction between "open fields" and "private dwellings" with more protection attaching to the latter than the former.[30] Using binoculars, flying thirty feet off the ground, recording everything with a digital camera, while focusing in on someone's house would bump up against Fourth Amendment protection and a reasonable expectation of privacy.[31] Engaging in these activities while focusing on a large backyard or an open field, however, would not.

In "One Hundred Years of Privacy"[32] Ken Gormley notes, "A reasonable expectation of privacy has been found, sufficient to ward off governmental intrusion, with respect to the use of . . . bugging devices; administrative searches of homes and businesses; searches of closed luggage and footlockers; sealed packages; . . . [and] random spot checks for automobiles to inspect drivers' licenses and vehicle registrations." On the negative side,

27. Omnibus Crime Control and Safe Streets Act of 1968, 42 U.S.C. secs. 2510–2520 (1994 and Supp. V 2000).

28. *Coolidge v. New Hampshire*, 403 U.S. 443 (1971).

29. Tom Bush, "Comment: A Privacy-Based Analysis for Warrantless Aerial Surveillance Cases," *California Law Review* 75 (1987): 1776.

30. See *Oliver v. United States*, 466 U.S. 170, 177 (1984), and *Kyllo v. United States*, 533 U.S. 27 (2001).

31. Bush, "Comment," 1781.

32. Ken Gormley, "One Hundred Years of Privacy," *Wisconsin Law Review* (1992): 1369.

"the court had found no reasonable expectation of privacy in an individual's bank records; in voice or writing exemplars; in phone numbers recorded by pen registers; in conversations recorded by wired informants; and a growing list of cases involving automobiles, trunks, glove compartments and closed containers therein."

More recently, and especially after the terrorist attacks of September 11, 2001, Fourth Amendment privacy has been further amended and refined. This area of law will be considered further in the final chapter on privacy, accountability, and government monitoring.

Statutory Privacy

Statutory privacy protections exist at the local, state, and federal levels. While a comprehensive overview of each level is beyond the scope of this chapter, I will mention several of the most important federal statutes and a few of the more interesting state statutes.[33]

The Omnibus Crime Control and Safe Street Act of 1968 regulates electronic surveillance and wiretaps.[34]

The Fair Credit Reporting Act of 1970 regulates the accuracy and use of personal information held by credit agencies.[35]

The Family Educational Rights and Privacy Act of 1974 regulates access to educational records.[36]

The Privacy Act of 1974 was enacted to promote fair information practices between citizens and the government.[37]

The Right to Financial Privacy Act of 1978 regulates access to personal financial records in reaction to the Supreme Court's ruling in *United States v. Miller*.[38]

33. See also the Cable Communications Policy Act of 1984, 47 U.S.C. sec. 521; the Video Privacy Protection Act of 1988, 18 U.S.C. sec. 2710; the Telephone Consumer Protection Act of 1991, 47 U.S.C. sec. 227; the Communications Assistance for Law Enforcement Act of 1994, 47 U.S.C. secs. 1001–1021; the Telecommunications Act of 1996, 47 U.S.C. sec. 222; and the Children's On Line Privacy Protection Act of 1999, 15 U.S.C. secs. 6501–6506.

34. Omnibus Crime Control and Safe Street Act of 1968, 42 U.S.C. secs. 2510–2520 (1994 and Supp. V 2000). Amendments to this act will be considered in Chapter 10.

35. The Fair Credit Reporting Act of 1970, 15 U.S.C secs. 1681–1681u (1996, 2003).

36. The Family Educational Rights and Privacy Act of 1974, 20 U.S.C. sec. 1232g.

37. The Privacy Act of 1974, 5 U.S.C. sec. 552a.

38. The Right to Financial Privacy Act of 1978, 12 U.S.C. sec. 3401 et seq.; *United States v.*

The Electronic Communications Privacy Act of 1986 expands the scope of federal wiretap laws to cover electronic communications and stored electronic communications.[39]

The Computer Matching and Privacy Protection Act of 1988 amended the Privacy Protection Act related to computer matching and information sharing across different federal agencies.[40]

Title V of the Gramm-Leach-Bliley Financial Modernization Act of 2000 regulates the sharing of personal information by giving data subjects the ability to opt-out of certain sharing practices used by financial institutions.[41]

The Health Insurance Portability and Accountability Act of 1996 protects the security, confidentiality, and accessibility of health information.[42]

The Video Voyeurism Prevention Act of 2004 protects individuals from intrusions via the use of miniature cameras, camera phones, and video recorders in public places.[43]

The states have also passed legislation designed to protect privacy.[44] Numerous states have prohibitions against Peeping Toms and voyeurism. Washington State's voyeurism statute prohibits the photographing of a person without that person's knowledge and consent in a "place where he or she would have a reasonable expectation of privacy."[45] California's antivoyeurism statute focuses on the intrusion rather than the place.

Miller, 425 U.S. sec. 435 (1976). In *Miller* the court rejected the view that bank customers had legal privacy rights to financial information held by financial institutions.

39. The Electronic Communications Privacy Act of 1986, 18 U.S.C. secs. 2510–2522. See *Smith v. Maryland*, 442 U.S. 735 (1979).

40. The Computer Matching and Privacy Protection Act of 1988, 5 U.S.C. sec. 552a.

41. Title V of the Gramm-Leach-Bliley Financial Modernization Act of 2000, Public Law 106–102, 113 Stat. 1338.

42. The Health Insurance Portability and Accountability Act of 1996, Public Law 104–91, 110 Stat. 1936.

43. The Video Voyeurism Prevention Act of 2004, Public Law 108–495, 18 U.S.C. sec. 1801 (2005).

44. For an overview of state privacy protections, see http://www.epic.org/privacy/consumer/states.html.

45. The Video Voyeurism Prevention Act of 2004.

Every person who commits any of the following acts is guilty of disorderly conduct, a misdemeanor: Any person who uses a concealed camcorder, motion picture camera, or photographic camera of any type, to secretly videotape, film, photograph, or record by electronic means, another, identifiable person under or through the clothing being worn by that other person, for the purpose of viewing the body of, or the undergarments worn by, that other person, without the consent or knowledge of that other person, with the intent to arouse, appeal to, or gratify the lust, passions, or sexual desires of that person and invade the privacy of that other person, under circumstances in which the other person has a reasonable expectation of privacy.[46]

One problem with the California statute is that it requires that the victim be identifiable—but in many cases the victim is not.[47]

Privacy torts, constitutional protections, and statutes control information flow and access. Via this "patchwork" of laws and judicial decisions, privacy is protected in numerous ways. In the next section I will consider just how thin these privacy protections actually are in practice.

PRIVACY UNDER SIEGE

Working in reverse order from the presentation above, I will consider the robustness of privacy protections related to statutory provisions, constitutional safeguards, and torts. Independent of the concerns mentioned later and in the remaining chapters are technological innovations that threaten privacy. In 2000 A. Michael Froomkin noted that "routine collection of transactional data, growing automated surveillance in public places, deployment of facial recognition technology and other biometrics, cell-phone tracking, vehicle tracking, satellite monitoring, . . . internet tracking, . . . and sense-enhanced searches" continue to threaten privacy and push beyond legal protections.[48] These trends have continued.

46. California Penal Code sec. 647(k)(1) (2000).
47. See also the Video Voyeurism Prevention Act of 2004.
48. A. Michael Froomkin, "The Death of Privacy," *Stanford Law Review* 52 (May 2000): 1461.

THE THINNESS OF STATUTORY-BASED PRIVACY

A brief glance at some of the statutory provisions already mentioned should be enough to demonstrate the general weaknesses of the statutory protections for privacy at the state and federal levels. The Omnibus Crime Control and Safe Street Act has been amended numerous times, relaxing its privacy protections—the several USA Patriot Act amendments to it will be considered in Chapter 10. The Privacy Act of 1974 was amended by the Computer Matching and Privacy Protection Act of 1988 to allow the sharing of information across government agencies—information gathered for one purpose may be used for different purposes by different agencies without the consent of the information target. Exemptions to the Right to Financial Privacy Act of 1978 have all but eliminated its privacy protections. Administrative subpoenas, authorized independently of judicial review, have opened up most financial records to monitoring.[49]

The Gramm-Leach-Bliley opt-out provision is fairly weak, given that most people do not know about it. Moreover, no data security measures are required, and sharing among affiliates is permitted independent of consent. Given the size of some multinational corporations with interests across different domains, information sharing among affiliates may allow massive data files to be compiled.[50] Moreover, administrative subpoenas allow government agencies to access these data files without probable cause or a warrant—this is also true of the Health Insurance Portability and Accountability Act, which contains some the strongest privacy protections. Finally, although the Video Voyeurism Prevention Act of 2004 is promising in that it protects privacy in public, it is very narrow in its scope.

CONSTITUTIONAL PRIVACY

While left relatively untouched by subsequent decisions, the right to choose enshrined in *Roe* is narrow in scope and only protects, however important, the privacy interests of a particular segment of the population. Conversely, as of 1960, every state had some sort of antisodomy law prohibiting anal or

49. See Christopher Slobogin, "Subpoenas and Privacy," *DePaul Law Review* 54 (2005): 805.
50. For example, Acxiom holds personal financial information about almost every consumer in the United States, United Kingdom, and Australia. See Ian Grayson, "Packer Sets up Big Brother Data Store," *Australian,* November 30, 1999.

oral sex between consenting adults in private places. In *Bowers v. Hardwick*,[51] the Supreme Court upheld as constitutional a Georgia antisodomy statute. Seventeen years later the *Bowers* decision was overturned in *Lawrence et al. v. Texas*.[52] Justice Kennedy wrote, "The petitioners are entitled to respect for their private lives. . . . The state cannot demean their existence or control their destiny by making their private sexual conduct a crime."[53] *Griswold*, *Roe*, and *Lawrence*, as well as the other cases mentioned, ground what some legal scholars have called "decisional privacy"—that is a right, in private places and between consenting adults, to decide what happens to and with our own bodies.

While acknowledging the privacy protection afforded by *Griswold*, *Roe*, and *Lawrence*, a broader view of the cases and laws that surround "decisional privacy" indicates just how narrow these decisions were and are.[54] Writing the dissent in the *Lawrence* case Supreme Court Justice Antonin Scalia claimed:

> The Court leaves strangely untouched its central legal conclusion: [R]espondent would have us announce . . . a fundamental right to engage in homosexual sodomy. This we are quite unwilling to do. . . . Countless judicial decisions and legislative enactments have relied on the ancient proposition that a governing majority's belief that certain sexual behavior is "immoral and unacceptable" constitutes a rational basis for regulation. See, e.g., *Williams v. Pryor*, 240 F. 3d 944, 949 (CA11 2001) (citing *Bowers* in upholding Alabama's prohibition on the sale of sex toys on the ground that "[t]he crafting and safeguarding of public morality . . . indisputably is a legitimate government interest under rational basis scrutiny"); *Milner v. Apfel*, 148 F. 3d 812, 814 (CA7 1998) (citing *Bowers* for the proposition that "[l]egislatures are permitted to legislate with regard to morality . . . rather than confined to preventing demonstrable harms"); *Holmes v. California Army National Guard* 124 F. 3d 1126, 1136 (CA9 1997) (relying on *Bowers* in upholding the federal statute and regulations banning from military service those who engage in homosexual conduct); *Owens v. State*, 352

---

51. *Bowers v. Hardwick*, 478 U.S. 186 (1986).
52. *Lawrence et al. v. Texas*, 539 U.S. 558 (2003).
53. Ibid.
54. It is also not true to claim that *Roe* hasn't been undermined in recent years. Mississippi, for example, has implemented numerous restrictions on the ability of women to obtain an abortion, among them mandatory waiting periods and counseling. See Anna Quindlen, "Connecting Up the Dots," *Newsweek*, January 2005.

Md. 663, 683, 724 A. 2d 43, 53 (1999) (relying on *Bowers* in holding that "a person has no constitutional right to engage in sexual intercourse, at least outside of marriage"); *Sherman v. Henry*, 928 S. W. 2d 464, 469–473 (Tex. 1996) (relying on *Bowers* in rejecting a claimed constitutional right to commit adultery).

In light of the *Lawrence* decision, and the overturning of *Bowers*, Scalia maintains that laws against same-sex marriage, prostitution, masturbation, and fornication will not be sustainable. Coming from a conservative justice, these sentiments are hardly surprising—allow acts of sodomy to occur and the floodgates of immorality and vice will be opened. Nevertheless, legislation against same-sex marriage is widespread, and laws against prostitution are firmly in place. My reason for mentioning these cases is not to broach the issue of legal moralism and paternalism, but to indicate the tenuousness of decisional privacy.

In addition, we cannot use recreational drugs,[55] and we lack the legal right to obtain physician assistance when committing suicide[56] or to engage in certain sorts of athletic events, such as extreme fighting.[57] State laws against viewing obscene material, adultery, and gambling are also regularly enforced.[58] In Alabama it is illegal to stimulate the wrong organs with self-pleasuring devices.[59] Apparently it is still the case that fornication, or sex

55. All fifty states have laws prohibiting the use of certain types of drugs. For example, in the state of Washington possession of less than forty grams of marijuana is punishable by up to 90 days in jail and a fine up to $1,000. For amounts of forty grams or more the penalties increase to up to five years in prison and a fine up to $10,000.

56. See, for example, *Washington et al. v. Glucksberg et al.*, 521 U.S. 702 (1997). For a privacy-based defense of euthanasia, see Tom Beauchamp, "The Right to Privacy and the Right to Die," *Social Philosophy and Policy* 17 (2000): 276–92.

57. For example, Missouri has banned extreme fighting. "Combative fighting is prohibited in the state of Missouri." Legislation defines "Combative Fighting," also known as "Toughman Fighting," "Toughwoman Fighting," "Badman Fighting," "Ultimate Fighting," "U.F.C.," and "Extreme Fighting," as "any boxing or wrestling match, contest or exhibition, between two or more contestants, with or without protective headgear, who use their hands, with or without gloves, or their feet, or both, and who compete for a financial prize or any item of pecuniary value, and which match, contest, tournament championship or exhibition is not recognized by and not sanctioned by any officially recognized state, regional or national boxing or athletic sanctioning authority, or any promoter duly licensed by the department of economic development." Mo. Rev. Stat. sec. 317.018 (1996).

58. See *Sherman v. Henry*, 928 S. W. 2d 464, 469–473 (Tex. 1996) (relying on *Bowers* in rejecting a claimed constitutional right to commit adultery).

59. Alabama Code now "makes it unlawful to produce, distribute or otherwise sell sexual devices that are marketed primarily for the stimulation of human genital organs." Ala. Code. sec. 13A-12–200.1. See also *Williams v. Pryor*, 240 F.3d 944, 949 (11th Cir. 2001) (citing *Bowers* in upholding Alabama's prohibition on the sale of sex toys on the ground that "the crafting and

between unmarried people, is legally prohibited in Idaho.[60] Even when these activities are done in private places between consenting adults, our government—federal, state, and local—has decided that we cannot make these decisions for ourselves. And if judges like Scalia have their way, all of these activities, including those mentioned in *Roe* and *Lawrence*, would be prohibited in the name of safeguarding public morality.

My own view is that arguments for "safeguarding public morality" are little more than impositions of power and preference—those who have power and find certain activities distasteful attempt to prohibit them. A real argument for "safeguarding public morality" would have to define "public morality," demonstrate that society has the right to safeguard it, and prove that this right outweighs individual rights to liberty and privacy—even between consenting adults in private places. Consider again Scalia's view that "countless judicial decisions and legislative enactments have relied on the ancient proposition that a governing majority's belief that certain . . . behavior is 'immoral and unacceptable' constitutes a rational basis for regulation."[61] What a spectacularly bad position. First, note that if individuals have moral privacy rights that are captured in the penumbras of the First, Third, Fourth, and Fifth Amendments or as a right retained by the people as codified in the Ninth Amendment, then we would have another canonical example of how individual rights trump majority preferences. The primary purpose of the Bill of Rights is to secure individual rights against the tyranny of the majority. Second, it is quite surprising to find someone adhering to the view that just because a majority of people believe X is true, their mere believing makes X true, and justifies legal prohibitions. A majority of people at one time thought that slavery was justified and that women shouldn't vote. To call the whims, desires, and preferences of a ruling majority a "rational basis for regulation" makes a mockery of the word "rational." Scalia has not made an argument; he has only made an appeal to tradition and what he calls majority preferences.[62]

---

safeguarding of public morality . . . indisputably is a legitimate government interest under rational basis scrutiny").

60. See Idaho Code sec. 18–6603 (enacted 1972).

61. Scalia, *Lawrence et al. v. Texas*, 539 U.S. 558 (2003).

62. I am not claiming that majority voting is an illicit method for limiting liberty in some cases. For example, see the "public sex" case below. For more about legal moralism, see Mill, *On Liberty*; Sir James Fitzjames Stephen, *Liberty, Equality, Fraternity* (New York: Henry Holt, 1873); Patrick Devlin, *The Enforcement of Morals* (London: Oxford University Press, 1965); H. L. A. Hart, *Law, Liberty and Morality* (Oxford: Oxford University Press, 1963); Ronald Dworkin, *Law's Empire* (Cambridge: Belknap Press of Harvard University Press, 1986); and Michael Sandel, *Democracy's Discontent: America in Search of a Public Philosophy* (Cambridge: Belknap Press of Harvard University Press, 1998).

Furthermore, it is also questionable whether the kinds of cases that have traditionally fallen under the heading "decisional privacy" are fundamentally about privacy rather than liberty. John Hart Ely, for example, argued that in *Roe v. Wade* "the court neither provides an alternative definition [of privacy] nor an account of why it thinks privacy is involved."[63] Louis Henkin notes that "the Court . . . does not distinguish between privacy and autonomy. . . . But they are, I think, different notions conceptually."[64]

Briefly, I have defined privacy as a right to control access to and uses of bodies and information. But the essential element at issue in *Griswold, Roe, Lawrence,* and the other cases is the liberty to engage in various activities—albeit, more often than not, in private places. A right to control access and use is distinct from a liberty to engage in certain actions. For example, a right to control access to a house does not include or allow a liberty to engage in spousal abuse. In this case, privacy rights are overridden by other considerations. In other cases, what one is free to do may be constrained by the privacy rights of others. For example, a right to liberty does not include hugging or kissing strangers without consent.

Nevertheless, given that enforcement of laws against sodomy, abortion, masturbation, fornication, and the like would have profound effects on individual privacy and government power, it is advantageous to retain the category of "decisional privacy." The liberties protected by *Griswold, Roe,* and *Lawrence* are linked to individual privacy rights in important and obvious ways. For example, few would deny that the state has a legitimate interest in regulating sexual behavior in public places—consider two adults having sex in plain view on a busy public street (although admittedly this is a culturally based norm). When such activity is moved to a private place, the legitimate state interest seems to vanish—privacy is the difference maker. Note as well that the notion of *control over use* includes an important element of liberty. In any case, it should be obvious that "decisional privacy" is a fairly narrow area.

FIRST AMENDMENT AND FOURTH AMENDMENT PRIVACY

As with decisional privacy, First Amendment privacy is fairly narrow in protecting anonymous speech, secrecy in one's associations, and confiden-

63. John Hart Ely, "The Wages of Crying Wolf: A Comment on *Roe v. Wade*," *Yale Law Journal* 82 (1973): 931; cited in DeCew, *In Pursuit of Privacy*, 35.
64. Henkin, "Privacy and Autonomy," 1424–25.

tiality in information access. As already noted, confidentiality in information access has not been upheld by the courts in some cases.[65] Moreover, anonymous speech and association have been and continue to be undermined by technological advances in information-gathering practices. A simple administrative subpoena issued without court oversight requiring the production of records held by third parties may completely undermine anonymity.

Fourth Amendment privacy protections will be considered more fully in Chapter 10; here I will simply note a few ways in which privacy has been undermined in this area of the law. The "open view" and "plain view" doctrines have shrunk the domain of privacy protected by the Fourth Amendment.[66] Moreover, administrative subpoenas are a problem. Christopher Slobogin writes:

> The Department of Justice (DOJ) not only relies on subpoenas to investigate antitrust violations, government fraud, and other organizational crimes, but also is authorized to use subpoenas to obtain records in connection with kidnapping, child pornography, false claims and bribery, health care fraud, racketeering, and possession or sale of controlled substances. And the DOJ is not shy about taking advantage of its authority. In 2001, it issued almost 1,900 subpoenas seeking Internet records concerning child exploitation and abuse, and a total of 2,102 subpoenas seeking bank, medical, and other records in connection with health care offenses. Since the attacks of September 11, 2001, government use of subpoenas directed at Internet Service Providers in attempts to identify national security threats has been particularly prolific.[67]

Beyond the government surveillance powers already noted, the U.S. Constitution grants the president broad surveillance powers in times of crisis and war.

UNDERMINING THE PRIVACY TORTS

A series of judicial decisions have all but eliminated the private facts tort except in rare instances—I'll mention only a few of the more prominent

---

65. *Urofsky v. Gilmore*, 995 F. Supp. 634, 634 (E.D. Va. 1998), rev'd en banc, 216 F.3d 401 (4th Cir. 2000), *cert. denied*, 121 S. Ct. 759 (2001).

66. See *Coolidge v. New Hampshire*, 403 U.S. 443 (1971); *Oliver v. United States*, 466 U.S. 170, 177 (1984); and *Kyllo v. United States*, 533 U.S. 27 (2001).

67. Slobogin, "Subpoenas and Privacy," 840.

cases. *Melvin v. Reid,* decided in 1931, set the stage for undermining privacy rights in public places.[68] In this case, Gabrielle Darley, a former prostitute who was also tried and acquitted of murder, married Bernard Melvin in 1919, left her old life behind, and began a respectable life with new friends. In 1925 the defendants, without permission, produced a movie entitled *The Red Kimono* based on the life of Gabrielle Darley. Moreover, the principal character was named Gabrielle Darley. Upon release of the film, Gabrielle's friends scorned and ridiculed her. She brought suit for the sum of fifty thousand dollars. The case was decided in favor of the defendants. Judge J. Marks writes:

> From the foregoing it follows as a natural consequence that the use of the incidents from the life of appellant in the moving picture is in itself not actionable. These incidents appeared in the records of her trial for murder which is a public record open to the perusal of all. The very fact that they were contained in a public record is sufficient to negate the idea that their publication was a violation of a right of privacy. When the incidents of a life are so public as to be spread upon a public record they come within the knowledge and into the possession of the public and cease to be private.[69]

While the court in *Melvin* allowed the use of the facts of the plaintiff's life, the court also held that the use of the plaintiff's name was actionable. This cause of action was upheld in *Briscoe v. Reader's Digest Association, Inc.* (1971)[70] but was later overturned in *Gates v. Discovery Communications, Inc.* (2004).[71]

The view that by entering the public domain individuals voluntarily relinquish privacy claims was further solidified as a principle of law in *Gill v. Hearst Publishing Company*[72] decided seven years before Prosser's four torts were explicated. In *Gill* a photograph was taken and published of the plaintiffs embracing and used to illustrate an article entitled "And So the World Goes Round." Citing *Melvin,* Judge J. Spence reaffirmed the view that privacy rights generally lapse in public places.

> By their own voluntary action plaintiffs waived their right of privacy so far as this particular public pose was assumed, for "there can be

68. *Melvin v. Reid,* 112 Cal. App. 285, 290 (1931).

69. Ibid.

70. *Briscoe v. Reader's Digest Association, Inc.,* 4 Cal. 3d 529, 483 P.2d 34, 93 Cal. Rptr. 866 (1971).

71. *Gates v. Discovery Communications, Inc.,* 34 Cal. 4th 679, 101 P.3d 552, 21 Cal. Rptr. 3d 663 (2004).

72. *Gill v. Hearst Publishing Co.,* 40 Cal. 2d 224 (1953).

no privacy in that which is already public." (*Melvin v. Reid*) The photograph of plaintiffs merely permitted other members of the public, who were not at plaintiffs' place of business at the time it was taken, to see them as they had voluntarily exhibited themselves. Consistent with their own voluntary assumption of this particular pose in a public place, plaintiffs' right to privacy as to this photographed incident ceased and it in effect became a part of the public domain.[73]

The death knell for private fact torts came in *Florida Star v. B. J. F.*[74] In this case a news agency published the name of a sexual assault victim after obtaining the name from a police report.[75] The Supreme Court, on appeal, decided in favor of the defendant, stating: "It was held that the imposition of civil damages on the newspaper, pursuant to the Florida statute, violated the First Amendment, because (1) the news article contained lawfully obtained, truthful information about a matter of public significance, and (2) imposing liability under the circumstances was not a narrowly tailored means of furthering state interests in maintaining the privacy and safety of sexual assault victims or encouraging such victims to report the offenses, since (a) the government itself failed to abide by the policy against disclosure."[76]

In the same case Justice White argued that "at issue in this case is whether there is any information about people, which—though true—may not be published in the press. By holding that only 'a state interest of the highest order' permits the State to penalize the publication of truthful information, and by holding that protecting a rape victim's right to privacy is not among those state interests of the highest order, the Court accepts appellant's invitation . . . to obliterate one of the most noteworthy legal inventions of the 20th century: the tort of the publication of private facts."[77]

Thus, in *Melvin, Gill,* and *Florida Star* we see a heavy judicial bias against informational privacy in public places.[78] In *Bartnicki v. Vopper*[79] the Su-

---

73. J. Spence, *Gill v. Hearst Publishing Co.*, 40 Cal. 2d at 231.

74. *Florida Star v. B.J.F.*, 491 U.S. 524 (1989).

75. For a lengthy analysis and critique of the private facts tort, see Diane L. Zimmerman, "Requiem for a Heavyweight: A Farewell to Warren and Brandeis's Privacy Tort," *Cornell Law Review* 68 (1983).

76. *Florida Star v. B.J.F.*, 491 U.S. 551 (1989).

77. Ibid.

78. See also *Cox Broadcasting Corp. v. Cohn*, 420 U.S. 469 (1975); *Jones v. Herald Post Co.*, 230 Ky. 227, 229 (1929); *Bazemore v. Savannah Hospital*, 171 Ga. 257 (1930); *Hubbard v. Journal Pub. Co.* 69 N.M. 473, 368 P.2d 147 (1962); and *Cape Publications, Inc. v. Bridges*, 423 So. 2d 426, 1982 Fla. App. (1982).

79. *Bartnicki v. Vopper*, 121 S. Ct. 1753 (2001).

preme Court ignored the "lawfully obtained" test mentioned in *Florida Star* and applied a balancing test, weighing the privacy interests involved against public interest. *Bartnicki* involved the recording of a cellular phone conversation in violation of state and federal statutes followed by the broadcasting of the conversations by a third party not involved with the initial illegal acquisition. The Supreme Court concluded that the public interest in obtaining the recorded information outweighed the privacy interests of the plaintiffs—in this case, independent of the fact that the information in question was not publicly available.

As noted by Patrick McNulty, "The public's right to receive news is nearly all encompassing. It extends to publicity about public figures who invite public attention by their activities, those who are involuntarily placed in the public eye such as crime victims, information as hard news, and information as entertainment."[80] This view was enshrined over forty years ago by the Third Circuit Court of Appeals:

> For present purposes news need be defined as comprehending no more than relatively current events such as in common experience are likely to be of public interest. . . . A large part of the matter which appears in newspapers and news magazines today is not published or read for the value or importance of the information it conveys. Some readers are attracted by shocking news. Others are titillated by sex in the news. Still others are entertained by news which has an incongruous or ironic aspect. . . . Few newspapers or news magazines would long survive if they did not publish a substantial amount of news on the basis of entertainment value of one kind or another. This may be a disturbing commentary upon our civilization, but it is nonetheless a realistic picture of society which courts shaping new juristic concepts must take into account. In brief, once the character of an item as news is established, it is neither feasible nor desirable for a court to make a distinction between news for information and news for entertainment in determining the extent to which publication is privileged.[81]

If such standards set the boundaries of "newsworthiness" or of "legitimate public concern" and if no legal action is warranted in cases where these

---

80. Patrick J. McNulty, "The Public Disclosure of Private Facts: There Is Life After Florida Star," *Drake Law Review* 50 (2001): 108.

81. *Jenkins v. Dell Publ'g Co.*, 251 F.2d 447, 451 (3d Cir. 1958); cited in McNulty, "Public Disclosure of Private Facts," 108.

terms apply, then the tort of private facts has been eviscerated. But what of Prosser's other torts—false light, appropriation, and intrusion? As we shall see, none of the other torts has fared any better.

The common law tort of false light has seemingly transformed into defamation and has little to do with privacy and more to do with a property claim in one's reputation. As with defamation, truth is seen as a defense against a false light charge.[82] Andrew McClurg notes, "False light, a sickly stepchild of defamation, has been rejected by several states and even where accepted, 'the chances of a plaintiff ultimately prevailing . . . are slim.'"[83]

Consider, for example, *Falwell v. Flynt*[84]—a case where an issue of *Hustler* magazine included a fake interview with Jerry Falwell concerning his first sexual experience. In the course of this fictitious interview Falwell states that his "first time" was "during a drunken incestuous rendezvous with his mother in an outhouse."[85] As a conservative religious leader and founder of the Moral Majority, *Hustler*'s portrayal of Falwell was seen by many to be quite humorous. Falwell was not amused and sued for false light invasion of privacy, libel, and infliction of mental distress. Reversing a mental distress judgment in favor of Falwell, the Supreme Court

> held (1) that the free speech guaranties of the First Amendment prohibit public figures and public officials from recovering for the tort of intentional infliction of emotional distress by reason of the publication of a caricature, such as the ad parody in question, unless it is shown that the publication contains a false statement of fact which was made with actual malice, that is, with knowledge that the statement was false or with reckless disregard as to whether it was true; and (2) that the minister in question thus could not recover for intentional infliction of emotional distress, since (a) he is a public figure, and (b) the Supreme Court accepted the jury's finding that the ad parody could not reasonably be understood as describing actual facts.[86]

Two basic details worked against Falwell in this case. First, he was a nationally known public figure outspoken across a range of political, cultural, and

---

82. See *Machleder v. Diaz*, 801 F.2d 46 (2d Cir. 1986); *cert. denied*, 479 U.S. 1088 (1987).

83. Diane Zimmerman, "False Light Invasion of Privacy: The Light That Failed," *N.Y.U. Law Review* 64 (1989): 366–67; cited in McClurg, "Bringing Privacy Law Out of the Closet," 1004.

84. *Falwell v. Flynt*, 485 U.S. 46 (1988).

85. Ibid.

86. Ibid.

religious issues. Second, by ensuring that everyone would understand that the fake interview was indeed fake, *Hustler* did not make any false claims about Falwell and could not thereby place him in a false light.[87]

The tort of appropriation, which prohibits the commercial use of someone's name or likeness without consent, has also broken free from protecting privacy interests. Typically, it is used by celebrities and public figures to protect commercial value in intangible property like names, likeness, and vocal quality.[88] Thus when a television commercial includes a song sung "in the voice" of a famous singer, the actual owner of said voice might sue for misappropriation.[89]

The scope and power of the intrusion tort has also been severely limited. Some jurisdictions require physical trespass, and virtually no violation can occur in public places. The invasion must be intentional, it must physically intrude, the plaintiff must have a reasonable expectation of privacy, and it must be highly offensive to a reasonable person.[90] Here again the cases pile up against privacy and in favor of free speech. *Melvin, Gill,* and *Florida Star* each rule out the possibility of an invasion tort because the private information disclosed in these cases was, in some sense, publicly available.

In *Shulman v. Group W. Productions*[91] we get more of the same except in this case the tort of intrusion was upheld—although in an odd and restricted way. On June 24, 1990, Ruth and Wayne Shulman were involved in an automobile accident that was filmed and ultimately broadcast. This film included footage of Ruth asking to die as well as other grisly footage of the accident scene. Deeming the facts newsworthy and truthful, the Court ruled against the plaintiffs' private facts charge. As for intrusion, the Court found that "cameraman Cooke's mere presence at the accident scene and filming of the events occurring there cannot be deemed either a physical or sensory intrusion on plaintiffs' seclusion. Plaintiffs had no right of ownership or possession of the property where the rescue took place, nor any actual con-

---

87. For more about false light privacy torts, see *Lerman v. Flynt Distributing Co., Inc.,* 745 F.2d 123, 135 (2d Cir. 1984), *cert. denied,* 471 U.S. 1054; *Cibenko v. Worth Publishers, Inc.,* 510 F. Supp. 761, 766 (D. N.J. 1981); *Time, Inc. v. Hill,* 385 U.S. at 374; *Cantrell v. Forest City Publishing Co.,* 419 U.S. 245, 248; *Philadelphia Newspapers, Inc. v. Hepps,* 475 U.S. 767 (1986); *Fogel v. Forbes, Inc.,* 500 F. Supp. 1081, 1088 (1988); and *Devlin v. Greiner,* 147 N.J. Super. 446, 462, 371 A.2d 380, 390 (Law Div. 1977).

88. See, for example, *Matthews v. Wozencraft,* 15 F.3d 432, 438 (5th Cir. 1994).

89. See *Young and Rebicam, Inc. v. Midler,* 112 S. Ct. 1513 (1992), concerning a suit brought by Bette Midler. See also *Carson v. Here's Johnny Portable Toilets, Inc.,* 698 F.2d 831, 834 (6th Cir. 1983).

90. Restatement (Second) of Torts 652B (1977).

91. *Shulman v. Group W. Productions,* 18 Cal. 4th 200, 955 P.2d 469 (1998).

trol of the premises. Nor could they have had a reasonable expectation that members of the media would be excluded or prevented from photographing the scene; for journalists to attend and record the scenes of accidents and rescues is in no way unusual or unexpected."[92]

Nevertheless, actionable issues of intrusion were found to exist when Cook accompanied the plaintiff in the rescue helicopter where more footage was obtained. Moreover, the Court held that an expectation of privacy was invaded "by placing a microphone on Carnahan's person [a nurse/ paramedic], amplifying and recording what she said and heard, defendants may have listened in on conversations the parties could reasonably have expected to be private."[93] All in all it would seem that Prosser's four privacy torts have fallen on hard times.

RESURRECTING THE PRIVACY TORT OF INTRUSION

Prosser defined the tort of intrusion as "intruding (physically or otherwise) upon the solitude of another in a highly offensive manner. For example, a woman sick in the hospital with a rare disease refuses a reporter's request for a photograph and interview. The reporter photographs her anyway, over her objection."[94] As mentioned above, the tort of intrusion has been undermined by a series of cases starting with *Melvin v. Reid*[95] and running through *Shulman v. Group W. Productions*[96] and more recent cases.

In an effort to revive the tort of intrusion, Andrew Jay McClurg's "Bringing Privacy Law out of the Closet: A Tort Theory of Liability for Intrusions in Public Places" offers a modified definition of intrusion as well as additional factors that are relevant in determining if a violation has occurred.[97] As McClurg defines it, the tort of intrusion has occurred when someone "intentionally intrudes, physically or otherwise, upon the private affairs or concerns of another, whether in a private physical area or one

92. *Shulman v. Group W. Productions*, 18 Cal. 4th 200 at 66.

93. *Shulman v. Group W. Productions*, 18 Cal. 4th 200, at 69. See also *Brownie Miller et al. v. National Broadcasting Company et al.*, 187 Cal. App. 3d 1463 (1986).

94. Prosser, "Privacy," 383, 384.

95. *Melvin v. Reid*, 112 Cal. App. 285, 290 (1931).

96. *Shulman v. Group W. Productions*, 18 Cal. 4th 200, 955 P.2d 469 (1998).

97. McClurg, "Bringing Privacy Law Out of the Closet." See Elizabeth Paton-Simpson, "Privacy and the Reasonable Paranoid: The Protection of Privacy in Public Places," *University of Toronto Law Journal* 30 (Summer 2000): 305. For a defense of photography and picture taking over privacy in public spaces, see "Note: Privacy, Photography, and the Press," *Harvard Law Review* 111 (1998): 1086. See also *United State v. Gugel*, 119 F.Supp. 897 (E.D. Ky. 1954).

open to public inspection, [and] . . . if the intrusion would be highly offensive to a reasonable person."[98]

Factors to be considered when determining whether an act is intrusive include:

1. the defendant's motive;
2. the magnitude of the intrusion, including the duration, extent, and the means of intrusion;
3. whether the plaintiff could reasonably expect to be free from such conduct under the habits and customs of the location where the intrusion occurred;
4. whether the defendant sought the plaintiff's consent to the intrusive conduct;
5. action taken by the plaintiff that would manifest to a reasonable person the plaintiff's desire that the defendant not engage in the intrusive conduct;
6. whether the defendant disseminated images of the plaintiff or information concerning the plaintiff that was acquired during the intrusive act; and
7. whether images of or other information concerning the plaintiff acquired during the intrusive act involve a matter of legitimate public interest.[99]

In brief, McClurg argues that motive is important in determining an actionable intrusion because of its relation to what would be highly offensive to a reasonable person. To intrude with pure motives is much better than intruding for economic gain or sexual gratification. Certainly motive would be a mitigating factor.[100] Consider the following cases.

1. Person A accompanies his family to the beach, bringing his video camcorder to record the event. While panning the beach with his camcorder, A pauses with the camera focused upon Person B, who is building a sand castle with her child. A records the scene because he is touched by the child's laughter and excitement.
2. A takes his video camcorder to the beach. He records B, who is sun-

---

98. McClurg, "Bringing Privacy Law out of the Closet," 1059.
99. Ibid.
100. See *Elmore v. Atlantic Zayre, Inc.*, 341 S. E.2d 905, 905 (Ga. Ct. App. 1986), and *Norris v. King*, 355 So. 2d 21 (La. Ct. App.), *cert. denied*, 439 U.S. 995 (1978).

bathing. A's purpose in filming B is to use the videotape for sexual gratification, which he later does.[101]

While an intrusion occurs in both cases, the one factor that makes a difference is motive. We may even go so far as to say that something wrong, however slight in the first case, has occurred in each case. Not every wrong need be codified in the law, however, and perhaps motives, in cases like these, could be the difference maker between legal and illegal conduct.

The magnitude of the intrusion is important as well. Slightly annoying or offensive action should not warrant legal relief. On the other hand, the greater the magnitude in terms of duration, extent, and means, the more likely the conduct would offend a reasonable person. McClurg writes,

> Creating a permanent record of the plaintiff by photography or videotape carries the potential for magnifying an intrusion in three important ways: (1) it allows the invader to, in effect, take a part of the victim with him, thereby allowing intrusive scrutiny of the victim to continue indefinitely; (2) a permanent photographic image may convey more information about the victim than would observation with the naked eye; and (3) a durable recording by whatever means has the potential to multiply the impact of the intrusion through dissemination. Use of mechanical or electronic means to record the plaintiff is a factor that should carry great weight in assessing whether the defendant's conduct was highly offensive to a reasonable person.[102]

Again consider two cases.

3. A, a nosy neighbor, spends a considerable amount of time watching B and his family through a crack in A's curtains as they go about their normal business.
4. The same facts as in case 3, except that A uses a video camcorder set up on a tripod to record the comings and goings of B and his family.[103]

101. McClurg, "Bringing Privacy Law Out of the Closet," 1063.
102. Ibid., 1064.
103. Ibid.

As with the first two cases, and even more so in 3 than in 1, we may find such actions morally suspicious. Nevertheless, legal action may be reserved for cases like 2 and 4 because of the motive and the magnitude of the intrusion.

The context of the action is also clearly relevant. In many public places information about us will likely be captured by some sort of recording device such as a camcorder, microphone, or camera. When someone snaps a picture of a building and inadvertently captures my likeness, the intrusion may be annoying but not legally actionable. Factors of motive and magnitude are relevant as well. A crowded street provides a very different context than a secluded public beach. Offensiveness and judicial relief would be mitigated by the context of the intrusion.

The consent of those being intruded upon or monitored would also be fairly decisive in deciding legal recourse. If someone has agreed to have their picture taken or their motions and sounds recorded, then they would have no legitimate cause of action, no matter the motive, magnitude, or context. Consent is closely connected with evasion. If someone makes an effort not to be seen, photographed, or recorded, then we may set the default position as if they have requested not to be included in these activities. Consider cases 5 through 7.

5. A uses his video camcorder to film persons sunbathing at the beach. B, a sunbather, requests that A not videotape her. A ignores her request.
6. Same facts as in 5, except that, instead of making an oral request, B covers herself with a towel and scowls at A.
7. A follows B about in a shopping mall. B requests that he desist, but A continues to follow him.[104]

In each of these cases, A may be liable for intrusion.

Dissemination of information is important especially when viewed in terms of magnitude, extent, and means. When pictures, video, and sounds are published or broadcast, the magnitude of the invasion is amplified considerably. While there may be many mitigating factors to consider, widespread dissemination of information would be clearly relevant to a reasonable person trying to determine if some action was highly offensive.

104. Ibid., 1070.

Without wider dissemination, in case 8 the photographer would not be liable, while in 9 he would.

8.   A photographs beach scenes while on vacation in Florida. Included in one photograph is B, who was sunbathing at the time.
9.   The same facts as 8, except that A later publishes the photograph of B in a men's magazine above a caption that makes sexual references concerning the photograph.[105]

Lastly, McClurg discusses whether or not the information acquired is of legitimate public concern. If it is, then as with consent, a mitigating factor would be present. The difficulty from the privacy rights perspective is that the notion of "legitimate" may be broadly defined so that just about any information would be captured under this heading. On the other side, if "legitimate" is defined too narrowly, then free speech is threatened.

Consider the table on the following page, which maps these factors on right-left scale. Behavior that falls on the left of each scale—the motives are pure, the infraction slight, the action was performed in an area where there was little expectation of privacy, the acquisition was consented to, and the matter was of great public importance—would clearly not be legally actionable. Behavior that falls on the right of each scale—the motives are suspicious, the invasion profound, the action was performed in an area where there was a high expectation of privacy, the acquisition was evaded, and the matter of little or no public importance—would warrant judicial action. The extremes are easy—that is, if along each dimension, an action falls clearly to the right or the left, then it is clearly the case that legal action is warranted or not. In these all-or-nothing examples, the dimensions of motive, magnitude, and the other factors operate as a set of sufficient conditions for or against judicial relief.

By itself, consent has great importance, in that behavior that falls clearly to the right in terms of motive, magnitude, context, and public interest would become legally excusable if consent was obtained. In this case, consent appears to be a sufficient condition for excluding legal culpability. Notice that this relationship does not hold when we slide to the other extreme on the consent scale. That is, if someone did not consent or evaded notice and yet there were pure motives, little magnitude, and so on, we should not conclude that legal action is warranted. By themselves, evasion or express nonconsent would not be a sufficient condition for legal action.

105. Ibid.

Table 1. Factors to be considered when determining whether an act of intrusion is actionable

	Nonactionable	Actionable
Motives	*Pure* A father takes a picture of his son and inadvertently captures someone else in the picture as well.	*Suspicious* A pedophile videotapes children at play with the intent to sell the images to other pedophiles.
Magnitude*	*Slight* Person A accidentally bumps into person B.	*Profound* A "Watcher" videotapes and uploads to the Web your every move while in public.
Context	*Little expectation of privacy* You and a date go to Times Square in New York to celebrate New Year's Eve.	*Reasonable expectation of privacy* You and a date find a secluded spot in a public park that is well off the beaten path.
Consent	*Consented to intrusion* A "Watcher" videotapes and uploads to the Web your every move while in public—with your consent.	*Evaded or did not consent to intrusion* A "Watcher" videotapes a person who is wearing a disguise and verbally requesting not to be videotaped.
Public interest	*Of great public importance* Taking pictures of a government official who is taking a bribe.	*Of little public importance* Taking pictures of a government official who is having a romantic dinner with his or her spouse.

*Concept of magnitude includes duration, extent, and means.

In this way consent is a "difference maker" while evasion or verbal nonconsent is not.

The public interest dimension has this form as well. If the matter is of great public importance, then even in cases of suspicious motives, profound invasions, and target evasion, there would not likely be an actionable cause. Notice as well that if the matter in question was of little public importance, and yet there were pure motives, little magnitude, and so on, we should not conclude that legal action is warranted. Like consent, a matter of great public importance is a "difference maker" when determining legal culpability.[106]

106. Someone may charge that what is of great public importance is a subjective matter determined by specific cultural arrangements. For example, what was of great public importance for German society of the Nazi era would be very different from what would be important to modern U.S. society. But if we cast this parameter as public interest—in terms of free speech

The magnitude of the invasion has a similar form to public interest and consent. If the infraction is slight, then judicial relief is unwarranted even if suspicious motives, evasion, and private contexts are present. Setting aside the dimensions of consent and public interest, if the invasion is profound, then purity of motive and contexts of diminished privacy would have little force. Assuming that consent is not present and that the matter is not of great public importance, magnitude becomes a "difference maker." In this case, a slight infraction would not be actionable while a profound one would—independent of motive and context.

Putting consent, public interest, and magnitude aside, motive appears to be a mitigating factor when compared to the dimension of context. That is, in cases where the motive is pure but there is a high expectation of privacy there would be little grounds for legal action. This kind of case is difficult because it is hard to imagine how consent, public interest, and magnitude would not be relevant. These other dimensions would play an important, if not deciding, role in any example.

Crudely put, when determining legal culpability it would appear that motive is more important than context, magnitude is more important than motive, public interest is more important than magnitude, and consent is more important than public interest. These relations appear transitive as well—that is, consent trumps everything, public interest is next, and so on.

INFORMATIONAL PRIVACY AND CRIMINAL TRESPASS

Assume that a wealthy individual or corporation simply pays whatever fines are levied against them in civil tort invasion cases. Or at the other extreme, suppose the person engaged in invasive behavior has nothing to seize and no way to pay fines or damages. Finally, it could be the case that intrusion was so severe that no compensation could rectify the situation. In such cases, I contend that criminal remedies should be available to prosecutors. Consider the case of video voyeurs.

> The Plaza security observed via the video surveillance system a subject carrying a shopping bag, riding the escalator up and down on several occasions. As security observed the subject, they noticed he was enter-

guaranteeing just democratic institutions—then an answer can be given. I would like to thank Kimberly Moore for the example.

ing the escalator to ride up to the second story behind women wearing skirts. The subject placed a shopping bag on the step below the female wearing the skirt, and would ride up the escalator until it reached the top floor. The subject would then ride down the escalator and wait [for] another female wearing a skirt. . . . Plaza security contacted the subject and found that he had an 8mm video camera hidden in a shoebox within the shopping bag . . . [and he] admitted to video taping the women wearing skirts in order to sell the videotape to an Internet website.[107]

Suppose we assume that the perpetrator in this case was extremely wealthy or extremely poor and thus, in a sense, had little to lose—the fines would either go unpaid or have no effect. Independent of effect, it may be a simple matter of justice that incarceration of some duration is appropriate. As with theft, assault, and criminal trespass, there are options open to judges and prosecutors beyond fines and community service. In the most egregious cases of privacy invasion, like the video voyeur example, criminal punishment should be available.[108]

In 2000, California recognized this problem and criminalized the following behavior: "Any person who looks through a hole or opening, into, or otherwise views, by means of any instrumentality . . . the interior of a bathroom, changing room . . . or the interior of any other area in which the occupant has a reasonable expectation of privacy, with the intent to invade the privacy of a person or persons inside is guilty of a crime."[109] The California Penal Code goes on to recognize that an expectation of privacy may exist in public spaces and criminalizes certain kinds of invasive behavior.[110] In 1999 a case of video voyeurism gained public attention in Louisiana and prompted the legislature to consider criminal penalties for such

107. Matthew Eaton, sex crime investigator, City of Montclair, California, to Assemblyman Dick Ackerman, California State Assembly, June 7, 1999; cited in Lance Rothenberg, "Re-Thinking Privacy: Peeping Toms, Video Voyeurs, and the Failure of the Criminal Law to Recognize a Reasonable Expectation of Privacy in the Public Space," *American University Law Review* 49 (June 2000): 1127. See also Lisa F. Wu, "Review of Selected 1996 California Legislation: Crimes: Peeping Tom Crimes," *Pacific Law Journal* 28 (1997): 705.

108. Lance Rothenberg agrees, "This comment argues that criminal law must break free from fallacious distinctions between public and private space and must specifically recognize an individual's legitimate expectation of privacy in the public space." Rothenberg, "Re-Thinking Privacy," 1127.

109. See Cal. Penal Code 647(k)(1) (West 1994 and Supp. 2000); cited in Rothenberg, "Re-Thinking Privacy," n. 153.

110. Ibid., n. 159. See note 46 and the associated text.

conduct. In this case two families agreed to watch each other's houses when one of them was away. One of the families discovered that their neighbor, a church deacon no less, had installed hidden video equipment throughout the house: "The neighbor drilled holes in the ceilings of the master bedroom and bathroom as well as the teenage daughter's bathroom and installed a video camera and television monitor hidden underneath the attic insulation."[111] In light of this case, the Louisiana legislature passed a statute prohibiting "the use of a camera . . . or any other image recording device for the purpose of observing, viewing, photographing, filming or videotaping a person where that person has not consented to the observing . . . or videotaping and it is for a lewd or lascivious purpose."[112] More recently, passage of the Video Voyeurism Prevention Act offers nationwide protection.[113] I would support stronger and broader legislation at both the state and federal level.

CONCLUSION

After surveying the legal foundations and history of privacy law in the United States, I have argued that the tort of intrusion should be resurrected and a criminal option of informational trespass offered. I will leave the issue of how to strengthen legal privacy in this area for the final chapter. Suffice it to say, if we are to take moral claims to privacy seriously—as we should, if the arguments presented in Chapters 2 through 5 are correct—then incursions into private domains must be severely restricted.

To conclude, I would like to test the tort and criminal model of invasion offered with a much discussed case—first presented at the end of Chapter 5.

On the night of October 30, 1979 . . . an NBC television camera crew entered the apartment of Dave and Brownie Miller in Los Angeles, without their consent, to film the activities of Los Angeles Fire Department paramedics called to the Miller home to administer lifesaving techniques to Dave Miller, who had suffered a heart attack in

111. Joanna Weiss, "Voyeur Prompts DA to Propose Peeping Tom Law," *New Orleans Times-Picayune*, January 10, 1999, A1.

112. See 1999 La. Sess. Law. Serv. 14:283(A)(1) (West) (codified at La. Rev. Stat. Ann. 283 [West Supp. 2000]) and La. Rev. Stat. Ann. 283(A)(1); cited in Rothenberg, "Re-Thinking Privacy," 1164.

113. Video Voyeurism Prevention Act of 2004.

his bedroom. The NBC television camera crew not only filmed the paramedics' attempts to assist Miller, but NBC used the film on its nightly news without obtaining anyone's consent. In addition, after it had received complaints from both Brownie Miller and her daughter, Marlene Miller Belloni, NBC later used portions of the film in a commercial advertising an NBC "mini-documentary" about the paramedics' work.[114]

We can assume that the motives of the camera crew were benign—perhaps their intentions were to get a good story and further their careers. The magnitude, however, was extreme. Not only did the crew film Dave Miller having a heart attack but the footage was aired more than once. Moreover, before the second broadcast, the Miller family expressed their wish that the footage not be used. Consent was thus absent as a mitigating factor. Context is also important, given that the event occurred in the Millers' home.

Last is the issue of public importance. As I will argue in the next chapter, we may have a right to know that the paramedics did a good job, or more broadly that our public officials and employees are performing adequately, but none of this sanctions invasions of the sort found in this case. We do not have the right to see Dave Miller taking his last breath or saying goodbye to family members. Thus in this case, I would argue that the Millers have an actionable cause of intrusion against NBC and the camera crew.

The question of whether or not *criminal* charges should be advanced in the Miller case is more difficult, and ultimately should be left to the discretion of prosecutors in possession of all the relevant facts—the camera crew may have been invited in by a family member, or perhaps the front door was open. Suppose Brownie Miller, in the middle of the event, noticed the camera crew entering and shouted, "Get out!" Had the crew stayed, filmed, and later broadcast the footage over the objections of the family, I believe criminal prosecution would have been warranted.

To conclude, in the paper-based world of our past, where information was stored in analog form, privacy concerns were more easily protected. Video or sound recordings and paper trails were difficult to collect, process, and disseminate. In recent times, digital technology and information networking have profoundly changed our notions of public and private. Indi-

---

114. *Brownie Miller et al., v. National Broadcasting Company et al.,* 187 Cal. App. 3d 1463 (1986).

vidual privacy is everywhere threatened. But this need not be so. There have been many technological advances in the past that forced changes in legal systems—the printing press and radio broadcasting are obvious examples. Within the current expansion of digital technology, we need to think more imaginatively about legal protections for privacy.

7

PRIVACY, SPEECH, AND THE LAW

If we assume that individuals have *moral* rights to free speech, and that privacy may restrict such expression, then there appears to be a conflict of rights—a conflict where speech or expression may trump privacy concerns. For example, when a musician offers up a song about a romantic affair for public consumption, privacy rights may run headlong into speech and expression rights. Andrew McClurg has noted that judges are not willing to protect privacy if doing so threatens free speech: "Of the forty-nine invasion of privacy cases reported by state courts in 1992, trial courts granted summary judgment to the defendant in twenty-one of the cases and granted the defendant's motion to dismiss the complaint in fifteen of the cases. In other words, in thirty-six of the forty-nine cases (73 percent) trial judges deprived plaintiffs the opportunity to have their privacy claims heard by a jury."[1] McClurg also mentions that the situation is nearly identical in the federal courts.[2]

1. McClurg, "Bringing Privacy Law Out of the Closet," 1000–1002. See also *Rawlings v. Kentucky,* 448 U.S. 98 (1980); *New York v. Belton,* 453 U.S. 454 (1981); *United States v. Ross,* 456 U.S. 798 (1982); *Michigan v. Long,* 463 U.S. 1032 (1983); and *Oliver v. United States,* 466 U.S. 170 (1984).

2. McClurg, "Bringing Privacy Law Out of the Closet," 1000–1002. See also James Goodale, Robert Sherman, Paul Schwartz, Deirdre Mulligan, and Steven Emmert, "Privacy Laws and the First Amendment: A Conflict?" panel discussion, *Fordham Intellectual Property, Media and Entertainment Law Journal* 11 (2000): 21, and Christopher Slobogin, "Public Privacy: Camera Surveillance of Public Places and the Right to Anonymity," *Mississippi Law Journal* 72 (2002): 213.

As I mentioned in Chapter 6, anonymous communication, online or otherwise, allows individuals to express themselves freely without fear of censure. Citing precedents dating back to the 1950s, Nadine Strossen, president of the American Civil Liberties Union, writes, "In all these cases, the Court has recognized that without the cloak of anonymity, many individuals simply will not exercise their First Amendment rights. They will not freely associate with controversial organizations, nor will they express controversial ideas or discuss sensitive subjects."[3] Privacy also reinforces free speech by supporting access to information. When Virginia mandated blocking software to deny access to pornographic materials online and required permission and public disclosure to turn off the blocking software, free speech was threatened. Professors and researchers across numerous disciplines were loath to disclose the subject matter of their studies—especially when such disclosures would occur "piecemeal" and unaccompanied by the final written document.[4]

While privacy may reinforce speech or expression in some cases, there are also numerous tensions. In this chapter I will argue that upon careful analysis there is little conflict between privacy and expression in the *moral* realm. Moreover, if legal systems are to reflect, promote, or protect basic rights, then it is not so clear that speech should nearly always trump privacy. The ascendancy of speech protection in the legal realm, I argue, is due to an expansive and unjustified view of the value or primacy of free expression—this is perhaps understandable, given that privacy has been understood as a mere interest, whereas speech rights have been seen as more fundamental. If the primary claims of earlier chapters are correct, we should not view privacy as any less important or fundamental than free speech.

Before offering a method for balancing privacy claims and speech protections, I will briefly consider several arguments—or strands of argument—purporting to justify free speech rights. While these arguments, taken together, establish that free speech is important, they do not support the view that speech should nearly always trump privacy. In the second part of this chapter, I will suggest a way to balance free speech and privacy claims.

ESTABLISHING A MORAL PRESUMPTION IN FAVOR OF SPEECH AND EXPRESSION

I am always surprised when legal scholars talk of the value of speech or privacy without giving any analysis of the concept of value itself. My sur-

---

3. Strossen, "Protecting Privacy," 2107.
4. Ibid., 2108.

prise grows as these same scholars move from *value* claims to *ought* claims—as if the one automatically follows from the other. Balancing free speech and privacy at the legal level without providing foundations for these values and obligations leaves the entire enterprise hanging in thin air. Paraphrasing Jeremy Bentham, such views appear to be "nonsense on stilts."[5]

The American system of government can be understood as a method of maximizing social utility within certain constraints. Thus it may be the case that some rights exist independent of governments, while others are simply created by governments or institutions. The first may be called "bottom-up" rights; the second "top-down" rights. Privacy rights are bottom-up because they exist independent of government or societal institutions. Many have claimed that intellectual property rights are top-down rights because they are created by an act of the state and do not exist prior to or independent of government.[6]

If we take the position that freedom of expression is a top-down right created and dependent on government or society, then it would seem that privacy rights advocates have won an important battle. For while it is the case that we sometimes sanction the overriding of basic rights in the name of social utility, the cases are rare and the burden of proof high. The right to property, for example, is a basic right; eminent domain laws place the burden of showing need on those who would override it, require just and fair compensation for the taking, and give the property owner recourse to the courts if she thinks she has been unjustly treated.[7] Ratified in 1791, the Fifth Amendment of the Constitution holds that "[No person] . . . shall . . . be deprived of life, liberty, or property, without due process of law; nor shall private property be taken for public use, without just compensation." Similarly, but not necessarily for the sake of promoting social utility, depriving an individual of life or liberty in terms of imprisonment or capital punishment puts the burden of proof squarely on those who would override these rights. Overriding basic rights within the Anglo-American tradition, or what I have called bottom-up rights, is serious business.

---

5. Jeremy Bentham, *Introduction to the Principles of Morals and Legislation* (New York: Garland, 1981). Even those who would defend legal positivism—the view that there is no necessary connection between morality and the law—appeal to moral norms by positing that the purpose of legal systems is to ameliorate the human condition and provide for security and stability. See, for example, H. L. A. Hart, *The Concept of Law* (Oxford: Clarendon Press, 1961).

6. I have argued at length that this view of intellectual property is false. See Moore, *Intellectual Property and Information Control.*

7. For an in-depth analysis of the "takings clause," see Richard Epstein, *Takings: Private Property and the Power of Eminent Domain* (Cambridge: Harvard University Press, 1985).

Viewing free speech rights as top-down, state-created entitlements and privacy rights as bottom-up, preexisting rights would turn much of the current debate between privacy rights and free speech on its head. Rather than talking about privacy limitations on speech with nearly all of the cards held by the speech side (see the relevant cases cited in Chapter 6), we would have privacy holding nearly all the cards. In this case social utility advanced by free speech and eminent domain would be constrained by the more basic rights of privacy and property. More minimally, it would be odd to maintain that free speech and expression should nearly always trump privacy.

The legal right to free speech, on the other hand, might be a reflection of more basic moral norms. If individuals have moral rights to speech and expression, then the playing field will have been leveled—neither set of rights would be, by their nature, more fundamental or weighty. There are at least seven promising strategies for establishing speech rights. After briefly considering and dismissing the absolutist position with respect to free speech, I will present each of these strategies in turn. While brief, this analysis is important because it supports my claim that we should not view speech rights as more important or fundamental than privacy rights.[8]

ABSOLUTISM VERSUS BALANCING: A FALSE DICHOTOMY?

The free speech absolutist maintains that there should be no restrictions on speech or expression. On this view, speech is an absolute value that cannot be traded away or balanced against competing values. Justice Hugo Black wrote: "It is my belief that there *are* 'absolutes' in our Bill of Rights, and that they were put there on purpose by men who knew what words meant, and meant their prohibitions to be 'absolutes.' . . . Our First Amendment was a bold effort to adopt this principle—to establish a country with no legal restrictions of any kind upon the subjects people could investigate, discuss and deny."[9]

8. For a nice analysis of many of these arguments and issues, see Amy E. White, *Virtually Obscene: The Case for an Uncensored Internet* (Jefferson, N.C.: McFarland, 2006).

9. Hugo L. Black, "The Bill of Rights," *New York University Law Review* 35 (1960): 866, 881; *Konigsberg v. State Bar*, 366 U.S. 36 (1961); *Whitney v. California*, 274 U.S. 357, 374–77 (1927). See also Jed Rubenfeld, "The First Amendment's Purpose," *Stanford Law Review* 53 (2001): 767; Alexander Meiklejohn, "The First Amendment Is an Absolute," *Supreme Court Review*, 1961, 245; Harry Kalven Jr., "Privacy in Tort Law—Were Warren and Brandeis Wrong?" *Law and Contemporary Problems* 31 (Spring 1966); Zimmerman, "Requiem for a Heavyweight," 291;

Alexander Meiklejohn, in "The First Amendment Is an Absolute," refined the absolutist position in light of several obvious and devastating problems.[10] Quid pro quo sexual harassment, blackmail, extortion, false advertising, and the like cannot be defended on free speech grounds, Meiklejohn concludes, noting that "the First Amendment does not protect a 'freedom to speak.' It protects the freedom of those activities of thought and communication by which we govern."[11]

The problem with Meiklejohn's view and this latter move is that the issue is merely sidestepped. It is not at all clear which thoughts and communications are necessary for self-government—or which expressions count as speech. Meiklejohn seems like less of an absolutist when he claims, "Congress may . . . 'regulate' the activities by which the citizens govern the nation. . . . A citizen may be told when and where and in what manner he may or may not speak, write, assemble, and so on. . . . We must recognize that there are many forms of communication which, since they are not being used as activities of governing, are wholly outside the scope of the First Amendment."[12] Some of these might be non-newsworthy speech that opens up private lives for public consumption, trade secrets and trademarks, or a "recipe" for creating an extremely lethal and easily transferable biological agent—I doubt that Justice Hugo Black would defend the expression or dissemination of such information. It would seem that absolutists do their balancing in coming up with the category of "speech" or "protected speech" while the balancers adopt an expanded definition of speech and balance afterward. My proposal could be considered a way to define what counts as speech or as a method for determining the correct balance between speech and privacy. Viewed one way, it could be considered absolutist; viewed another, balancing.

TRUTH DISCOVERY

Presumptive claims to free speech and expression are essential for truth discovery. John Stuart Mill argued, "The peculiar evil of silencing the ex-

Solveig Singleton, "Privacy Versus the First Amendment: A Skeptical Approach," *Fordham Intellectual Property, Media and Entertainment Law Journal* 11 (2000): 97; and Volokh, "Freedom of Speech and Information Privacy," 1049.

    10. Meiklejohn, "First Amendment," 245.

    11. Ibid., 255.

    12. Ibid., 257, 258.

pression of an opinion is, that it is robbing the human race; posterity as well as the existing generation; those who dissent from the opinion, still more than those who hold it. If the opinion is right, they are deprived of the opportunity of exchanging error for truth: if wrong, they lose, what is almost as great a benefit, the clearer perception and livelier impression of truth, produced by its collision with error."[13] If we view truth discovery as a social process whereby ideas are freely traded, checked, and analyzed, then we should view speech regulations with suspicion. No one is immune to error, and the "collision of ideas" associated with free speech is the best method we have for determining truth or justified belief.

At best though, Mill's argument does not support the view that free speech is an overriding value—a value that trumps all others. As Sir James Fitzjames Stephen puts it, "If . . . the object aimed at is good, if the compulsion employed such as to attain it, and if the good obtained overbalances the inconveniences of the compulsion itself, I do not understand how, upon utilitarian principles, the compulsion can be bad."[14] In short, other values or strategic rules—like privacy—may trump expression in certain cases. Moreover, it is questionable that in the "marketplace of ideas" the truth will win in the end. As a hypothetical case, suppose that God, of whatever form, does not exist. It is doubtful, given our propensity to believe, that truth will triumph over falsehood in this case, regardless of how much discussion we give to the topic.

THE ARGUMENT FROM INTRINSIC VALUE

The argument from intrinsic value holds that having a sense of dignity, obtaining security, developing one's abilities to a consistent and harmonious whole, and liberty are each intrinsically valuable. Thus, liberty is not related to flourishing as a cause to an effect but as a part to a whole. On this account any interference with the liberty of thought and expression is necessarily a lessening of human flourishing or well-being.

As with the truth discovery argument, the argument from intrinsic value doesn't show that on balance the best consequences cannot be obtained by interfering with free speech and expression. When liberty conflicts with other elements of well-being, it may still be that interference with liberty is justified on consequentialist grounds.

13. Mill, *On Liberty*, 16–17.
14. Sir James Fitzjames Stephen, *Liberty, Equality, Fraternity*.

A CHECK ON POWER

A third well-known argument supporting presumptive claims to free speech has to do with accountability and checks on those in power.[15] First, in having their actions scrutinized by a free press and a robust exchange of ideas those in power are less likely to abuse power. Second, when an official does commit a crime or abuses power, the press may expose the wrong and force corrective actions to be taken. The sentiment of this view was captured nicely by Supreme Court Justice Louis Brandeis when he wrote, "A little sunlight is the best disinfectant."[16]

As with truth discovery, this argument does not support the view that free speech is an overriding value. A free press may indeed be an important check on governmental power, but freedom of the press does not have to be extended to sanction intrusions into the private lives of ordinary citizens. Furthermore, privacy itself may be an important check on governmental power and control.

SELF-GOVERNMENT

Free speech and expression are also important in relation to self-government and democracy—this is Meiklejohn's view. To be an active citizen and take part in public life, one must be informed about a wide range of issues, policies, and disputes. Conscientious voting, for example, requires information and understanding. Information access is also important for efficient and just democratic institutions.

An often-mentioned variation of Mill's consequentialist argument in favor of expression is that free speech is necessary for democracy and an open society. Representative government requires a robust information flow between voters and public officials. Moreover, suppression and censorship are typically practiced by those in power, and more often than not, in ways that extend, promote, and stabilize the prevailing power relations. A free press works as a check on government run amok and on other information sources.

Michael Curtis has argued convincingly that such considerations have

15. See Vincent Blasi, "The Checking Value in First Amendment Theory," *American Bar Foundation Research Journal*, 1977, 521.

16. Louis Brandeis, *Other People's Money, and How the Bankers Use It* (New York: Frederick A. Stokes, 1914), 92.

been undermined by current mass-media practices.[17] Curtis notes that in the 1800s, the press provided a wide range of viewpoints, ownership was decentralized, and newspapers typically printed entire debates and covered political issues in great detail. In modern times, media is dominated by television and ownership has become centralized: "At the end of World War II, 80 percent of American newspapers were independently owned. When Ben Haig Bagdikian published *Media Monopoly* (Beacon Press) in 1982, 50 corporations owned almost all of the major media outlets in the United States. That included 1,787 daily newspapers, 11,000 magazines, 9,000 radio stations, 1,000 television stations, 2,500 book publishers and seven major movie studios. By the time Bagdikian put out the revised edition in 1987, the number was down to 29 corporations. And now there are nine. They own it all."[18]

Moreover, unlike the media outlets of the 1800s, modern media sources devote an ever decreasing amount of time to political, philosophical, and theological positions and issues. "In 1968 the average presidential campaign sound bite on network news was forty-three seconds. In the 1996 election, it dropped to 8.2 seconds."[19] We hear less and less from the candidates themselves, and more from analysts and "talking heads," who focus on the polls and the "horse race" rather than important content. For example, George W. Bush's arrest for drunk driving, an event that happened twenty-five years before the 2000 election, received more coverage than all the foreign policy issues combined.[20]

Curtis also notes that as serious news coverage has been replaced with trivial fluff, political advertising has increased. In lieu of getting their message out through news services, candidates simply buy television and radio time and fill the airways with political advertisements. This trend makes it difficult for newcomers to enter the political arena because of the vast amount of money needed to become noticed. Furthermore, a cozy relationship emerges between incumbents—who typically have less trouble raising the cash necessary to run a modern campaign—and media sources, who rake in billions in advertising revenue.

17. Michael Kent Curtis, "Democratic Ideals and Media Realities: A Puzzling Free Press Paradox," *Social Philosophy and Policy* 21 (2004): 385–487.

18. Molly Ivins, "Three New Books Offer Suggestions for Fixing the Media Mess," *Charleston Gazette,* November 2, 1999, A-4; cited in Curtis, "Democratic Ideals and Media Realities," 406.

19. Steven Hill, *Fixing Elections: The Failure of America's Winner Take All Politics* (New York: Routledge, 2002), 68; cited in Curtis, "Democratic Ideals and Media Realities," 407.

20. Thomas E. Patterson, *The Vanishing Voter: Public Involvement in an Age of Uncertainty* (New York: Knopf, 2002), 48; cited in Curtis, "Democratic Ideals and Media Realities," 408.

The situation appears worse when considering issues connected to corporate interests. Curtis continues: "When the tobacco industry decided to oppose the amended version of the McCain tobacco bill, the industry spent 35 million dollars in television ads attacking the bill. Viewers were regaled with pictures of a cuckoo bird coming out of a clock while an announcer solemnly announced that it was cuckoo time in Washington—with huge taxes on working people, 60 new bureaucracies, etc."[21]

While there were many inaccuracies and falsehoods in the advertisements, few media sources made note of them, and CNN, which aired most of the ads, failed to comment at all. As with paid political ads, the checking function of media outlets appears to be near nonexistent—although there is some hope that Internet-based sources will provide this service.[22]

Curtis continues with case after case, each undermining the view that modern media practices provide a checking function against government and other media sources. If such contentions are plausible, then our modified version of Mill's argument is suspect.[23]

For those who continue to doubt, consider the following thought experiment. Imagine a society with numerous media sources and no government restrictions on speech. Each source, however, decides to publish fluff and avoid political and philosophical issues. In this case we could have total freedom of speech and shoddy democratic institutions built upon false information or no information. Unrestricted freedom of speech is not sufficient to guarantee a robust democracy. It is also not necessary. There are numerous restrictions on freedom of speech currently in place, and even more were in place in the 1800s, yet then and now, our democratic institutions seem fairly robust.

21. Bill Moyers, "Free Speech for Sale," PBS Television, June 8, 1999; cited in Curtis, "Democratic Ideals and Media Realities," 410.

22. While Internet sources may be able to provide a checking function on government, these same sources may become relatively useless if governments control the pipeline or the initial disclosure of information. A government that keeps its secrets safe while employing censorship-enhancing technologies may be able to minimize the effects of a free Internet-based press.

23. McClurg notes, "At the end of Clinton's first year in office, when the clamor concerning his sex life had quieted down, an article in *The American Spectator* reignited the furor. The article detailed lurid accusations of sexual misconduct made by two Arkansas state troopers who served on Clinton's security detail while he was governor of Arkansas. A NEXIS computer search revealed an astounding 13,210 newspaper articles written about President Clinton and his sex life, as well as 1,394 magazine articles. To appreciate the magnitude of these figures, consider that print coverage of the Brady Bill, involving a controversial public policy issue that generated fierce debate for seven years before its passage, has produced a comparatively meager 5,733 newspaper articles and 328 magazine articles." McClurg, "Bringing Privacy Out of the Closet," 1013.

ADVANCING AUTONOMY AND PROMOTING TOLERANCE

Like the self-government argument, the "advancing autonomy" argument holds that free speech is an important part of individual growth and self-realization. Forming our own beliefs, taking stands on issues we find important, and defending our commitments promote autonomy. The claim is not that insisting on free speech will produce maximally autonomous individuals but that such policies will produce agents with more autonomy compared to systems where speech is suppressed.

Adopting a policy of free speech and expression also promotes tolerance in obvious ways. For example, when individuals are confronted with views, opinions, and ways of living that are different from their own, it is difficult to remain unhesitatingly sure of one's own views. It becomes even more difficult when those with foreign views are successful, happy, and well adjusted. Moreover, in dealing with others, friendships—or at least the basis of respect—will inevitably form.

As with the other views, these arguments do not support the claim that free speech is an overriding value. Privacy also promotes autonomy, toleration, and diversity. As I noted in Chapter 3, it is behind the walls of privacy that individuals grow and experiment with new ways of living. These differences provide the background for tolerance.

THE BEST POLICY ARGUMENT

John Stuart Mill's "best policy" argument seeks to show that even if interference with liberty may, in principle, be justified, we ought on consequentialist grounds to adopt the sort of absolute principle he endorses. Mill says: "The strongest of all the arguments against the interference of the public with purely personal conduct is that when it does interfere, the odds are that it interferes wrongly and in the wrong place."[24] When government interferes with speech and expression, it will likely mess things up horribly. Thus, the best policy will be to severely restrict the government's role in this area.

But privacy advocates will quickly note that publishing or broadcasting sensitive personal information about others is not "purely personal conduct"—not on any defensible meaning of that phrase. It would seem that

24. Mill, *On Liberty*, chap. 4.

privacy is embedded in the notion of "the public" and "purely personal conduct." Moreover, consider Mill's harm principle: "The sole end for which mankind are warranted, individually or collectively, in interfering with the liberty of action of any of their number, is self-protection. The only purpose for which power can be rightfully exercised over any member of a civilized community, against his will, is to prevent harm to others."[25]

If privacy is valuable, then speech that violates privacy may indeed harm—and if individuals have privacy rights, then the harm may be magnified. It seems that in the end Mill's arguments in support of free speech and expression will not provide the near absolute status that speech advocates desire. Mill's justification of moral rights to speech may provide a foundation for legal speech rights. Nevertheless, such justifications open up the possibility that free speech should be traded for more privacy.

THE PARETO ARGUMENT

We may be able to provide for free speech rights in the same way we argued for privacy rights in earlier chapters. If the disclosure of some bit of information does not worsen an individual's level of material well-being compared to the appropriate base point of comparison, then the act of disclosure is permitted. If interfering with such acts does worsen that level of material well-being, then rights have been established. Moreover, speech or expression that may worsen others at the level of acts may be overbalanced by the goods that flow from a system or institution of free speech. Like the utilitarian we are concerned with good and bad consequences. Unlike the utilitarian, we are not trying to *maximize* social utility or progress. If the harm that occurs by publishing private facts is overbalanced by other values provided by the system or institution of free speech, then no worsening has occurred and the act is permitted.

Like the other arguments offered to this point, however, the Pareto argument fails to elevate free speech over privacy. In light of the arguments offered in Chapter 3, privacy emerges as a core human value necessary for human well-being or flourishing. While free speech and expression may end up being equally weighty in terms of promoting human flourishing, it would be difficult to maintain that speech is somehow more primary or fundamental. If anything, the reverse appears to be true. Without bodily

25. Ibid., 1.

privacy at least, free speech is impossible. Or to put the point another way, there can be both strong privacy rights and speech rights, so long as the latter do not cross into private domains. Informational privacy, on the other hand, would be completely eradicated if there were no restrictions on speech or access.

The upshot of this discussion is that we should challenge the assumption that expression is more valuable when compared to other values like privacy. It is not clear that any of the arguments given in support of free speech, taken individually or together, are strong enough to establish the claim that speech is more important than privacy or other important values like security or property.

BALANCING PRIVACY AND FREE SPEECH

In determining the correct balance between free speech and individual informational privacy John Rawls's notion of placing individuals behind a veil of ignorance may be of some service.[26] Imagine that we are trying to determine if some bit of information unnecessarily crosses into private domains—here we are trying to produce a method that will mark appropriate from inappropriate domains of free speech and expression. Behind this veil of ignorance individuals do not know any specific facts about themselves, such as age, race, gender, political affiliation, life goals, profession, subjective desires, and the like. What individuals do know, however, is that freedom of expression is valuable and important for stable democratic institutions and that privacy is valuable and necessary for human flourishing. From this vantage point we can ask two important questions. What information is necessary for stable democratic institutions and what speech or expression violates informational privacy? Some may argue that these questions do not mark out distinct kinds—that is, some information may fall into both domains. For example, Republicans may argue that character is an important consideration related to stable democratic institutions, and thus the speech about former president Clinton's extramarital activity was justified. But the objectivity forced upon us by Rawls's veil of ignorance would seemingly rule out such reasoning. Countless personal vices have been a part of the political landscape at all levels of government since the founding of this country, and they have not destabilized its institutions in

26. Rawls, *A Theory of Justice*, 136–42.

any obvious way. An elected official breaking the law would be another matter. To refine and further clarify this view, consider the following cases.

Case 1. *Cape Publications, Inc. v. Bridges*

> A woman is kidnapped, taken to an apartment, stripped, and terror-ized. The police—and the media—surround the apartment. The po-lice eventually overcome the kidnapper and rush the woman, who clutches a dish towel in a futile attempt to conceal her nudity, to safety. A photograph of her escape is published in the next day's newspaper. She sued for invasion of privacy and eventually lost the case.[27]

From an unbiased position we can easily split the information found in this case into two types. First, there is a host of information surrounding the good deeds and works of the police and other public officials. Facts like "the attacker was subdued," "the victim was unharmed," and "the police lieutenant Jane Smith organized the rescue" are each appropriate items for publication and discussion. On the other hand, facts like the information found in the photo of the escape and the sex, name, address, and workplace of the victim and the names of the victim's family clearly invade private domains and are not obviously important in maintaining democratic insti-tutions. To put the point another way, if we were to consider this case from behind the veil of ignorance, remembering that privacy and speech are important human values, then perhaps an unbiased vantage point will have been obtained—we have no compelling need to access personal infor-mation about the victim.

Case 2. *DeGregorio v. CBS, Inc.*

> Two construction workers, male and female, were walking hand in hand down Madison Avenue in New York City when they noticed that they were being filmed by a television crew. The couple told the television crew to stop filming, as they were both involved in other relationships. Nevertheless, the film aired twice on a CBS broadcast entitled "Couples in Love." The suit brought by the couple was dis-

---

27. *Cape Publications, Inc. v. Bridges,* 423 So. 2d 426 (Fla. Dist. Ct. App. 1982); cited in Alderman and Kennedy, *Right to Privacy,* 171.

missed. The court held that the subject matter—romance—was of public interest.[28]

Assuming that the identities of the couple were discernible from the footage, we may wonder what socially important information was being made available in this case. The idea that romance was alive and kicking in our society, hardly something that anyone would need convincing of, could have been conveyed without disclosing the identities of the individuals involved. Identifying markers could have been blurred or not shown at all. Moreover, the notion of "public interest" employed in the decision is troubling. It is as if the court reasoned that just because a bunch of people find romance interesting, content providers have a blank check on gathering and publishing such information—especially when the information is captured in a public setting.

Given that interests can be manipulated, manufactured, and arbitrary, it seems suspect at best to base law on such a test. Furthermore, such a test would allow the dissemination of information that has little to do with truth discovery, autonomy, self-government, or the other rationales for free speech. Finally, in Chapter 3, several arguments were presented for why "interest," "preferences," or "desire satisfaction" accounts of moral value are unworkable.

Following *Paulsen v. Personality Posters*[29] the court in *DeGregorio* adopted an extremely liberal notion of "public interest," going well beyond what might be considered newsworthy.

> The scope of the subject matter which may be considered of "public interest" or "newsworthy" has been defined in most liberal and far-reaching terms. The privilege of enlightening the public is by no means limited to dissemination of news in the sense of current events but extends far beyond to include all types of factual, educational and historical data, or even entertainment and amusement, concerning interesting phases of human activity in general.

> An even more liberal view of the permissible limits of such privileged expression has recently been enunciated by the United States Supreme Court in *Time, Inc. v. Hill* (385 U.S. 374) which involved the

28. *DeGregorio v. CBS, Inc.*, 473 N.Y.S.2d 922 (N.Y. Sup. Ct. 1984); cited in Alderman and Kennedy, *Right to Privacy*, 220.

29. *Paulsen v. Personality Posters*, 59 Misc. 2d 444, 299 N.Y.S.2d 501 (Sup. Ct. 1968).

application and construction of the New York "Right of Privacy" statute here relied upon. The court there made clear that such statute must be construed in light of the primacy of the far-reaching constitutional protections for speech and press which afford immunity even to false or fictional reports of matters of public interest unless published with knowledge of their falsity or in reckless disregard of the truth. Its expansive construction of the vast range of matter, both informative and entertaining and irrespective of timeliness or importance of the ideas seeking expression, which comes within the ambit of constitutional protection is consistent with its conviction that, "A broadly defined freedom of the press assures the maintenance of our political system and an open society." (*Time, Inc. v. Hill, supra*, 389)[30]

Clearly such an expansive definition of "public interest" and "newsworthiness" is not necessary for the maintenance of our political system or for an open society. No one would argue that the chilling effect of prohibiting certain kinds of speech and expression—such as sexual harassment, child pornography, and publishing trade secrets—undermines the stability of government and freedom of thought and discussion. Robust defenders of free speech would have us believe that each speech restriction erodes the very foundations of our society. Arguably Western democracies promote open societies because such openness is thought to secure individual liberty and rights. A free press may be an essential check on government run amok, but when that power is used to open up private lives for public consumption, it would seem that privacy rights are violated, media agencies make money, certain individuals get a "gossip fix"—and nothing more.

Case 3. *Sipple v. San Francisco Chronicle Inc.* (1975)

> In a split second, a decorated Vietnam veteran deflects a gun aimed at President Gerald Ford. The media celebrates the man as a hero. A reporter discovers that the man is a homosexual, a fact of which his family was not aware. A motion to suppress is denied, and the reluctant hero's sexuality becomes part of the national story.[31]

30. Ibid. See *Gautier v. Pro-Football*, 304 N.Y. 354 (1952); *Julian Messner, Inc. v. Warren E. Spahn*, U.S. Supreme Court, May 22, 1967, 87 S. Ct. 1706; 387 U.S. 239; 18 L.Ed.2d 744; *Dallesandro v. Holt and Co.*, 4 A.D.2d 470 [1st Dept 1957], 166 N.Y.S.2d 805; and *Goelet v. Confidential, Inc.*, 5 A.D.2d 226 [1st Dept 1958], 171 N.Y.S.2d 2235 A.D. 2d 226.

31. *Sipple v. San Francisco Chronicle, Inc.* (1975). This case is cited in Alderman and Kennedy, *Right to Privacy*, 171.

As with the first two cases the information found in this case is easily split into two categories. Facts like "an assassination attempt on the president occurred" and "James Smith, a Secret Service agent, did his job removing the president from a potentially dangerous situation" are certainly appropriate to disseminate and would be deemed as such from an unbiased position. Sensitive personal information about the citizen-hero—his sexual preferences, home address, favorite place to eat, and medical history—would be categorized as "personal" and not relevant to stable democratic institutions or an open society.

Case 4. Video Voyeurs
The Video Voyeurs case from Chapter 6 bears repeating here.

> The Plaza security observed via the video surveillance system a subject carrying a shopping bag, riding the escalator up and down on several occasions. As security observed the subject, they noticed he was entering the escalator to ride up to the second story behind women wearing skirts. The subject placed a shopping bag on the step below the female wearing the skirt, and would ride up the escalator until it reached the top floor. The subject would then ride down the escalator and wait [for] another female wearing a skirt. . . . Plaza security contacted the subject and found that he had an 8mm video camera hidden in a shoebox within the shopping bag . . . [and he] admitted to video taping the women wearing skirts in order to sell the videotape to an Internet website.[32]

As I noted in Chapter 6, it is shocking that such activity was neither criminally nor civilly prohibited in many states. To push things a bit further though, some may object to such activity on the grounds of the commercialism involved—imagine that the subject published the tapes on the Internet along with the names of those taped and a story entitled "Information Availability in Public Places." Would such a linkage between the tapes and the story in any way mitigate the wrongness found in the privacy violation? I believe the answer is no. Again, if there was any important content to the expression, it could have been conveyed in a noninvasive manner. Moreover, when placed behind the veil of ignorance, we could more readily determine the kinds of information important for upholding individual rights from information that undermines these rights.

32. Eatonto Ackerman, June 7, 1999; cited in Rothenberg, "Re-Thinking Privacy," 1127.

While contested by many legal scholars, the courts have recognized a distinction between low-value and high-value speech or expression.[33] In *Barns v. Glen Theater, Inc.*[34] the court noted that while nude dancing is expressive, it is "marginally and on the outer perimeters" of First Amendment protection. Such expression is "low-value" expression—low-value in terms of promoting an open society and stable democratic institutions. Commercial speech is also protected less vigorously than political speech.[35]

On my view, speech that is low-value and violates informational privacy rights should be more readily liable to prior restraint and, once broadcast, should expose its publishers to civil and criminal damages. Given that we have no general moral right not to be offended, low-value speech that simply offends would still be protected. When censorship is based on "offensiveness" standards, we should proceed with great caution. When censorship is based on rights violations, as with restrictions placed on divulging trade secrets or on child pornography, we should proceed aggressively.[36]

Case 5. Photographs and the Protest Against the War in Vietnam

On June 8, 1972, the nightly news broadcast the photograph of several screaming Vietnamese children fleeing a napalm strike in South Vietnam. The little girl in the center of the photograph was stark naked and badly burned; she had torn off all of her clothes in a futile attempt to escape the searing effects of the napalm. This photograph became "the last major icon" of the antiwar movement and "probably did more to increase public revulsion against the war than a hundred hours of televised barbarities."[37]

To be sure, this sort of case is extremely difficult. Here we have an expression that had a profound political impact on the course of the war pressing against the rights of the girl not to be violated and exploited in a

33. See, for example, Alex Kozinski and Stuart Banner, "Who's Afraid of Commercial Speech," *Virginia Law Review* 76 (1990).

34. *Barns v. Glen Theater, Inc.*, 501 U.S. 560 (1991).

35. Alex Kozinski and Stuart Banner, "The Anti-History and Pre-History of Commercial Speech: A Problem in the Theory of Freedom," *Iowa Law Review* 62 (1976). See also *Valentine v. Chrestensen*, 316 U.S. 52, 42, 54 (1942).

36. One could also talk of low-value and high-value privacy. For example, controlling access to one's body would be high-value privacy, whereas controlling access to the fact that one is an adult might be low value. As I noted in Chapter 2, what would count as high-value and low-value privacy would depend, in part, on cultural norms.

37. Vicki Goldberg, *The Power of Photography: How Photographs Changed Our Lives* (New York: Abbeville Press, 1991), 7; cited in T. Allen et al., "Privacy, Photography, and the Press."

moment of great pain and agony. If there were no identifying features, nothing that would link the photograph to the girl in later life, then there may be no privacy violation. Moreover, this result may be achieved by manipulating the image in some way. This is exactly what happened in a recent case dealing with Iraqi prisoners at Abu Ghraib prison outside Baghdad. In a shocking turn of events, shocking because the United States, in part, invaded Iraq to liberate Iraqi citizens from rights abuses, numerous U.S. guards were photographed attacking, humiliating, and torturing bound Iraqi prisoners. In addition, many of these prisoners were rounded up without probable cause. Without diminishing the power and effect of the photographs, the identities of the Iraqi prisoners were shielded through the use of blurring and white-out techniques.

To return to the case of the napalm strike in Vietnam, if the political impact somehow rested on the identifying markers found in the photograph and if no consent was given by the girl or her legal guardians, then I believe we should proceed with great caution. American democracy is founded on the notion that individuals are not to be sacrificed in terms of life, liberty, or property for mere increases in social utility—no matter how great the benefit, society does not get to kill or incarcerate individuals without first guaranteeing due process and recourse to the courts. To put the point another way, those in the Rawls's original position would likely forgo the benefits of publishing an uncensored photograph in favor of a modified version that protects the privacy and life prospects of a minor.

A right to free speech and expression is not a license to do or say whatever one wills. Other individuals have rights that restrict the kinds of expressions that we may create and broadcast. Finally, from an unbiased vantage point, behind the veil of ignorance, few would so clearly come down on the side of free expression in this case and similar ones. The refrain "What if you were the girl in the photograph?" and assuming what we know about the value of privacy, would silence all but the most fanatic defenders of free speech.

CONCLUSION

Consider once again the table presented at the end of Chapter 6 mapping privacy intrusions along several dimensions. Included with motive, magnitude, context, and consent, the dimension of "public interest" appears. It was noted that if the disclosure of information was of great public importance, then suspicious motives, profound invasions in areas where there is a high expectation of privacy, and so on would not lead to an actionable cause. Notice as well that if the information in question was of little public importance and yet there were pure motives, little magnitude, and so on, we should not conclude that legal action is warranted. Like consent, a matter of great public importance is a "difference maker" when determining legal culpability.

To determine whether or not an event or disclosure of information is newsworthy and of public importance, I have used Rawls's notion of the original position. Again, we are to ask from an unbiased position, "Is the information or access in question necessary or clearly relevant to the maintenance or promotion of democracy, autonomy, self-government, and so on?" If not, then motive, magnitude, context, and consent will be the deciding factors. If so, we should not hastily conclude that dissemination or access is automatically justified independent of privacy considerations. Perhaps the matter could be published without identifying markers—allowing both privacy and speech to flourish.

It is clear that my view runs counter to prevailing attitudes about the First Amendment. I would place more prohibitions on speech or expression than are currently found in the law. Not only should we be prohibited from yelling "fire" in a crowded theater when there is no fire, we should be prohibited from publishing sensitive personal information without permission.

Politicians and entertainers, in a sense, sanction a more limited sphere of privacy by choosing a certain career path, and a similar point can be made with respect to criminals. While the sphere of privacy protection may be more limited in these cases, there are still boundaries that cannot be crossed. Becoming a "public figure" does not sanction continual harassment for autographs, pictures, and interviews. Access, in many ways, is still left to the individual—and this is how it should be.

On my view, an important part of a right to privacy is the right to control personal information; "control" in the sense of deciding who has access to this information and the uses to which such information can be put; "personal" in the sense of being about some individual as opposed to being about inanimate objects, corporations, institutions, and the like.

Against this backdrop, what sense can be made of the public's "right to know"? A newspaper may publish information about a kidnapping and rescue, but this does not sanction publishing sensitive personal information about the victim. Right-to-know arguments may carry some weight in cases where public funds are being spent or when a politician reverses his stand on a particular issue, but they seem to be suspect when used to justify intrusions. Sissela Bok echoes these concerns when she writes,

> Taken by itself, the notion that the public has a "right to know" is as quixotic from an epistemological as from a moral point of view, and the idea of the public's "right to know the truth" even more so. It would be hard to find a more fitting analogue to Jeremy Bentham's characterization of talk about natural and imprescriptible rights as "rhetorical nonsense—nonsense upon stilts." How can one lay claim to a right to know the truth when even partial knowledge is out of reach concerning most human affairs, and when bias and rationalization and denial skew and limit knowledge still further?
>
> So patently inadequate is the rationale of the public's right to know as a justification for reporters to probe and expose, that although some still intone it ritualistically at the slightest provocation, most now refer to it with a tired irony.[38]

The social and cultural benefits of free speech and free information are generally cited as justification for a free press and the public's right to know. But information technology has changed the playing field, and such arguments seem to lose force when compared to the overwhelming loss of privacy that we now face. The kinds of continual and systematic invasions by news services, corporations, data-mining companies, and other individuals that is now possible is quite alarming.

Judge Cooley, in *Atkinson v. Detroit Free Press Company,* stressed that everyone must exercise their rights with due regard for the rights of others. "This is as true of the right to free speech as it is of the right to the free enjoyment of one's property."[39] Just as there is no tension between liberty rights and property rights—your liberty rights do not include the freedom to use someone else's property—there is no tension between free speech and informational privacy rights. Your freedom of speech, within obvious exceptions, does not include the liberty to shout someone else's credit card number from the mountaintop or broadcast private facts about their life without consent.

---

38. Sissela Bok, *Secrets* (New York: Vintage Books, 1984), 254.
39. *Atkinson v. Detroit Free Press Company*, 46 Michigan 341; 376, 9 N.W. 501, 520 (1881) (Judge Cooley dissenting).

DRUG TESTING AND PRIVACY IN THE WORKPLACE

Being required, as a condition for continued employment, to submit a urine sample might strike many as a mild privacy intrusion—a necessary evil to be endured as part of one's work life. Being watched while providing such a sample may seem more intrusive—but again, necessary because of the numerous ways to defeat such a test. Consent to such surveillance is a prominent justification. As with the consent argument in favor of allowing publicly available information to be published, discussed in Chapter 6, we may question the strength of the consent argument in favor of workplace drug testing.

At a more general level, there is a lot of ground between our current national policy, aptly called the "war on drugs," and total unrestricted legalization—although few advocate this latter view. Criminalization of drug use, "three strike" rules, incarceration of those found with forbidden substances, asset seizures, and demonizing those who use and distribute drugs are features of current U.S. national drug policy. Aside from throwing more money at the problem, incarcerating an even higher percentage of the population, and making punishments harsher, it seems that we have reached the extreme end of prohibition views.[1] In any case, taking the war on drugs into the workplace has given license to a wide range of intrusive practices.

1. The United States incarcerates a higher percentage of its population compared to other countries because of invasive antidrug laws. "More than 5.6 million Americans are in prison or

To be blunt, I think that these policies are nonsense and amount to little more than the sentiment "What you are doing makes me uncomfortable, so we are going to put you in jail or fire you—for your own good." It is as if those folks who use drugs might somehow overpower the rest of us and take us down the road to abuse and dependency. But few want to ask the question, "Given current drug policy and the associated costs, how many users are also dependent?" Alas, the central issue is not use. There are lots of individuals who use all kinds of drugs who are not drug dependent. Let's pick a high number—say 20 percent. Suppose 20 percent of the users of any drug are also dependent on that drug and that we as a nation (at the federal, state, and local levels) are spending 50 billion dollars per year to fight this war.[2] Now we weren't fighting the war on drugs and spending 50 billion dollars per year (even adjusted for inflation) in 1950. My guess is that use and dependency rates in 1950 were much lower—and even if they weren't lower, suppose the dependency rates were the same or slightly higher, the costs are not comparable. All other things being equal, would a defender of the current war on drugs maintain that it is worth 50 billion dollars a year to save a small fraction of the population from becoming addicted—the difference between the number of addicts with or without the current war? Suppose X is the current number of addicts, while N is the number of additional addictions that would occur if the war on drugs ceased. Are those who champion policies of criminalization, "three strike" rules, incarceration, and asset seizures going to maintain that N would still be a sizable number if we stopped the war on drugs and spent 25 billion on drug rehabilitation and maintenance programs? That is a 25 billion dollar a year savings! The economics of U.S. drug policy do not make much sense, which is why most Western governments have either not adopted or moved away from the kind of religious war the U.S. government is fighting.

The costs to individual liberty are also staggering. From military raids in

have served time there, according to a new report by the Justice Department released Sunday. That's 1 in 37 adults living in the United States, the highest incarceration level in the world. . . . The prison population has quadrupled since 1980. Much of that surge is the result of public policy, such as the war on drugs and mandatory minimum sentencing. Nearly 1 in 4 of the inmates in federal and state prisons are there because of drug-related offenses, most of them nonviolent." Gail Russell Chaddock, "U.S. Notches World's Highest Incarceration Rate," *Christian Science Monitor*, August 18, 2003, http://www.csmonitor.com/2003/0818/p02s0-usju.html/.

2. Reports indicate that globally 5 percent of the population between ages fifteen and sixty-five use illegal drugs each year. This would mean 200 million individuals use illegal drugs annually. Of this population only 6 percent (12 million) are identified as drug dependent or "problem drug users." See "2007 World Drug Report," United Nations Office on Drugs and Crime, 15, http://www.unodc.org/pdf/research/wdr07/WDR_2007.pdf (accessed January 22, 2008).

foreign lands to knocking down doors in suburban America there has been an unrelenting assault on privacy and liberty in the name of this war. Aside from the overt losses of liberty and privacy involved in interdiction and the like, the price tag itself hides a loss of liberty. We are spending between 30 and 50 billion dollars a year (with somewhere between 30 and 60 cents of each dollar lost in overhead) to prosecute a war on forbidden chemicals. This is not free money—it represents, in large part, the time and effort of hard-working Americans and creates huge downstream burdens on developing countries. Moreover, as already noted, there are opportunity costs involved. We could be doing something else with this money.

An important component of the national "war on drugs" is found in the more mundane practice of employee drug testing. Few would deny that monitoring employees is a necessary part of doing business. The very act of paying someone for services would necessitate, in a competitive environment, that the product produced or time spent working be observed. Continued employment, raises, and profit-sharing awards require employers to monitor their employees. Moreover, surveillance may be necessary to diminish corporate liability for sexual harassment claims, employee theft, and other illegal activities that take place at work. Nevertheless, we may wonder at the efficacy and moral legitimacy of employee drug testing. In this chapter several of the most prominent arguments in support of employee drug testing will be considered. As we shall see, none of the arguments typically offered are particularly compelling.

ARGUMENTS IN FAVOR OF DRUG TESTING

As I noted in Chapter 2, a right to privacy can be understood as a right to limit public access to the "core self," personal information that one never discloses, and information that one discloses only to family and friends. Privacy also extends to use claims over bodies and locations. There are five major strands of argument justifying employee drug testing—and overriding employee privacy rights. First, employee drug use is said to cause accidents, both to other employees and to customers. Second, drug users may have increased medical problems and cause undue strain on the ability to provide high-level health coverage for each employee. Third, there are productivity issues, in that drug users may not be as productive on the job when compared to nonusers. Fourth, society, by engaging in a broad-based effort against drug use, sends the much-needed message to our children that such behavior is undesirable. Finally, employees typically waive their privacy rights in return for a job.[3]

SAFETY CONCERNS

Those in favor of employee drug testing often mention safety as a primary justification. Employees who use drugs at work are more likely to hurt themselves, their coworkers, and customers. Employees who use drugs during nonworking hours are more likely to come to work "hung over" and tired and thereby present safety risks. An often-cited statistic is that drug users are 3.6 times more likely to be involved in workplace accidents.[4] Furthermore, in certain work environments drug use is especially risky—for example, bus drivers, airline pilots, and nuclear power plant technicians. Given that drug use causes these increased risks, businesses, companies, and employers, the ones who will bear the costs of these risks, are justified in administering drug tests.

HEALTH CARE ISSUES

On-the-job or after-hours drug use may cause an increase in medical problems for users. Drug use can suppress the immune system, lead to mental or physical addiction, and cause the employee to take more sick days than their peers. In each of these cases there will likely be a corresponding increase in medical costs subsidized by the employer and other employees in the form of higher premiums. Drug users are five times more likely to file workers' compensation claims and use three times more health care benefits.[5] Since these increased medical costs will be distributed across nonusers and owners, drug testing is justified.

3. I am indebted to Judith Wagner DeCew's analysis and presentation of these issues. See her *In Pursuit of Privacy*, 125–44.

4. This statistic comes from what has become known as the "Firestone Study." As I explain later, this study does not exist and the claim has not been verified. For more about the "Firestone Study," see Lewis Maltby, "Drug Testing: A Bad Investment," ACLU Report (1999), 5–7, http://www.workrights.org/issue_drugtest_dt_drugtesting.pdf.

5. "Firestone Study." For more about the "Firestone Study," see Maltby, "Drug Testing," 5–7.

PRODUCTIVITY ISSUES

Independent of safety concerns and health care costs or sick days, drug use, it is claimed, causes a decrease in on-the-job productivity. The resulting loss in profits affects other employees and stockholders, ultimately undermining the value of the company and decreasing profit-sharing pools. Alcoholics and heroin addicts tend to produce less than their unimpaired counterparts. In addition, losses in short-term memory, muscle control, concentration, and the like will result in a decrease in quality. For example, not only will phone calls not be returned, but when they are, important content will be forgotten. Poor decisions can cost lots of money. As with increased health care expenses and safety concerns, the costs of decreased productivity will impact numerous individuals in negative ways.

FIGHTING THE WAR ON DRUGS—THE MORAL ARGUMENT

Some advocates of workplace drug testing adopt a moral stance based on the illegal status of drug use and its moral reprehensiveness. For example, Bishop Brent, the Anglican bishop of the Philippines (1901), wrote:

> The question is first and foremost a moral one. The use of the drug otherwise than medicinally is a vice. . . . The opium traffic stands in the category of crime except so far as it is imported for purely medicinal purposes. It cannot be ranked with the liquor trade, for, as every temperate man acknowledges, in this latter there is a legitimate consumption as a beverage, however much the liberty may be abused, whereas there is no unvicious use of opium or its immediate products as a foodstuff or beverage. The consumption of opium is not merely a personal weakness; it is a social vice, i.e. a crime.[6]

Moreover, we must fight this war on drugs, which includes workplace drug testing, to send the right message to our children. A "druggie" lifestyle does not lead to a good life but rather to dependence, depravity, and stagnation.

---

6. Alexander Zabriskie, *Bishop Brent: Crusader for Christian Unity* (Philadelphia: Westminster Press, 1948), 98; quoted in David Richards, *Sex, Drugs, Death, and the Law: An Essay on Human Rights and Overcriminalization* (Lanham, Md.: Rowman and Littlefield Publishers, 1982), chap. 4. James Q. Wilson, in "Against the Legalization of Drugs," *Commentary* 89 (February 1990): 21–28, argues that using drugs destroys the user's humanity and is thus immoral on Kantian grounds.

As a society we have a moral obligation to deter individuals from using drugs and becoming addicted. This justifies the war on drugs in general and workplace drug testing in particular.

THE CONSENT ARGUMENT

One of the most common arguments used to justify employee drug testing is based on the notion of a contract or agreement. When a prospective employee agrees to sell her productive efforts for a wage, she may also consent to drug testing. In this sort of case, the employee freely trades privacy for other benefits like a wage, profit sharing, or a vacation package. Given that the employee didn't have to agree to relinquish privacy and no one was physically forcing the employee to consent, drug testing is justified.

Related to these arguments are a host of dire claims about the effects of drug use. For example:

- Among full-time workers aged 18 to 49 in 2000, 8.1 percent reported past month heavy alcohol use, and 7.8 percent reported past month illicit drug use.
- "7.4 percent of these workers were dependent or abusing alcohol, and 1.9 percent were dependent or abusing illicit drugs."[7]
- Occupations and industries with higher concentrations of males, such as construction and mining, had higher rates of substance use than other occupations and industries, such as professional services.
- "In 1997, those who reported current illicit drug use were more likely than those who reported no current illicit drug use to have worked for three or more employers in the past year (9.3% vs. 4.3%), to have skipped one or more days of work in the past month (12.9% vs. 5.0%), or to have voluntarily left an employer in the past year (24.8% vs. 15.4%)."[8]

---

7. "Substance Use, Dependence or Abuse Among Full-time Workers," NHSDA Report, September 6, 2002, http://oas.samhsa.gov/2k2/workers/workers.htm/.

8. Substance Abuse and Mental Health Services Administration, Office of Applied Studies, "Worker Drug Use and Workplace Policies and Programs: Results from the 1994 and 1997," NHSDA, OAS Series A#11, DHHS Publication No. (SMA) 99-3352, Rockville, Md., 1999, http://oas.samhsa.gov/NHSDA/A-11/TOC.htm/.

A CRITIQUE OF THE PRO–DRUG TESTING ARGUMENTS

Putting aside the moral argument and the consent argument for now, let us assume that individuals have privacy rights and that employers, employees, and society have a legitimate interest in employee drug use based on safety, health care, and productivity worries—that is, we have two competing legitimate interests. Suppose that there was some way to obtain the information necessary to alleviate safety, health care, and productivity concerns while at the same time limiting incursions into private domains.[9] There are different ways of gathering information about employees. Given the nature of drug testing and how the tests are administered, it is arguably the case that this way of gathering information is fairly intrusive. A report provided by Substance Abuse and Mental Health Services Administration noted: "Analysis of the 1994 and 1997 NHSDA (National Household Survey on Drug Abuse) provides continued evidence that workplace policies about drug and alcohol use are associated with lower prevalence rates of current illicit drug use and heavy alcohol use among workers."

But the question is not "Does drug testing lower workforce use rates?" I suppose that we could lower drug use even further if employees were monitored around the clock via universal video surveillance coupled with automatic shock therapy. The question should be, "Are there any less invasive methods that are cost effective and yield the same sorts of information?"

One method that would not require accompanied trips to the bathroom, the drawing of blood, or the harvesting of hair or tissue would be a simple agility test administered by a licensed technician. Perhaps randomly, as many drug tests are now administered, the technician would test an employee before the beginning of a shift. In addition, an agility test could be tailored to the employee position. Tests for pilots, bus drivers, and life guards would be more involved and have higher standards for passing than tests for gardeners, cooks, and grocery clerks.[10]

Another benefit of agility testing is that it will catch other employee impairments that drug testing does not. For example, lack of sleep, independent of drug use, decreases employee productivity and increases safety

9. In *Samuel K. Skinner v. Railway Labor Executives' Association*, 489 U.S. 602 (1989), the court determined that blood and urine tests were minimally intrusive and did not constitute a serious harm. But harm in this case seems irrelevant. If individuals have privacy rights, then they have justified control over access to themselves independent of harm—the Peeping Tom may not harm and yet still violate a right.

10. Other, less invasive alternatives to employee drug testing are reference checking, supervisor training, and employee drug assistance programs.

concerns. An airline pilot who is plagued by insomnia is as much or more of a safety risk as a pilot who smokes marijuana in his off-duty hours. The severe alcoholic may easily pass drug tests—all he has to do is come to work sober. Physical and mental impairments caused by severe alcoholism, however, would be easily determined by agility testing, especially if employee-specific baselines were first determined.

Thus, if we assume that the arguments from safety, health care, and productivity are compelling and that individuals have privacy rights, then we should abandon drug testing in favor of agility testing or some other process. Agility testing would be less invasive, immediately relevant to "same day" employee performance, and sensitive to a wide variety of impairments related to safety, health care, and productivity issues.

Before moving on to consider the merits of the moral argument and the consent argument, I would like to more forcefully critique the arguments from safety, health care, and productivity—they are not as compelling as one might think. These arguments are both too strong and too weak. They sanction unnecessary incursions into private domains, they are not job specific, and simply miss employee impairments that are as serious as on-the-job drug use.

First, the arguments from safety, health care, and productivity are too strong. While they may justify drug testing, they would also justify a host of policies and procedures that most would find objectionable. For example, having children, along with the associated loss of sleep, increased sickness, and numerous parental obligations, causes these employees to produce less and cost more. Moreover, such costs will be shared by other employees, stockholders, and owners. None of this would justify mandatory employee attendance at company sponsored "anti-child" seminars. Or more minimally, these considerations do not appear to generate a legitimate corporate or public interest in monitoring employees.

Obese employees may also produce less and cost more than their thinner counterparts. Similarly with smokers, the elderly, the young, and even left-handers. Smokers as a group will likely cost more in terms of health care.[11] The elderly will probably not produce as much when working at jobs that require robust physical activity. The young may not have the experience or mental capacity to make correct decisions. Left-handers may be more acci-

---

11. This claim has been recently disputed—smokers are more likely to die younger and quicker than their nonsmoking counterparts.

dent prone.[12] Judith Wagner DeCew continues: "Besides confirming or disconfirming the presence of drugs in the body, analysis of blood and urine samples may reveal numerous physiological facts about the party being tested that he or she may not want shared with others. Tests can reveal such conditions as the use of contraceptives, pregnancy, epilepsy, manic depression, diabetes, schizophrenia, and heart trouble, for example."[13]

As DeCew notes, these arguments are too strong in a second sense as well—they permit the gathering and use of sensitive personal information that is independent of drug use.

The arguments from safety, health care, and productivity are also too weak. Drug testing does not affect "same day" performance, given that there is typically a time lag between the test and employee performance. Thus a bus driver may be severely inebriated, receive a drug test, and still take a seat behind the wheel. Lewis Maltby of the ACLU writes, "Drug tests mainly identify drug users who may have used a drug on the weekend, as they might use alcohol, and who are not under the influence of a drug while at work or when tested. Moreover, because it takes several hours for drug metabolites to appear in urine, drug tests may miss drug users who are under the influence of drugs at the time the test is given."[14] As already noted, drug tests do not even test for a wide variety of employee impairments that are as serious as drug use.

Drug testing is also inefficient in other ways. Darold Barnum and John Gleason claim that even when drug tests are accurate, they may yield a high "false accusation rate."

> The proportion of positive drug tests that are false, that is, the false accusation rate, can be high even when the tests themselves are judged to be extremely accurate by contemporary laboratory measures. In such cases, positive drug tests do not provide credible evidence of drug use. Our estimates of drug use, false positive rates, and true positive rates, all of which are based on recently published empirical evidence, indicate that under common circumstances, drug test results have high false accusation rates and hence low credibility.

12. Charles J. Graham, Rhonda Dick, Vaughn I. Rickert, and Robert Glenn, "Left-handedness as a Risk Factor for Unintentional Injury in Children," *Pediatrics* 92 (December 1993): 823–26.

13. Judith Wagner DeCew, "Drug Testing: Balancing Privacy and Public Safety," *Hastings Center Report* 24 (1994).

14. Maltby, "Drug Testing," 9.

. . . [I]f a drug-testing process that produces only one false positive per 2000 drug-free specimens, and no false negatives, is administered to a population in which 0.1% of the people use the targeted drugs, one-third of those identified as drug users will be falsely accused.[15]

By themselves these results, if accurate, cast doubt on the entire practice of employee drug testing.

Additionally, drug tests are easily avoided or defeated. "Those who practice timed abstinence or who ingest large amounts of fluid can dilute the concentration of a drug in urine to below the cutoff amount. Adding salt, vinegar, bleach, liquid soap, blood, or another interfering substance can adulterate samples and produce false negative results that do not rule out abuse."[16] Users can also switch to drugs that are difficult to detect or are not tested for at all.

Drug testing is not cost-effective either. One government study indicated that it costs $77,000 to find one drug user.[17] If one out of ten users was an actual drug abuser, then the cost of identifying that individual would be $770,000. The aviation industry reported spending $14 million per year on drug testing.[18] Texas Instruments reported spending $1 million per 10,000 workers on drug tests.[19] In the United States there are approximately two million hard-core drug abusers distributed primarily across entry-level and blue-collar jobs.[20] In addition, a substantial number of these abusers are chronically unemployed or underemployed. The proponent of drug tests would be quick to counter—we are not only after the drug abusers, mere use impacts safety, health care, and productivity. Or does it?

Two studies show that drug users were no more likely to be involved in workplace accidents than nonusers.[21] After reviewing several other studies,

15. Darold Barnum and John Gleason, "The Credibility of Drug Tests: A Multi-Stage Bayesian Analysis," *Industrial Relations Review* 47 (July 1994).

16. DeCew, "Drug Testing," 9.

17. Bureau of National Affairs, "Focus on Federal Drug Testing," *Individual Employment Rights* (April 1991): 4; cited in Maltby, "Drug Testing," 14.

18. Robert Wick, "Why Pilot Drug Tests Don't Improve Safety Record," *Flying*, December 1992, 68–71; cited in Maltby, "Drug Testing," 4.

19. Mark Rothstein, "Workplace Drug Testing: A Case Study in the Misapplication of Technology," *Harvard Journal of Law and Technology* 5 (1991): 65–93; cited in Maltby, "Drug Testing," 4.

20. Maltby, "Drug Testing," 14.

21. Jacques Normand et al., "An Evaluation of Preemployment Drug Testing," *Journal of Applied Psychology* 75 (1990): 926–39; Craig Zwerling et al., "The Efficacy of Preemployment Drug Screening for Marijuana and Cocaine in Predicting Employment Outcomes," *Journal of the American Medical Association* 264 (1990): 2639–43.

the National Academy of Sciences concluded that "illicit drugs contribute little to the overall rate of industrial accidents" and "were no more profound than the effects of sleep deprivation in the absence of drug use."[22] A study by Jacques Normand noted that moderate doses of cocaine as well as other stimulants yielded "slight performance enhancing effects."[23] Surprisingly, the claim that drug users are 3.6 times more likely to be involved in a workplace accident, a statistic that has been widely cited, cannot be substantiated. The source usually given for it is the "Firestone Study," which wasn't a study at all but rather a lunchtime address given to Firestone Tire and Rubber executives.[24]

It is also not true that drug use entails a decrease in workplace productivity or an increase in health care claims. As Normand asserts, "It is often assumed rather than proven that those who use alcohol and other drugs away from work will also do so on the job or in close enough proximity to affect workplace performance."[25] In a study of employees at Utah Power and Light, drug users were actually found to file fewer claims and cost less than their nonusing counterparts.[26] Moreover, once age and gender are considered, rates of absenteeism between drug users and nonusers are negligible.[27] As with the claim about accidents, the assertions that drug users are five times more likely to file worker compensation claims and use three times more health care benefits are unsubstantiated—again, the citation given for these claims is the nonexistent "Firestone Study."

Lewis Maltby also notes several negative effects of drug testing. Drug testing deters highly qualified workers from applying, has a negative impact on workplace morale, diverts funds from drug treatment programs, and has been indicated in reduced productivity.[28] This last report deserves mention.

22. Maltby, "Drug Testing," 9.

23. Jacques Normand, *Under the Influence? Drugs and the American Workforce* (Washington, D.C.: National Academy Press, 1994), 107; Maltby, "Drug Testing," 9.

24. Maltby, "Drug Testing," 6.

25. Normand, *Under the Influence*, 89.

26. Denis Crouch et al., "A Critical Evaluation of the Utah Power and Light Company's Substance Abuse Management Program: Absenteeism, Accidents, and Costs," in *Drugs in the Workplace: Research and Evaluation Data*, ed. S. Gust and J. Walsh (Rockville, Md.: National Institute on Drug Abuse, 1989).

27. Maltby, "Drug Testing," 11: "In other words, those workers who are most likely to use drugs (young males) are also more likely to be absent from work, whether they use drugs or not. Thus the statistical difference between drug users and non-users may actually be due to age and sex differences in drug-using and non-using samples rather than to drug use *per se*."

28. Ibid., 16–21. This point seems more generally true as well. As a graduate student I worked at a now defunct catalog distribution center for a major retail store. When hired I was told to work hard and that if the managers who walked the floor caught us goofing around we would be written up and fired. This system of monitoring was soon replaced with a computer

"Companies that relate to employees positively with a high degree of trust are able to obtain more effort and loyalty in return. Drug testing, particularly without probable cause, seems to imply lack of trust."[29] Maltby writes: "A recent study applied a standard productivity analysis to 63 'high tech' firms in the computer equipment and data processing industry—some having drug-testing programs and some not. Overall, the researchers found that drug testing 'reduced rather than enhanced productivity.' Firms with pre-employment testing, compared to firms with no drug testing at all, scored 16 percent lower on productivity measures. For firms with both pre-employment and random testing, productivity was 29 percent lower."[30]

In light of all of this, it would seem that the arguments from safety, health concerns, and productivity are not overly compelling—certainly not compelling enough to override individual rights to privacy.

PROBLEMS FOR THE MORAL ARGUMENT IN FAVOR OF EMPLOYEE DRUG TESTING

The moral argument in favor of workforce drug testing holds that businesses have a moral obligation to administer drug tests because drug use is immoral. We must fight the war on drugs in every sector in order to send the right message to our children. A "druggie" lifestyle does not lead to a good life, and we as a society should fight this war.

I have always been somewhat perplexed by this sort of argument for the following reasons. First, what is the argument for the claim that drug use is immoral? It does not follow from the claim that "X is bad" that "we ought not to do X." In addition, even if it did, it does not follow that society ought to interfere with such activity. For example, we cannot jump, without further argument, from the claim that "lying is disvaluable" to the claim that "we ought not to lie." And even if "we ought not to lie," we cannot jump, without further argument, to "society ought to prohibit lying and take appropriate measures to punish liars."

Why do we think that drug use necessarily leads to a depraved life?

---

surveillance system and a per hour work quota. Our response to the ever-increasing levels of surveillance was to figure out ways to defeat the monitoring and simply appear to be good employees.

29. Edward Shepard and Thomas Clifton, "Drug Testing: Does It Really Improve Labor Productivity?" *Working USA*, November–December 1998, 76; cited in Maltby, "Drug Testing," 20.

30. Maltby, "Drug Testing," 17.

Addiction and abuse *may* lead to a depraved life, but this is true of any activity or behavior performed in excess. Laziness, overactivity, eating too much, eating too little, reading too much, never learning to read, and so on would each lead to a nonflourishing life—and yet I doubt that the defender of the moral argument in favor of workforce drug testing would marshal similar arguments against these other activities. There is no outcry that businesses have a moral obligation to stamp out after-work laziness—after all, such laziness may lead to on-the-job laziness.

Finally, this argument smacks of unjustified moral paternalism and places an undue burden on corporations. While becoming addicted and abusing drugs is irrational, stupid, and perhaps even immoral, these value statements are not in themselves sufficient for requiring businesses to administer drug tests that override individual privacy rights.

AGAINST THE CONSENT ARGUMENT IN FAVOR OF EMPLOYEE DRUG TESTING

Advocates of workforce drug testing typically offer the consent argument as a discussion stopper. What justifies drug testing is employee consent. Most would agree that absent such consent, drug testing represents a serious violation of privacy. But under what conditions does consent or agreement yield the appropriate sort of permission? The initial bargaining situation must be fair if we are to be morally bound by the outcome.

Please do not take what follows as a general view about coercion, wage offers, and liberty. My goal here is to indicate the force of relinquishing privacy in certain conditions. If consent is offered under certain conditions—assume that there are lots of jobs and few workers or that a specific type of surveillance is necessary for doing business—then privacy claims may be justifiably waived. When conditions do not favor the employee—suppose there are lots of workers and no jobs—and the monitoring is unnecessary, counterproductive, and violates a basic right, then we should proceed with great caution. It is not so clear that in this latter case consent is sufficient for waiving privacy rights.[31]

31. For more about coercion, see David Zimmerman, "Coercive Wage Offers," *Philosophy and Public Affairs* 10 (1981): 121; C. B. Macpherson, "Elegant Tombstones: A Note on Friedman's Freedom," *Democratic Theory* (London: Oxford University Press: 1973); Robert Nozick, "Coercion," in *Philosophy, Science and Method*, ed. S. Morgenbesser et al. (New York: St. Martin's Press, 1969), 440–72; David Lyons, "Welcome Threats and Coercive Offers," *Philosophy* 50 (1975): 427; and Harry Frankfurt, "Coercion and Moral Responsibility," in *Essays on Freedom of Action*, ed. T. Honderich (London: Routledge and Kegan Paul, 1973), 71.

Justifying employee drug testing in light of privacy rights begins with what I call thin consent. A first step in justifying a kind of monitoring is employee notification. The notification takes the following form: "If your employment is to continue, then you must agree to such-and-so kinds of surveillance," or "If you would like to obtain employment, then. . . ." This is appropriately called "thin consent" because it assumes that jobs are hard to find and the employee in question needs the job. Nevertheless, quitting remains a viable option. The force of such agreements or contracts is noted by Ronald Dworkin.

> If a group contracted in advance that disputes amongst them would be settled in a particular way, the fact of that contract would be a powerful argument that such disputes should be settled in that way when they do arise. The contract would be an argument in itself, independent of the force of the reasons that might have led different people to enter the contract. Ordinarily, for example, each of the parties supposes that a contract he signs is in his own interest; but if someone has made a mistake in calculating his self-interest, the fact that he did contract is a strong reason for the fairness of holding him nevertheless to the bargain.[32]

An employee cannot consent, even thinly, to drug testing if it is unknown to her—suppose the employer obtains biological samples from an employee's work area without her consent. Given a fairly strong presumption in favor of privacy, thin consent would seem obligatory. The employee would be notified of the different sorts of drug testing that will be administered. Individual instances of drug testing, however, would not require notification—thus users would not be notified to stop using or to take countermeasures.

It should be clear, however, that thin consent is not enough to justify employee drug testing—not in every case. When jobs are scarce, unemployment high, and government assistance programs swamped, thin consent becomes thin indeed. In these conditions employees will be virtually forced to relinquish privacy because of the severe consequences if they don't. But notice what happens when we slide to the other extreme. Assume a condition of negative unemployment where there are many more jobs than em-

---

32. Ronald Dworkin, *Taking Rights Seriously* (Cambridge: Harvard University Press, 1977), 150–51.

ployees and where changing jobs is relatively easy. In circumstances such as these, thin consent has become quite thick. And if employees were to agree to drug testing in these favorable conditions, most would think it justified.

As we slide from one extreme to the other, from a pro-employer environment with lots of workers and few jobs to a pro-employee environment with lots of jobs and few workers, this method of justification becomes more plausible. What begins looking like a necessary condition ends up looking like a sufficient condition. To determine the exact point where thin consent becomes thick enough to bear the justificatory burden required is a difficult matter. The promise of actual consent depends on the circumstances. Minimally, if the conditions favor the employee, then it becomes plausible to maintain that actual consent would be enough to override a presumption in favor of privacy.

As I have noted, thick consent is possible when employment conditions minimize the costs of finding a comparable job for an employee. Put another way, an employee who doesn't have to work, but agrees to anyway, has given the right kind of consent—assuming of course they have been notified of the different types of drug testing that will occur. What justifies a certain type of surveillance is that it *would be agreeable* to a worker in a pro-employee environment. If thin consent is obtained and the test of hypothetical thick consent is met, then we have reason to think that a strong presumption in favor of privacy has been justifiably overridden.

We will also have to assume that the hypothetical worker making the choice is modestly interested in maintaining control over private information. If this constructed individual has nothing to hide and a general attitude of openness, then any type of surveillance will pass the test. And if I am correct about the value of privacy, anyone would be interested in retaining such control. If the individual agreeing did not know whether she was a worker, manager, or owner and if we assume that anyone would be interested in retaining control over private domains, then the correct vantage point for determining binding agreements will have been attained.[33]

The force of hypothetical contracts has been called into question by Dworkin and others—"A hypothetical contract is not simply a pale form of an actual contract; it is no contract at all."[34] Here I agree with Dworkin.

---

33. This method for ensuring an unbiased standpoint is similar to Rawls's original position. See Rawls, *A Theory of Justice*, 136–42.

34. Dworkin, *Taking Rights Seriously*, 151.

The moral bindingness of hypothetical contracts has to do with the reasons for why we would choose to do this or that. Viewed this way, hypothetical contracts are simply devices that enable us to more clearly understand the reasons, moral or otherwise, for adopting a particular institution or process. Dworkin notes: "There must be reasons, of course, why I would have agreed if asked in advance, and these may also be reasons why it is fair to enforce these rules against me even if I have not agreed. But my hypothetical consent does not count as a reason, independent of these other reasons, for enforcing the rules against me, as my actual agreement would have."[35]

Thus the test of hypothetical thick consent can be understood as a way of clarifying, and allowing us to arrive at, a position that is fair and sensible. Hereafter, when I talk of hypothetical consent and the moral force of such agreements, be aware that this is simply a tool or device to notify us when privacy rights may be justifiably relaxed.

I take a virtue of hypothetical thick consent to be that satisfaction is determined by imagining a pro-employee situation and then asking what an employee would do in the face of drug testing. Some may charge that I am stacking the deck. Why not imagine a pro-employer situation and then ask what an employee would do? We wouldn't have to do much imagining though; and employee consent in such conditions wouldn't justify anything. Moreover, if I am correct in positing privacy rights for each of us, then the deck is already stacked. There is a presumption in favor of individuals having control over personal information and rights to control access to their own bodies—we have privacy rights. Since workforce drug testing may cross into private domains, we must consider under what conditions a privacy right may be waived. In relatively few cases is thin consent thick enough to handle the justificatory burden. Hence, the use of hypothetical thick consent. We are imagining a case where the bargaining situation favors the employee, and if agreement is offered in these conditions, then we may have binding consent.

In general, even in a pro-employee environment there would be certain kinds of employee monitoring that would be necessary for any business. Punching a time clock or measuring time spent working, for example, would occur in almost any business or company. Even in a pro-employee market theft would have to be minimized. It is not as if McDonalds would become so desperate for workers that they would leave the register drawers open, allow employees to come and go as they please, and continue to pay

35. Ibid.

wages. The market demands that businesses make a profit or at least break even. Given this, there will be certain kinds of employee monitoring that every business will use.

This method of determining employee consent also works well for different types of jobs. For example, airlines will have to monitor, and perhaps drug test, pilots no matter which job a pilot takes. This kind of surveillance may be required by the market—after all, who would want to fly with a carrier who did not monitor its pilots in some fashion? In addition there may be laws that require certain licenses that make businesses liable for noncompliance. The hypothetical or constructed airplane pilot, no matter where he goes, will be subject to certain kinds of monitoring. So, even in a pro-employee environment certain kinds of surveillance will be justified—those kinds that are necessary for doing business.

If I am correct, thin consent will justify certain kinds of monitoring when employment conditions favor the employee. Absent such conditions, we can imagine what an employee would choose if she were in a pro-employee environment. If she would agree to a type of monitoring from this vantage point, or because every business in her field will monitor in the way she is considering, then the monitoring is permitted.

TEST CASES AND ILLUSTRATIONS

Let us begin with an easy case. Suppose that one day an employee is approached by his boss and is informed that a new drug-testing policy is being initiated. Randomly, but at least once a month, each employee will submit a urine sample obtained under direct observation. The employee complains and asks what conceivable purpose such a policy could have at an insurance company. Management replies that "only someone with something to hide would object." By my lights the fact that an employee should have nothing to hide is irrelevant. It is her private life that is being monitored, and so it is up to her to deny access. Whether or not she has something to hide is nobody's business.

Assuming that there are lots of jobs and few workers, we may ask if this type of drug testing is justified in relation to hypothetical thick consent. I think it is clear that an individual who is modestly interested in protecting privacy and in a pro-employee environment would leave, other things being equal, and find similar employment elsewhere. The "other things being equal" exception is important because if management were to double employee salaries, then maybe a deal could be made—no privacy at work for lots of cash.[36] Outside such offers, however, the presumption in favor of privacy rights would not have been surpassed for this type of drug testing.

Consider a slightly modified version of this case. Suppose we are considering college professors. Given that no lives are at stake in the execution of typical academic work, it would seem that our hypothetically constructed individual interested in maintaining private domains would not agree to such testing. It would appear that even random agility testing would not be justified in this case. What kinds of "impairment" testing would be justified—you might ask? I cannot see how someone could reasonably object to agility testing coupled with reasonable suspicion—suppose the teacher was slurring his speech or falling down drunk. Still, little is lost if an impaired teacher slips by the monitoring net for a day or a week. No lives hang in the balance. It is not as if hearing a bad lecture will kill you.

The case in favor of monthly urine testing under direct observation does not get much better if we consider bus drivers, airplane pilots, or food inspectors. While employee impairment in these occupations could have much more serious consequences, less invasive methods exist for gathering the requisite information. Agility testing, direct supervision, redundant systems, and the like would likely provide better information in a more timely fashion than monthly urine testing under direct observation or blood tests.

In addition an individual who did not know whether she was the pilot, navigation officer, attendant, or airline owner, and who was interested in maintaining private domains, would not agree to drug testing, assuming a pro-employee environment. If there were no other options and employee impairment could threaten lives, then perhaps drug testing would be justified. But we simply don't live in that world.

THE CANADIAN MODEL

In the area of workplace drug testing it seems that Canada has seized on a more appropriate model. Consider the following strictures on drug testing: The following types of testing are not acceptable:

---

36. Employment agreements grant rights, powers, liberties, and duties to both parties. Thus an employee may trade privacy for some kind of compensation like time off. When trade-offs such as these have occurred, we may take the obligations, generated by the agreement, as binding. If I am correct, fairness of conditions and binding agreements that justifiably relax rights are guaranteed when the tests of thin and hypothetical thick consent are passed.

- Pre-employment drug testing
- Pre-employment alcohol testing
- Random drug testing
- Random alcohol testing of employees in non-safety-sensitive positions

The following types of testing may be included in a workplace drug and alcohol testing program, but only if an employer can demonstrate that they are *bona fide* occupational requirements:

- Random alcohol testing of employees in safety-sensitive positions. Alcohol testing has been found to be a reasonable requirement because alcohol testing can indicate actual impairment of ability to perform or fulfill the essential duties or requirements of the job. Random drug testing is prohibited because, given its technical limitations, drug testing can only detect the presence of drugs and not if or when an employee may have been impaired by drug use.
- A safety-sensitive job is one in which incapacity due to drug or alcohol impairment could result in direct and significant risk of injury to the employee, others, or the environment. Whether a job can be categorized as safety-sensitive must be considered within the context of the industry, the particular workplace, and an employee's direct involvement in a high risk operation. Any definition must take into account the role of properly trained supervisors and the checks and balances present in the workplace.
- Drug or alcohol testing for "reasonable cause" or "post-accident," e.g., where there are reasonable grounds to believe there is an underlying problem of substance abuse or where an accident has occurred due to impairment from drugs or alcohol, provided that testing is a part of a broader program of medical assessment, monitoring and support.
- Periodic or random testing following disclosure of a current drug or alcohol dependency or abuse problem may be acceptable if tailored to individual circumstances and as part of a broader program of monitoring and support. Usually, a designated rehabilitation provider will determine whether follow-up testing is necessary for a particular individual.
- Mandatory disclosure of present or past drug or alcohol dependency or abuse may be permissible for employees holding safety-sensitive positions, within certain limits, and in concert with accommodation

measures. Generally, employees not in safety-sensitive positions should not be required to disclose past alcohol or drug problems.[37]

In general the Canadian model seems much more sensible than current U.S. legal or corporate policy. When asked why random drug testing is prohibited, champions of the Canadian model say things like random testing is not time sensitive and it gathers personal information that is not the concern of employers. Identifying "safety-sensitive" positions, insisting on "reasonable cause" for testing, and restricting required disclosures of past drug dependency problems by employees each seem defensible from a pro-employee choice situation.

CONCLUSION

In summary, it is not so clear that employee consent should be a "discussion stopper" for advocates of employee drug testing. Actual consent will only have normative force in pro-employee conditions. In pro-employer conditions where there are lots of workers and few jobs, actual consent is almost meaningless. If we imagine a pro-employee environment and ask, given the occupation in question what type of "impairment" testing would be agreeable, it is doubtful that many currently used drug-testing programs would be justified.

The arguments from safety, health care, and productivity have been undermined as well. Even if we assume that employers have a legitimate interest in gathering information about employee drug use, there will be less invasive ways of achieving this goal. Furthermore, it is not so clear that the arguments from safety, health care, and productivity generate a legitimate corporate interest in testing for employee drug use. Employers do sometimes have a legitimate interest in employee impairment—especially when lives are at stake. But once we change the discussion to one of detecting employee impairment, the issue of drug testing begins to weaken. Political ideologies no longer drive the debate—Democrats and Republicans don't typically have ideological axes to grind when it comes to those who suffer from sleep deprivation or back pain.

A positive argument in favor of permitting some drug use might run as

37. "Canadian Human Rights Commission Policy on Alcohol and Drug Testing: Executive Summary,"   http://www.caw.ca/en/services-departments-substance-abuse-canadian-human-rights-commission-policy-on-alcohol-and-drug-testing.htm/ (accessed on December 20, 2008).

follows. There are a substantial number of automobile drivers who cannot safely operate a motor vehicle. Some of these individuals are "speed nuts," while others may lack, for whatever reason, the requisite eye, hand, and foot coordination. We don't, as a society, take away everyone's liberty to drive because of those who don't or can't drive responsibly. More controversially, we don't take away everyone's liberty to gamble just because there are those who can't gamble responsibly. In these types of cases, it is better to restrict the liberties of the offending class of individuals than to insist on blanket prohibitions. Why don't we adopt this sort of policy with drugs? Those who recreationally use drugs and do not break any laws would be left alone—it is my understanding that the vast majority of drug users are of this type. Those who demonstrate that they cannot use drugs responsibly, by driving under the influence or committing property crimes to support a habit for example, would be legally prohibited from using.

A hidden assumption in this argument is that recreational drug use does not necessarily lead to dependency, abuse, and serious impairment. This empirical claim is demonstrably supported by the facts—there are vastly more drug users than abusers, vastly more individuals who use drugs as an infrequent escape than those who are dependent. As the United Nations "World Drug Report" notes: "While a large share of the world's population uses illicit drugs each year (about 5 per cent of the population between the ages of 15 and 64), only a small share of these can be considered 'problem drug users' (0.6%)."[38] Worldwide approximately 200 million individuals use illegal drugs annually, while only 12 million of these actually have a "drug problem."

Consider the differences between illegal drug possession rules in the United States and Portugal. In the United States the mere possession of small amounts of illegal drugs will lead to arrest and incarceration. In 2001 Portugal decriminalized the possession of up to ten daily doses (determined by weight) of all "illegal" drugs. Thus an individual in Portugal could have ten doses each of cocaine, heroin, marijuana, and ecstasy and not be subject to arrest or incarceration. Probably the most important aspect of Portugal's 2001 drug policy change is the surprising effect on use rates. Overall, there has been an "increased use of cannabis, decreased use of heroin, increased uptake of treatment, and a reduction of drug related deaths."[39] Cocaine use

38. United Nations Office on Drugs and Crime, "2007 World Drug Report," 2007, 15, http://www.unodc.org/pdf/research/wdr07/WDR_2007.pdf.

39. Caitlin Hughes and Alex Stevens, "The Effects of Decriminalization of Drug Use in Portugal," International Drug Policy Consortium, 9, http://www.idpc.info/php-bin/documents/BFDPP_BP_14_EffectsOfDecriminalisation_EN.pdf.

rates appeared to stay the same between 2001 and 2007 as well.[40] Perhaps the decrease in drug-related deaths and the use of heroin in Portugal were caused by funneling the resources that would have been spent on prosecution and incarceration into treatment and prevention. In any case, if these statistics hold up, we would have a powerful argument for changing drug possession laws in the United States. Even more minimally—we could at least make a "new mistake."

When in conflict with speech and security, we have too often been willing to sacrifice privacy for other values. The balance between corporate drug policy and individual privacy has also been ill struck. There are many ways to protect individual privacy rights while testing for workplace impairment that do not include accompanied trips to the bathroom or the harvesting of hair, tissue, and blood.

40. Ibid., 3.

EVALUATING FREE ACCESS ARGUMENTS: PRIVACY, INTELLECTUAL PROPERTY, AND HACKING

Those who have grown up with digital technology—the so-called digital natives—have some novel views about information flow and access.[1] Along with freely sharing copyrighted material and in spite of the security risks, these individuals are willing to provide vast amounts of personal information on various social networking sites.[2] Much of this information is mined and available to anyone who cares to look. For example, companies increasingly search for information about prospective employees that might indicate questionable past decisions or information that goes against the core values of the corporation.[3] One view regarding this openness with respect to personal information is that digital natives are pushing us toward a paradigm that considers information hoarding a thing of the past. My own view is that the new openness has more to do with the indiscretions of youth than some profound shift in views about privacy and information flow.

Nevertheless, at a more theoretical level the debate over access to information and intellectual property has been waged by two factions. Standing in the way of the digital natives, cyberpunks, and hackers, who claim that

1. See John Palfrey and Urs Gasser, *Born Digital: Understanding the First Generation of Digital Natives* (Philadelphia: Basic Books, 2008).
2. For example, see Ralph Gross and Alessandro Acquisti, "Information Revelation and Privacy in Online Social Networks," Association for Computing Machinery Workshop on Privacy in the Electronic Society (2005).
3. Ibid., 46.

"information wants to be free," are the defenders of Anglo-American copyright, patent, trade secret, and privacy law. Those who defend a model of restricted access to information argue that authors and inventors have rights to control the intellectual works they produce and individuals have privacy rights that shield private information from public consumption. In both cases, accessing, trading, or manipulating the information in question is seen as a kind of trespass—a zone of control has been violated without justification.

Champions of free access argue that an "author-centered" paradigm of intellectual property gives undue credit to innovators. If we view information as a social product, then it is not clear why individuals and corporations should be allowed to hoard and control content at the expense of society. Hackers have held that information belongs to everyone and that access to computer systems should be nearly unlimited and unrestricted. Support for this view is found in current attitudes related to file sharing. It is estimated that for every legitimate copy of software there are between two and ten illegal copies, which translates into vast amounts of lost revenue for software producers.[4] The justification typically given for such pirating and sharing is that "owners still have their copies."

Hacking networks rather than software is also a common occurrence. Automated attack tools have progressed so that meaningful analysis of network hacking attempts is impossible. Computers and networks of all sorts are being probed nearly around the clock. Many of those who engage in these activities argue that they are performing a public service by finding security flaws.

Before considering the "free access" position, I will sketch two arguments in support of intellectual property. If these arguments are compelling, then a moral presumption in favor of controlling intangible works will have been established—the arguments in Chapters 2 through 5 should be sufficient to establish a presumption in favor of privacy. Next, three arguments typically given by hackers and those who champion the "free access" view will be considered. After a presentation and analysis, I will argue that the modern digital native position about information access and control is not strong enough to override the moral presumptions in favor of intellectual property and privacy—"information should not be free."

---

4. Business Software Alliance, Software and Information Industry Association, "Pirates Raid World Businesses," *Mobile Computing and Communications*, August 1999, 24. See also Geoffrey James, "Organized Crime and the Software Biz," *MC Technology,* January 2000; cited in Darryl Seale, "Why Do We Do It If We Know It's Wrong?" in *Ethical Issues of Information Systems*, ed. A. Salehnia (London: IRM Press, 2002), 120.

ESTABLISHING A PRESUMPTION IN FAVOR
OF INTELLECTUAL PROPERTY

Anglo-American systems of intellectual property are typically justified on utilitarian grounds.[5] Article 1 of the Constitution grants limited rights to authors and inventors of intellectual property "to promote the progress of science and the useful arts." Beginning with the Patent Act of 1790 and continuing through the adoption of Berne Convention Standards in 1989, the basis given for Anglo-American systems of intellectual property is utilitarian in nature, and not grounded in the natural rights of the author or inventor.[6] Thomas Jefferson, a central figure in the formation of American systems of intellectual property, expressly rejected any natural rights foundation for granting control to authors and inventors over their intellectual work. William Francis and Robert Collins summarize Jefferson's position as follows: "The patent monopoly was not designed to secure the inventor his natural right in his discoveries. Rather, it was a reward, and inducement, to bring forth new knowledge."[7] Society seeks to maximize utility in the form of scientific and cultural progress by granting rights to authors and inventors as an incentive toward such progress. In general, patents, copyrights, and trade secrets are devices, created by statute, designed to prevent

5. See the *Revision of the U.S. Copyright Act of 1909*, H. R. Rep. No. 2222, 60th Cong., 2nd sess. 7 (1909). The courts have also reflected this theme: "The copyright law . . . makes reward to the owner a secondary consideration." *United States v. Paramount Pictures*, 334 U.S. 131, 158 (1948). "The limited scope of the copyright holder's statutory monopoly, like the limited copyright duration required by the Constitution, reflects a balance of competing claims on the public interest: Creative work is to be encouraged and rewarded, but private motivation must ultimately serve the cause of promoting broad public availability of literature, music, and other arts." *Twentieth Century Music Corp. v. Aiken*, 422 U.S. 151 (1974).

6. This view is echoed in the following denials of a common law right to intellectual property. "Wheaton established as a bedrock principle of American copyright law that copyright, with respect to a published work, is a creature of statute and not the product of the common law." See Sheldon Halpern, David Shipley, and Howard Abrams, *Copyright: Cases and Materials* (St. Paul, Minn.: West Publishing, 1992), 6. The General Court of Massachusetts (1641) adopted the following provision, "There shall be no monopolies granted or allowed among us, but of such new inventions as are profitable to the country, and that for a short time." See "Walker on Patents," in *Early American Patents*, ed. A. Deller (Mt. Kisco, N.Y.: Voorhis Publishing, 1964). "The monopoly did not exist at common law, and the rights, therefore, which may be exercised under it cannot be regulated by the rule of common law. It is created by the act of Congress; and no rights can be acquired in it unless authorized by statute, and in the manner the statute prescribes." Chief Justice Taney, *Gayler et al. v. Wilder*, 10 How. (51 U.S.) 477, 493, 13 L.Ed. 504 (1850). See also *Sony Corp. of America v. Universal Studios, Inc.*, 464 U.S. 417, 78 (1984); *Wheaton v. Peters*, 33 U.S. (8 Pet.) 591, 660–1 (1834); and *Graham v. John Deere Co.*, 383 U.S. 1, 9 (1966).

7. William Francis and Robert Collins, *Cases and Materials on Patent Law: Including Trade Secrets, Copyrights, Trademarks*, 4th ed. (St. Paul, Minn.: West Publishing, 1995), 93.

the diffusion of information before the author or inventor has recovered profit adequate to induce such investment. Restricted initial access to intellectual works creates incentives so that more intellectual goods are created or discovered. Moreover, utilitarian justifications of intellectual property are elegantly simple. Control is granted to authors and inventors of intellectual property because granting such control provides incentives necessary for social progress. If we couple this justification with the theoretical claim that society ought to maximize social utility, we arrive at a simple yet powerful argument.[8]

A SECOND ARGUMENT IN FAVOR OF THE
INTELLECTUAL PROPERTY PRESUMPTION

Independent of social progress or utility maximization arguments, John Locke offered what has become known as the "labor theory of acquisition"—the outlines of this view as it relates to privacy were presented in Chapters 4 and 5. If we build on the Lockean claim that labor establishes prima facie claims to control and show through a "no harm, no foul" rule that when these prima facie claims remain undefeated, we arrive at a different argument in favor of intellectual property.[9] Consider the simplest of cases. After weeks of effort and numerous failures, suppose I come up with an excellent recipe for spicy Chinese noodles—a recipe that I keep in my mind and do not write down.[10] Would anyone argue that I do not have at

8. Please note that it is possible that neither of the arguments offered in support of intellectual property may end up sanctioning particular rules or practices found in current Anglo-American institutions of copyright, patent, and trade secret. For example, the incentives-based social-utility argument would not likely support the current term limits on copyrights and patents—there is no reason to think that incentives and utility have been maximized by insisting on copyrights that last the lifetime of the author plus seventy years or twenty years for patents. See Moore, "Intellectual Property, Innovation, and Social Progress," and *Intellectual Property and Information Control,* chap. 3. Also, the Lockean/Pareto argument that follows would not support exclusive patent rights—those who independently invent an already patented intellectual work would be worsened by exclusive patent monopolies.

9. I present lengthier analyses of intangible property rights in *Intellectual Property and Information Control,* "Intangible Property," and "Toward a Lockean Theory of Intellectual Property," in *Intellectual Property: Moral, Legal, and International Dilemmas,* ed. A. Moore (Lanham, Md.: Rowman and Littlefield, 1997), chap. 5.

10. Ken Himma notes that "content creation involves the expenditure of moments of our lives, something that we all tend to value intrinsically. Intellectual property protection might be justified as a matter of respect for this precious and limited resource." See Ken Himma, "Justifying Intellectual Property Protection: Why the Interests of Content-Creators Usually Win Over Everyone Else's," in *Information Technology and Social Justice,* ed. Emma Rooksby and John Weckert (Hershey, Pa.: Information Science Publishing, 2006), 47.

least some minimal moral claim to control the recipe? Suppose that you sample some of my noodles and desire to purchase the recipe. Is there anything morally suspicious with an agreement between us that grants you a limited right to use my recipe provided that you do not disclose the process? After all, you didn't have to agree to my terms, and no matter how tasty the noodles, you could eat something else. A slightly different way to put this Lockean argument for intellectual property rights is:

Step 1. The generation of prima facie claims to control. Suppose Ginger creates a new intangible work. Her efforts yield her prima facie claims to control.

Step 2. Locke's proviso. If the acquisition of an intangible object makes no one (else) worse off in terms of their level of well-being compared to how they were immediately before the acquisition, then the taking is permitted.

Step 3. From prima facie claims to property rights. Prima facie claims to control an intangible work are undefeated when the proviso is satisfied.

Conclusion: As long as the proviso is satisfied, the prima facie claims that labor and effort may generate turn into property claims.[11]

As with the arguments for physical and informational privacy found in Chapters 4 and 5 the linchpin of this argument is the use of the proviso, which includes a measure of harm or bettering and worsening and a baseline of comparison. An individual's level of material well-being is the measure of moral bettering and worsening or harm. The baseline of comparison is how Fred would be when Ginger possesses and excludes an intangible work to his level of well-being immediately before Ginger's acquisition. Prior to the act of creation or discovery Fred did not have access to the

---

11. Ken Himma, in correspondence, has suggested that this argument could succeed without defending initial prima facie claims to control. "Suppose I have no prima facie claim to X, but my taking X leaves no one worse off in any respect. Since they have no grounds to complain, what could be wrong with my taking it? If, however, there is a prima facie claim on my part, much more would be needed to defeat it than just pointing out that someone is made worse off by it. That's how [moral] claims work, it seems to me—and why they're needed: to justify making others worse off." My worry, though, is that without establishing initial prima facie claims to control there would be no moral aspect to strengthen into rights by application of the proviso. In any case, this is an interesting line of inquiry.

intellectual work in question, so he is not worsened when we compare this state to how he is after Ginger's act of creation and exclusion. Notice, in both states—as with the spicy Chinese noodles example—Fred is free to come up with his own intellectual creation.

If correct, this account points toward a second justification for rights over intangibles like genetic enhancement techniques, movies, novels, and information. When an individual creates an intangible work and fixes it in some fashion, then labor and possession create a prima facie claim to the work. Moreover, if the proviso is satisfied, the prima facie claim remains undefeated and moral claims or rights are generated.

OVERRIDING THE PRIVACY AND INTELLECTUAL PROPERTY PRESUMPTIONS: ARGUMENTS IN FAVOR OF HACKING

If the argument so far has been compelling, then moral presumptions in favor of intellectual property and privacy have been established. I will now consider three arguments offered by hackers and the "free access" community that purport to override these presumptions.

THE SOCIAL NATURE OF INFORMATION ARGUMENT

As I noted in the introduction, many hackers and digital natives have held that information belongs to everyone and that access to computer systems should be nearly unlimited and unrestricted.[12] According to this view, information is a social product and enforcing access restrictions unduly benefits authors and inventors.[13] Individuals are raised in societies that endow them with knowledge, which these individuals then use to create intellectual works of all kinds. Individuals should not have exclusive and perpetual ownership of the works that they create because these works are built upon the shared knowledge of society. Allowing rights to intellectual works would be similar to granting ownership to the individual who placed the last brick in a public works dam. The dam is a social product, built up by the efforts

12. Often this argument is linked to the claim that "information should be free." For an in-depth analysis of the "information should be free" argument, see Ken Himma, "Information and Intellectual Property Protection: Evaluating the Claim That Information Should Be Free," http://repositories.cdlib.org/cgi/viewcontent.cgi?article = 1013andcontext = bclt.

13. Parts of this section draw from material published in Moore, *Intellectual Property and Information Control*, chap. 7.

of hundreds, and knowledge, upon which all intellectual works are built, is built up in a similar fashion.

Similarly, the benefits of market interaction are social products. It is not clear that the individual who discovers crude oil in his or her backyard should obtain the full market value of their find. And why should the inventor who produces the next technology breakthrough be allowed to harvest full market value when such value is actually created through the interactions of individuals within a society? A. John Simmons writes: "Locke himself uses examples that point to the social nature of production (*The Second Treatise of Government*, II 43). But if the skills, tools, or invention that are used in laboring are not simply the product of the individual's effort, but are instead the product of a culture or a society, should not the group have some claim on what individual laborers produce? For the labor that the individual invests includes the prior labor of many others."[14]

A mild form of this argument may yield a justification for limiting the ownership rights of authors and inventors. A more radical form of this argument may lead to the elimination of intellectual property rights. If market value and knowledge are, in a deep way, social products, then the creator-centered paradigm that grounds Anglo-American systems of intellectual property cannot be justified.

The social nature of information argument is, however, suspect for several reasons. First, it is doubtful that the notion of "society" employed in this view is clear enough to carry the weight that the argument demands. In some vague sense, we may know what it means to say that Lincoln was a member of American *society* or that Aristotle's political views were influenced by ancient Greek *society*. Nevertheless, the notion of "society" is conceptually imprecise—one that it would be dubious to attach ownership or obligation claims to. Those who would defend this view would have to clarify the notions of "society" and "social product" before the argument could be fully analyzed.

But suppose for the sake of argument that supporters of this view come up with a concise notion of "society" and "social product." We may ask further, why think that societies can be *owed* something or that they can

14. A. John Simmons, *The Lockean Theory of Rights* (Princeton: Princeton University Press, 1992), 269. Ruth Grant, in *John Locke's Liberalism* (Chicago: University of Chicago Press, 1987); Ian Shapiro, in "Resources, Capacities, and Ownership: The Workmanship Ideal and Distributive Justice," *Political Theory* 19 (February 1991); and others have argued along these lines. For earlier and more general defenses of this sentiment, see Karl Marx and Friedrich Engels, *The Communist Manifesto*, and P. J. Proudhon, *What Is Property? An Inquiry into the Principles of Right and of Government*, trans. D. Kelly and B. Smith (New York: Cambridge University Press, 1994).

own or *deserve* something?[15] Surely, it does not follow from the claim that X is a social product that society owns X. Likewise, it does not follow merely from the claim that because Ginger produced X, Ginger owns X. It is true that interactions between individuals may produce increased market values or add to the common stock of knowledge. What may be denied is that these by-products of interaction, market value, and shared information are in some sense owned by society or that society is owed for their use. This should not be assumed without argument. It is one thing to claim that information and knowledge is a social product—something built up by thousands of individual contributions—but quite another to claim that this knowledge is owned by society or that individuals who use this information owe society something in return.[16]

Suppose that Fred and Ginger, along with numerous others, interact with and benefit me in the following way. Their interaction produces knowledge that is then freely shared, and allows me to create some new value, V. Upon creation of V, Fred and Ginger demand that they are owed something for their part. But what is the argument from third-party benefits to demands of compensation for these benefits? Why think that there are "strings" attached to *freely* shared information? And if such an argument can be made, it would seem that burdens create reverse demands. Suppose that the interaction of Fred and Ginger produces false information that is freely shared. Suppose further that I waste ten years trying to produce some value based, in part, on this false information. Would Fred and Ginger, would society, owe me compensation? The position that "strings" are attached in this case runs parallel to Robert Nozick's benefit "foisting" example. In Nozick's case a benefit is foisted on someone, and then payment is demanded. This seems an accurate account of what is going on in this case as well.

One cannot, whatever one's purposes, just act so as to give people benefits and then demand (or seize) payment. Nor can a group of

15. Do notions of *ownership*, *owing*, or *deserving* even make sense when attached to the concept of society? If so and if different societies can *own* knowledge, do they not have the problem of original acquisition? See Nozick, *Anarchy, State, and Utopia*, 178.

16. Lysander Spooner argued that one's culture or society plays almost no role in the production of ideas. "Nothing is, by its own essence and nature, more perfectly susceptible of exclusive appropriation, than a thought. It originates in the mind of a single individual. It can leave his mind only in obedience to his will. It dies with him, if he so elect." Lysander Spooner, "The Law of Intellectual Property," in *The Law of Intellectual Property; or, An Essay on the Right of Authors and Inventors to a Perpetual Property in Their Ideas*, 58, in *The Collected Works of Lysander Spooner*, ed. C. Shively (Weston, Mass.: M & S Press, 1971).

persons do this. If you may not charge and collect for benefits you bestow without prior agreement, you certainly may not do so for benefits whose bestowal costs you nothing, and most certainly people need not repay you for costless-to-provide benefits which yet *others* provided them. So the fact that we partially are "social products" in that we benefit from current patterns and forms created by the multitudinous actions of a long string of long-forgotten people, forms which include institutions, ways of doing things, and language, does not create in us a general free floating debt which the current society can collect and use as it will.[17]

Arguably this is also true of market value. Given our crude oil example, the market value of the oil is the synergistic effect of individuals freely interacting. Moreover, there is no question of desert here. The individual who discovers the oil does not *deserve* full market value any more than the lottery winner deserves her winnings.

On my view, common knowledge, market value, and the like are the synergistic effects of individuals freely interacting. If a thousand of us *freely* give our new and original ideas to all of humankind, it would be illicit for us to demand compensation, after the fact, from individuals who have used our ideas to create things of value. It would even be more questionable for individuals ten generations later to demand compensation for the current use of the now very old ideas that we freely gave. Lysander Spooner puts the point succinctly: "*What* rights society have, in ideas, which they did not produce, and have never purchased, it would probably be very difficult to define; and equally difficult to explain *how* society became possessed of those rights. It certainly requires something more than assertion, to prove that by simply coming to a knowledge of certain ideas—the products of individual labor—society acquires any valid title to them, or, consequently, any *rights* in them."[18]

But once again, suppose for the sake of argument that the defender of this view can justify societal ownership of general pools of knowledge and information. It could be argued that we have already paid for the use of this collective wisdom when we pay for education and the like. When a parent pays, through fees or taxation, for a child's education, it would seem that the information—part of society's common pool of knowledge—has

---

17. Nozick, *Anarchy, State, and Utopia*, 95.
18. Spooner, *Law of Intellectual Property*, 103.

been fairly purchased. And this extends through all levels of education and even to individuals who no longer attend school.

Finally, in many contexts where privacy interests are at stake, an appeal to the social nature of intellectual property and information seems unconvincing—assuming that this view can be saved from the points already discussed. The fact that sensitive personal information about an individual's medical history is a social product may have little force when it comes to questions of access and control. This is also true of information related to national security and financial information.

BUT THEY STILL HAVE THEIR COPY!

A common argument given by hackers and others who defend "free access" is that making a copy does not deprive anyone of their possessions.[19] Intangible works are nonrivalrous, meaning that they can be used and consumed by many individuals concurrently. Edwin Hettinger argues,

> The possession or use of an intellectual object by one person does not preclude others from possessing or using it as well. If someone borrows your lawn mower, you cannot use it, nor can anyone else. But if someone borrows your recipe for guacamole, that in no way precludes you, or anyone else, from using it. This feature is shared by all sorts of intellectual objects. . . .
>
> This characteristic of intellectual objects grounds a strong prima facie case against the wisdom of private and exclusive intellectual property rights. Why should one person have the exclusive right to possess and use something that all people could possess and use concurrently? . . . [T]he unauthorized taking of an intellectual object does not feel like theft.[20]

Consider a more formal version of this argument.

P1. If a tangible or intangible work can be used and consumed by many individuals concurrently (nonrivalrously), then maximal access and use should be permitted.

19. For an interesting analysis of this argument, see Ken Himma, "Abundance, Rights, and Interests: Thinking About the Legitimacy of Intellectual Property" (paper presented at the International Conference of Computer Ethics—Philosophical Enquiry, May 1, 2005); available at http://ssrn.com/abstract=727469.

20. Edwin Hettinger, "Justifying Intellectual Property," in *Intellectual Property: Moral, Legal, and International Dilemmas*, ed. A. Moore (Lanham, Md.: Rowman and Littlefield, 1997), 20.

P2. The content of intellectual works falling under the domains of copyright, patent, and *trade secret protection* are nonrivalrous.

C3. So it follows that there is an immediate prima facie case against intellectual property rights and for allowing access to intellectual works.

The weak point in this argument is the first premise—especially given that the second premise is generally true.[21] Again, consider sensitive personal information. It seems patently false to claim that just because this information can be used and consumed by many individuals concurrently that there is a prima facie moral claim that this be so. Information related to national security, personal financial information, and private thoughts are each nonrivalrous. Nevertheless, this fact does not, by itself, generate prima facie moral claims for maximal access and use.

Hettinger would likely reply that these sorts of examples would violate a "no harm, no foul" rule that underlies this argument. Taking personal information from someone harms them in a way that copying intellectual works does not. This view lies at the heart of the second argument establishing a presumption in favor of intellectual property rights.

But consider a case first mentioned in Chapter 4.

> Dr. Demento . . . has discovered a drug that will put people into a trance for eight hours and rejuvenate their bodies so that they need no sleep. The fiendish doctor realizes that he has a way to use the bodies of others without making them any worse off than they would have been in his absence. . . . In addition to making his temporary zombies work in his lab at night, he engages in vile and disgusting sex acts with them which he videotapes . . . [and] sells at great profit in foreign countries.[22]

Arguably Demento's actions are immoral even though, *ex hypothesi*, no harm has been done to his subjects. Similarly, a Peeping Tom may engage in immoral activity without harming his victims—perhaps there will be no consequences to the victims and they will never know of the peeping.

More forcefully, however, if Demento's victims have moral claims to control their own bodies, then they will be worsened by his activity—a

21. Some kinds of information are rivalrously consumed—for example, stock tips, trade secrets, new football defensive schemes, and so on.

22. Hubin and Lambeth, "Providing for Rights," 495.

moral claim or obligation will have been violated and certain risks imposed without consent. In summary, the claim that maximal access should be allowed and perhaps promoted for goods that are nonrivalrous is without merit. Intangible works of all sorts are nonrivalrous, including sensitive personal information, financial records, and information related to national security. It may even be the case that our bodies could be nonrivalrously used by others. This feature of most intangible goods, and perhaps some tangible goods, does not obviously justify free access and use.

THE SECURITY AND SOCIAL BENEFITS ARGUMENT

According to the security and social benefits argument, presumptions in favor of privacy and intellectual property are overridden because of the social benefits that occur when hackers crack software and networks. David Dittrich and Ken Himma note: "By gaining insight into the operations of existing networks, hackers develop a base of knowledge that can be used to improve those networks . . . [and] break-ins themselves call attention to security flaws that could be exploited by crackers or, worse, cyber-terrorists."[23]

In many cases hackers who, without authorization, access systems do no damage to files or programs and simply look around as a matter of curiosity. Viewing a file and making copies does no obvious damage. Moreover, by hacking systems and software hackers are able to alert administrators and owners of potential security flaws. Nonmalicious hacking of this sort provides social benefits by strengthening computer networks and software packages against cyberterrorists.

Such behavior is often likened to neighborhood "crime watch" programs or innocently walking on someone else's property. In an interview with a hacker, Richard Spinello asks about trespass. An unnamed hacker replied, "I don't see the problem here. What's wrong with snooping around especially if I do not alter any data or screw up some commands or programs . . . [w]here is the damage? It is the same as walking across Farmer Brown's field—as long as I leave the animals and crops alone what harm

---

23. David Dittrich and Ken Himma, "Hackers, Crackers, and Computer Criminals," in *The Handbook of Information Security*, vol. 2, ed. H. Bidgoli (Hoboken, N.J.: John Wiley and Sons, 2005), 156.

have I done?"[24] In many of these cases a "no harm, no foul" sentiment is included within a social benefits or security argument.

But consider the following case. Suppose Ginger comes home to find that Fred, someone she has never met, is in her house looking around. Before Ginger can scream or call for help, Fred exclaims, "Hey now, I have done no damage, I am only looking, and moreover, I have found several security flaws with your doors and windows." My guess is that few of us would find Fred's position tenable—but why? Arguably, Fred has harmed Ginger by foisting certain risks upon her. She cannot be sure of his intentions, goals, or ambitions. Without being able to trust Fred, Ginger's security is threatened in a profound way. Fred could attack her directly or take away information that could be used as the basis for a later attack.

Similar considerations apply to hacking software. When Crusoe cracks Friday's software program or simply obtains a copy he wouldn't have otherwise purchased, he opens Friday up to unforeseen and unconsented-to risks. A "black hat" hacker may crack Crusoe's machine, obtain a copy of Friday's program, and market a pirated copy at a lower price. When Crusoe legitimately buys a copy, Friday consents to certain risks—among them the risk that someone may break in to Crusoe's computer. But this is not the case when unauthorized copies are made or when security protections are cracked.

Moreover, the very existence of walls, doors, fences, firewalls, and passwords makes a difference. All of these are basically "keep out" signs erected, more often than not, by those who have legitimate moral claims to control access and use. Farmer Brown may put up fences to keep his animals in but also to keep others out. Curtains, firewalls, and passwords serve a similar function.

CONCLUSION

If correct, Chapters 2 through 5 establish a moral presumption in favor of privacy. A moral presumption in favor of intellectual property may be grounded in incentives to innovate or via a Lockean model. According to the former, control is granted to authors and inventors of intellectual property because granting such control provides incentives necessary for social

---

24. Richard Spinello, "Interview with a Hacker," in *Information and Computer Ethics*, ed. R. Spinello (Upper Saddle River, N.J.: Prentice Hall, 1997), 182.

progress. On the Lockean view, moral claims to intellectual works are grounded in desert or merit along with a "no harm, no foul" rule.

Three prominent "free access" arguments have been discussed and dismissed on the grounds that they are not forceful enough to override the presumptions in favor of privacy and intellectual property. The social nature of information argument trades on an imprecise notion of "society" or that society can own or deserve something. Even if society had some claim on certain pools of knowledge, individuals have fairly purchased such information through education fees and the like. Moreover, where privacy interests are at stake, an appeal to the social nature of intellectual property and information seems unconvincing.

The nonrivalrousness of information argument fails because, among other things, it is not at all apparent that just because something can be used and consumed by numerous individuals concurrently that it should be. Private sensitive information and national secrets are two obvious examples.

The security and social benefits argument is problematic because it does not consider the hidden costs of foisting risks on others. When hackers break into systems or software, they impose morally relevant risks on others without consent. As with the Peeping Tom or the home intruder, we cannot be sure of the intentions of unauthorized hackers. Moreover, we must shoulder the costs of reestablishing the security and trustworthiness of our systems.

10

PRIVACY, SECURITY, AND PUBLIC ACCOUNTABILITY

In times of national crisis citizens are often asked to trade liberty and privacy for security. And why not, it is argued, if we can obtain a fair amount of security for just a little privacy. The surveillance that enhances security need not be overly intrusive or life altering. It is not as if government agents need to physically search each and every suspect or those connected to a suspect. Advances in digital technology have made such surveillance relatively unobtrusive. Video monitoring, global positioning systems, and biometric technologies, along with data surveillance, provide law enforcement officials monitoring tools without also unduly burdening those being watched.

Against this view are those who maintain that we should be worried about trading privacy for security. Criminals and terrorists, it is argued, are nowhere near as dangerous as governments.[1] There are too many examples for us to deny Lord Acton's dictum that "power tends to corrupt, and

---

1. Terrorists are nowhere near as dangerous as governments. "From 1980 to 2000, international terrorists killed 7,745 people according to the U.S. State Department. Yet, in the same decades, governments killed more than 10 million people in ethnic cleansing campaigns, mass executions. . . . In the 1990's, Americans were at far greater risk of being gunned down by local, state, and federal law enforcement agents than of being killed by international terrorists." James Bovard, *Terrorism and Tyranny: Trampling Freedom, Justice, and Peace to Rid the World of Evil* (New York: Palgrave Macmillan, 2003), 8.

absolute power corrupts absolutely."[2] If information control yields power and total information awareness radically expands that power, then we have good reason to pause before trading privacy for security.

In this final chapter I will consider a number of issues related to governmental and societal control of information. More specifically, I will focus on the question of when rights to control certain kinds of information may be justifiably overridden in the name of public security and how easily balancing arguments go awry. I will argue that one way to appropriately balance privacy and security is to insist upon establishing probable cause for an intrusion, robust judicial discretion on issuing warrants, and public oversight of the process and the reasoning involved.

OVERVIEW OF SURVEILLANCE IN THE UNITED STATES

Within the U.S. legal system there are four ways that law enforcement agents can conduct surveillance.[3] First, there are warrants authorizing the interception of communications. Second, there are warrants authorizing the search of physical premises. Third, there are provisions that allow trap-and-trace devices and pen registers—trap-and-trace devices allow law enforcement agents to trace outgoing and incoming telephone numbers. Finally, there are subpoenas requiring the production of goods such as telephone logs or e-mail records. Unlike the first two methods of surveillance, the last two require a lower standard of justification. Trap-and-trace devices only require a sworn declaration that the information being sought is relevant to an investigation. Court orders for records require that agents show that the information being sought is relevant and material to an ongoing investigation.[4] Moreover, each of these requirements applies only to domestic surveillance—monitoring individuals who are not American citizens is another matter.

Surveillance of American citizens is carried out by several agencies, including city, county, and state police departments and the Federal Bureau of Investigation (FBI). The National Security Administration (NSA) and the Central Intelligence Agency (CIA) are forbidden by law from monitor-

2. Lord Acton to Bishop Mandell Creighton, April 3, 1887, in *The Life and Letters of Mandell Creighton* (New York: Longmans, Green, 1904).

3. For a nice overview, see Jacob Lilly, "National Security at What Price? A Look into Civil Liberty Concerns in the Information Age Under the USA Patriot Act of 2001 and a Proposed Constitutional Test for Future Legislation," *Cornell Law Journal* 12 (2003): 457.

4. See 17 U.S.C. sec. 512 (2002).

ing domestic activities and are responsible for conducting surveillance outside the United States.[5]

To clarify the intelligence gathering abilities of the FBI, CIA, and NSA, Congress enacted the Foreign Intelligence Act of 1978 (FISA). Judicial oversight of FISA warrants was given to a newly created court called the Foreign Intelligence Surveillance Court (FISC).[6] To obtain a FISC order allowing surveillance of a U.S. citizen the government must show that the target is a foreign power or is the agent of a foreign power. Since the information is not related to a criminal investigation, there is no requirement of probable cause—that is, government agents do not need to show that the target will commit a crime. If the target is not a U.S. citizen, then no court order is necessary and only authorization from the attorney general is required.[7] It should also be noted that applications for FISC orders are submitted in secret, the decisions are almost never published, and only government agents are allowed to appear before the court.[8]

The USA Patriot Act made numerous changes to the surveillance methods already mentioned. Below is a list of some of the changes. The Patriot Act:

1. Expands the government's ability to conduct covert "sneak and peek" searches. Government agents may take photographs, seize property, and not notify the target until a later time.[9]
2. Allows the inclusion of DNA information into databases of individuals convicted of "any crime of violence."[10]
3. Increases government surveillance abilities of suspected computer

---

5. See Executive Order No. 12,333 1.14, 3 C.F.R. 200 (1982); reprinted in U.S.C. 50, 401.

6. "FISA essentially allows electronic surveillance and physical searches of foreigners and U.S. citizens when there is 'probable cause to believe that . . . the target . . . is a foreign power or an agent of a foreign power.' Still standards for obtaining a warrant are much less rigorous than under Title III." Lee, "USA Patriot Act and Telecommunications," 375; citing U.S.C. 50 (2000), 1805(a)(3)(A), 1824(a)(3)(A).

7. U.S.C. 50, 1802(a)(1).

8. "The eagerness of many in law enforcement to dispense with the requirements of the Fourth Amendment was revealed in August 2002 by the secret court that oversees domestic intelligence spying (the 'FISA Court'). Making public one of its opinions for the first time in history, the court revealed that it had rejected an attempt by the Bush Administration to allow criminal prosecutors to use intelligence warrants to evade the Fourth Amendment entirely. The court also noted that agents applying for warrants had regularly filed false and misleading information. That opinion is now on appeal." ACLU Report, "Surveillance Under the USA PATRIOT Act," http://www.aclu.org/SafeandFree/SafeandFree.cfm?ID=12263andc=206.

9. USA Patriot Act (U.S. H.R. 3162, Public Law 107–56), Title II, sec. 213.

10. Ibid., 503.

trespassers—any target suspected of violating the Computer Fraud and Abuse Act may be monitored without a court order.[11]

4. Increases the government's ability to access records held by third parties.[12] By expanding the use of FISA, targets "whose records are sought need not be an agent of a foreign power. United States citizens could be . . . investigated on account of activities connecting them to an investigation of international terrorism."[13] In addition, FISC judges must issue a warrant if the application satisfies the requirements of Section 215.

Before the Patriot Act law enforcement agents could obtain records but could only seize physical items in rare cases. Records from libraries, Internet service providers, businesses, and hospitals are now subject to search and seizure. Individuals who are not U.S. citizens can be investigated solely because of their First Amendment activity—"because they wrote a letter to the editor criticizing the government, or because they participated in a particular political rally."[14] U.S. citizens, on the other hand, cannot be investigated solely on First Amendment grounds—other conditions must be satisfied before legal surveillance can occur.[15]

Moreover, FISC judges and magistrate judges have the authority to rule on these surveillance applications, although they have little power to reject them. "The FBI need not show 'probable cause' or any reason at all to believe that the target of the surveillance order is engaged in criminal activity. All the FBI needs to do is 'specify' that the records are 'sought for' an authorized investigation."[16] Note that as long as this requirement is satisfied, the specification that the records are "sought for" an authorized investigation, U.S. citizens are also covered.

Beyond the government surveillance powers already noted, the U.S. Constitution grants the president broad powers in times of crisis and war. As an example, in early 2002 President Bush implemented a secret program that allowed the NSA to conduct warrantless searches of U.S. citizens. This

11. Ibid., 217.

12. Ibid., 215.

13. Lee, "USA Patriot Act and Telecommunications," 381.

14. Ann Beeson and Jameel Jaffer, "Unpatriotic Acts: The FBI's Power to Rifle Through Your Records and Personal Belongings Without Telling You," ACLU Report, July 2003, 4, http://www.aclu.org/FilesPDFs/spies_report.pdf.

15. USA Patriot Act (U.S. H.R. 3162, Public Law 107–56), Title II, sec. 213.

16. ACLU, "Unpatriotic Acts," 5.

program authorized the NSA to search international phone calls from U.S. citizens, thus sidestepping FISA.

"JUST TRUST US"—TRADING CIVIL RIGHTS FOR SECURITY

A common view is that we should give the benefit of the doubt to those in power and assume that officials will not violate individual rights without just cause. Public officials typically seek office to promote the public good and are generally well meaning and sincere people—we should trust them to do what is right and fair.

Arguably, there are good reasons to distrust this method of establishing an appropriate balance between privacy and security. Justice Brandeis, dissenting in *Olmstead v. United States,* wrote: "Experience should teach us to be most on our guard to protect liberty when the government's purposes are beneficent. Men born to freedom are naturally alert to repel invasion of their liberty by evil-minded rulers. The greatest dangers to liberty lurk in insidious encroachment by men of zeal, well-meaning but without understanding."[17]

Below are several examples that suffice in demonstrating the perils of letting those in power set the guidelines for surveillance.

Emergency Powers and the Civil War

At the beginning of the Civil War President Abraham Lincoln declared a state of emergency and suspended the legal rights of citizens in the border states of Maryland, Kentucky, Missouri, and Tennessee. "In addition to using federal troops to intimidate state legislators and influence their decisions, Lincoln imprisoned 13,000 civilians and suspended the writ of habeas corpus so that no inquiry could be made into the validity of their detainment."[18] Lincoln also arrested nineteen members of the Maryland state legislature and encouraged civilians in Missouri to disperse gatherings of those who supported the Confederate cause. Additionally, the president established military tribunals that tried and punished civilians who offered aid and comfort to Southern sympathizers—thus denying these individuals the constitutional guarantees of a public trial by an impartial jury.

17. *Olmstead v. United States,* 227 U.S. 438 (1928).
18. Lilly, "National Security at What Price?" 451.

The appropriate test, Lincoln argued, was whether the president should "risk . . . losing the Union that gave life to the Constitution because that charter denied him the necessary authority to preserve the Union."[19] Arguably, the notion of a president exercising "emergency powers" in a time of crisis based on his own subjective assessment of the issues at stake sets a bad precedent.

Japanese-American Internment During World War II

Shortly after the attack on Pearl Harbor on December 7, 1941, Executive Order 9066, signed by President Roosevelt on February 19, 1942, authorized U.S. Attorney General Francis Biddle to have the FBI arrest "dangerous enemy aliens," including German, Italian, and Japanese nationals.[20] Over a hundred thousand people of Japanese descent were rounded up and incarcerated. Several Japanese-Americans who protested the internment and several who tried to escape were shot and killed.

The Supreme Court, in *Korematsu v. United States,*[21] found the internment constitutional, arguing that there was no way to distinguish Japanese agents from loyal Americans and that "hardships are a part of war."[22] Frederick Korematsu, an American citizen of Japanese descent, refused to leave a prohibited area and enter an internment camp. In 1983 the Court of Appeals overturned the conviction: "Fred Korematsu, Gordon Hirabayashi, and Minoru Yasui, who had challenged the constitutionality of the internment, reopened their landmark federal cases through writs of error *coram nobis*. Their wartime convictions for defying the internment policy were vacated, based on evidence that the government had misrepresented and suppressed evidence that racial prejudice, not military necessity, motivated the internment of Japanese Americans."[23]

In addition, a special commission appointed by President Carter to investigate Japanese internment during World War II concluded that the decision to detain and incarcerate Japanese Americans was based on "race

19. Ibid., citing Debora K. Kristensen, "Finding the Right Balance: American Civil Liberties in Time of War," *The Advocate*, December 2001, 21.

20. *Japanese Americans, from Relocation to Redress,* ed. Roger Daniels, Sandra Taylor, and Harry Kitano (Salt Lake City: University of Utah Press, 1986).

21. *Korematsu v. United States,* 323 U.S. 214 (1944).

22. *Korematsu,* 323 U.S. at 235; cited in Lilly, "National Security at What Price?" 452.

23. *Korematsu v. United States,* 584 F. Supp. 1406 (N.D. Cal. 1984); *Hirabayashi v. United States,* 627 F. Supp. 1445 (W.D. Wash. 1986), aff'd in part and rev'd in part, 828 F.2d 591 (9th Cir. 1987); *Yasui v. United States,* 83–151 BE (D. Or. 1984), remanded, 772 F.2d 1496 (9th Cir. 1985).

prejudice, war hysteria, and a failure of political leadership."[24] By 1988 Congress had granted $20,000 compensation to each internment survivor. It seems that once the crisis had passed those who thoughtfully considered the issue of trading Japanese-American freedom for security found that the balance was ill struck.

McCarthy and the House Un-American Activities Committee

The passage of the Taft-Hartley Act[25] in 1947 and the McCarran Act[26] in 1950 provided justification for the "red scare" and the ensuing McCarthyism of the early 1950s.[27] Reaffirming the "clear and present danger" test established in *Schenk v. United States* (1919),[28] the Supreme Court maintained that "mere membership in the Communist Party was sufficient to justify government action."[29] Thus began one of the worst periods of government abuse. Below is a brief summary and timeline of some of the events.

> 1947 The first wave of hearings of the House Committee on Un-American Activities (HUAC) occur. During this time novelist Ayn Rand testifies regarding the pro-communist slant of the film *Song of Russia* (1944). It is in these hearings that the "Hollywood Ten" are blacklisted and sentenced to prison terms for contempt of Congress.

> 1950 On February 9th in Wheeling, West Virginia, McCarthy gives his first public speech against communism. He opens with the sentence, "I have in my hand a list of 205 cases of individuals who appear to be either card-carrying members or certainly loyal to the Communist Party."

> 1950 The McCarran Act, or Internal Security Act of 1950, is passed. Among other things, it authorizes the creation of concentration

---

24. U.S. Commission on Wartime Relocation and Internment of Civilians, *Personal Justice Denied* (Washington, D.C.: U.S. GPO, 1983), summary.

25. Taft-Hartley Act of 1947, Public Law 80–101, 61 Stat. 136 (1947).

26. Internal Security (McCarran) Act of 1950, Public Law 81–831, 64 Stat. 987 (1950).

27. This was not the first event of its type in U.S. history. Recall the "red scare" and the Palmer raids in 1917. See http://www.duncanentertainment.com/timeline.php (accessed December 20, 2008). See also Robert Murray, *Red Scare: A Study in National Hysteria, 1919–1920* (Minneapolis: North Central Publishing, 1955), and Edwin Hoyt, *The Palmer Raids, 1919–1920: An Attempt to Suppress Dissent* (New York: The Seabury Press, 1969).

28. *Schenk v. United States*, 249 U.S. 47, 52 (1919). See *Dennis v. United States* 341 U.S. 494 (1951).

29. Lilly, "National Security at What Price?" 454.

camps "for emergency situations." Though Truman originally vetoes the legislation, the Senate overrides him by a vote of 89–11.

1951 The second wave of HUAC hearings begins with McCarthy leading the charge. Over the next three years McCarthy is a mainstay in the public eye, and he subpoenas some of the most prominent entertainers of the era (e.g. Orson Wells, Lucille Ball, Dashiell Hammett, and Lillian Hellman) before HUAC, demanding "the naming of names."

1954 After a confrontation with secretary of the army, Robert Stevens, McCarthy soon afterward convenes the Army-McCarthy hearings to investigate communism in the army. With the help of President Eisenhower and Edward Murrow's unedited footage of the hearings, the army is vindicated and the true nature of McCarthyism becomes evident to the American public.[30]

Consider the experience of Melvin Rader—a professor of philosophy at the University of Washington from 1930 to 1981.[31] In 1948 Rader was charged with subversive activities by the Canwell Committee—Washington State's equivalent of the U.S. Congress's Un-American Activities Committee. The committee produced a witness who accused Rader of attending a communist strategy seminar in Kingston, New York, during the summer of 1938. The unsubstantiated accusations of this witness put Rader's career in jeopardy and caused him to spend a number of years trying to clear his name. Later he wrote of the hearing that "the freedoms of the First and Fifth Amendments were violated. . . . There was no judge or jury, no right of cross examination of hostile witnesses, no right to subpoena evidence or introduce witnesses in one's own defense."[32] Rader contended that the Canwell Committee had suppressed evidence and that his accuser had lied, ultimately proving that he was in fact in Washington State that entire summer. Frank Donner, writing for the *Nation,* said that Rader "triumphed over his ordeals because he was able and willing to fight back: he was supported by the powerful tradition of northwest liberalism and his own strong faith in the democratic process."[33] Nevertheless, the Canwell Committee

---

30. See http://huac.tripod.com/ (accessed February 17, 2005).

31. Adam D. Moore, "Melvin Rader," in *American National Biography,* ed. Mark Carnes and John Garraty (New York: Oxford University Press, 1997).

32. Melvin Rader, *False Witness* (Seattle: University of Washington Press, 1979).

33. Frank J. Donner, "Melvin Rader: Obituary," *Nation,* October 27, 1969.

did not end its investigations. Other witnesses claimed that Rader was a communist or "fellow traveler," and he spent a good part of his life defending himself.

Laird v. Tatum (1972)—Military Surveillance of Civilian Activity

In response to aiding local authorities in dealing with civil disorders, U.S. Army Intelligence established a data-gathering system during the 1960s. Laura Murphy of the ACLU noted: "In total violation of the American tradition of preventing the armed forces from engaging in law enforcement and domestic surveillance, the U.S. military ran this cloak-and-dagger operation designed to monitor civilian political activity and dissent. [It] collected and maintained files on upwards of 100,000 political activists and used undercover operatives recruited from the Army to infiltrate these activist groups and steal confidential information and files for distribution to federal, state and local governments."[34]

Supreme Court Chief Justice Burger in *Laird v. Tatum* found that such activity "does not constitute a justiciable controversy" and did not cause "objective harm or threat of specific future harm."[35] Writing in dissent, Justice Douglas replied,

> The surveillance of the Army over the civilian sector—a part of society hitherto immune from its control—is a serious charge. It is alleged that the Army maintains files on the membership, ideology, programs, and practices of virtually every activist political group in the country, including groups such as the Southern Christian Leadership Conference, Clergy and Laymen United Against the War in Vietnam, the American Civil Liberties Union, Women's Strike for Peace, and the National Association for the Advancement of Colored People. The Army uses undercover agents to infiltrate these civilian groups and to reach into confidential files of students and other groups. The Army moves as a secret group among civilian audiences, using cameras and electronic ears for surveillance. The data it collects are distributed to civilian officials in state, federal, and local governments and to each military intelligence unit and troop command under the Army's juris-

---

34. Laura W. Murphy, director, ACLU Washington National Office, "ACLU Looks at Domestic Surveillance," ACLU Report, http://www.aclu.org/FreeSpeech/FreeSpeech.cfm?ID = 9790&c = 86 (last visited October 25, 2009).

35. *Laird v. Tatum*, 408 U.S. 1 (1972).

diction (both here and abroad); and these data are stored in one or more data banks.

Those are the allegations; and the charge is that the purpose and effect of the system of surveillance is to harass and intimidate the respondents and to deter them from exercising their rights of political expression, protest, and dissent "by invading their privacy, damaging their reputations, adversely affecting their employment and their opportunities for employment, and in other ways." Their fear is that "permanent reports of their activities will be maintained in the Army's data bank, and their 'profiles' will appear in the so-called 'Blacklist' and that all of this information will be released to numerous federal and state agencies upon request."[36]

One can easily understand how the use of the military might be necessary and justified in times of crisis. Quelling a riot, preventing a race war, and aiding in disaster relief efforts are obvious examples. But none of this requires gathering data on civilians or sharing information with other government agencies. Perhaps the loss of liberty associated with identification checkpoints, enforced curfews, and travel limitations is something we are willing to tolerate in the context of riots and race wars. Allowing military intelligence agents to circumvent constitutional protections, with no civilian oversight and no "sunlight" rules opening up procedures and processes to public scrutiny, seems suspect at best. Again, it would be hard to maintain that the appropriate balance was struck in this case.

COINTELPRO: The FBI's Covert Action Programs Against American Citizens

From the late 1950s through the early 1970s the FBI engaged in numerous operations designed to infiltrate, disrupt, and if possible eliminate groups that were deemed to be enemies of the American way of life. After a lengthy investigation of COINTELPRO operations, the Church Committee noted numerous abuses including:

- United States intelligence agencies have investigated a vast number of American citizens and domestic organizations. FBI headquarters alone

36. Ibid.

has developed over 500,000 domestic intelligence files, and these have been augmented by additional files at FBI Field Offices. The FBI opened 65,000 of these domestic intelligence files in 1972 alone. . . .

- Anonymously attacking the political beliefs of targets in order to induce their employers to fire them.
- Anonymously mailing letters to the spouses of intelligence targets for the purpose of destroying their marriages.
- Falsely and anonymously labeling as Government informants members of groups known to be violent, thereby exposing the falsely labeled member to expulsion or physical attack.
- The FBI mailed Dr. King a tape recording made from microphones hidden in his hotel rooms which one agent testified was an attempt to destroy Dr. King's marriage. The tape recording was accompanied by a note which Dr. King and his advisors interpreted as threatening to release the tape recording unless Dr. King committed suicide.
- For approximately 20 years the CIA carried out a program of indiscriminately opening citizens' first class mail. . . .
- In several cases, purely political information (such as the reaction of Congress to an Administration's legislative proposal) and purely personal information (such as coverage of the extra-marital social activities of a high-level Executive official under surveillance) was obtained from electronic surveillance and disseminated to the highest levels of the federal government.
- Warrantless break-ins have been conducted by intelligence agencies since World War II. During the 1960's alone, the FBI and CIA conducted hundreds of break-ins, many against American citizens and domestic organizations. In some cases, these break-ins were to install microphones; in other cases, they were to steal such items as membership lists from organizations considered "subversive" by the Bureau.[37]

A federal court, in *Socialist Workers Party v. Attorney General*,[38] found that "COINTELPRO was responsible for at least 204 burglaries by FBI agents, the use of 1,300 informants, the theft of 12,600 documents, 20,000 illegal wiretap days and 12,000 bug days."[39]

37. U.S. Senate, *Final Report of the Select Committee to Study Governmental Operations with Respect to Intelligence Activities*, 94th Cong., 2d sess., 1976, bk. 2, pp. 6 and 10–13; hereafter cited as "Church Committee Report."
38. *Socialist Workers Party v. Attorney General*, 642 F.Supp. 1357 (S.D.N.Y. 1986).
39. Murphy, "ACLU Looks at Domestic Surveillance."

Interestingly enough, the Church Committee also noted that while costing over $80 million per year these activities produced little in terms of security. "Not a single individual or group has been prosecuted since 1957 under the laws which prohibit planning or advocating action to overthrow the government. . . . A recent study by the General Accounting Office has estimated that of some 17,528 FBI domestic intelligence investigations of individuals in 1974, only 1.3 percent resulted in prosecution and conviction, and in only 'about 2 percent' of the cases was advance knowledge of any activity, legal or illegal, obtained."[40]

More recent cases come from abuses related to the Patriot Act and the terrorist attacks of 9/11—for example, Sami al-Hussayen's detainment for more than a year related to "providing expert advice and assistance" to terrorist organizations,[41] the incarceration of numerous individuals without trial at Guantánamo Naval Base, or the acts of rendition carried out by the CIA.[42] These cases, along with numerous others, are sufficient to show that balancing tests for suspending civil liberties frequently go wrong.[43]

40. Church Committee Report.

41. "The Department of Justice also used the material support provisions of the Patriot Act to prosecute Muslim student Sami al-Hussayen for engaging in First Amendment activities. Section 805 of the Patriot Act made it a crime to provide material support in the form of 'expert advice and assistance' to a designated foreign terrorist organization. Al-Hussayen, a 34-year old doctoral candidate at the University of Idaho and a computer expert, was charged with providing 'expert advice and assistance' because, among other things, he volunteered as a Webmaster for the Islamic Assembly of North America—an organization the government had not put on its list of foreign terrorist organizations. The government charged that this volunteer activity constituted expert advice and assistance.

Al-Hussayen's web pages provided many links, including links to 'fatwas' that advocated criminal activity and suicide operations, but that were not written by al-Hussayen. Essentially, he was reporting what others said—something journalists do every day. Al-Hussayen's lawyer also established that Reuven Paz, a prosecution witness, admitted that he had posted much of the same information on his own Web site and that the BBC did as well. The Justice Department did not stop this abuse of the Patriot Act, and detained al-Hussayen for one and one-half years on minor immigration charges. It was a jury that stopped this abuse by finding al-Hussayen not guilty of all terrorism charges leveled against him. He was later deported on immigration charges." Anthony D. Romero, "ACLU Letter to Senator Feinstein Addressing the Abuses of the Patriot Act by the Government," ACLU Report (April 4, 2005), http://www.aclu.org/safefree/general/17563leg20050404.html.

42. Ibid.

43. One of the more humorous examples comes from P. J. O'Rourke. "The United States Department of Agriculture has over 106,000 employees . . . [and] they are busy doing things like administering the Federal Wool and Mohair Program. According to the U.S. General Accounting office report to Congress on the 1990 farm bill, 'The government established a wool and mohair price-support program in 1954 . . . to encourage domestic wool production *in the interest of national security*.' Really, it says that. . . . From 1955 to 1980, 1.1 billion was spent on wool and mohair price supports, with 80 percent of that money going to a mere six thousand shepherds and (I guess) moherds. This is 146,000 per Bo Peep." P. J. O'Rourke, *Parliament of Whores* (New York: Grove Press, 1991), 144; italics mine.

"Just trust us" sentiments might have more force if they were accompanied by robust accountability provisions. But FISA courts meet in secret, their findings are almost never published, and only government officials appear before the court.[44] President George W. Bush's program authorizing the NSA to monitor international phone calls of U.S. citizens was secret—even more alarming to some, information about the program was withheld for a year by a "free press."[45] "The Bush administration refuses to say—in public or in closed session of Congress—how many Americans in the past four years have had their conversations recorded or their e-mails read by intelligence analysts without court authority. Two knowledgeable sources placed that number in the thousands; one of them, more specific, said about 5000."[46] One can only wonder what other secret programs are currently in place. Moreover, a generally recognized principle embedded in the Constitution is due process of law. Secret courts and search programs that include no accountability provisions violate this basic principle.[47]

I would like to conclude this section by considering an interesting argument offered by James Stacy Taylor.[48] Expanding on Taylor's example, suppose technology has advanced to the point where miniaturized robots roam everywhere, recording everything. Not only do they record everything you say or do from numerous angles, they also record your very thoughts. This entire vast amount of information is uploaded to an ever growing database. Taylor argues that "rather than opposing such an expansion of surveillance technology, its use should be encouraged—and not only in the public realm. Indeed, the State should place all of its citizens under surveillance at all times and in all places, including their offices, classrooms, shops—and even their bedrooms."[49] The mere existence of this database should not be worrisome and has clear benefits, among them unbiased access to the truth, better equality within the justice system between the rich and the poor, and

44. ACLU, "Surveillance Under the USA PATRIOT Act."

45. One theory about why Bush would sidestep FISA, which has never rejected a warrant application, is that the information used as the basis of the search was obtained by U.S. operatives torturing prisoners outside the United States.

46. Barton Gellman, Dafna Linzer, and Carol D. Leonning, "Spying on Overseas Calls Yields Scant Terror Leads," *Seattle Times,* February 5, 2006, A3.

47. Secret courts and search programs may also violate "equal protection" guarantees when specific groups are targeted. "Every thing secret degenerates, even the administration of justice; nothing is safe that does not show how it can bear discussion and publicity." Lord Acton to Newman and the Council of Trent, January 23, 1861, in *Lord Acton and his Circle,* Letter 74, ed. Abbot Gasquet (London: G. Allen, 1906).

48. Taylor, "In Praise of Big Brother."

49. Ibid., 227.

deterrence. In brief, Taylor argues that once specific conditions are met related to the accessing of information—those cases where the government is morally permitted to access information about individuals—then having more information available would be best, given that it is difficult to determine what information will be needed beforehand. The primary thrust of Taylor's argument is that the mere existence of such a database is value neutral.[50] The important questions are those surrounding access to this information.

Putting aside the supposed benefits of having such a system—in fact, there are numerous cases demonstrating how monitoring of this sort does not deter crime[51]—I will present two general problems for Taylor's account. First, if controlling access to our bodies and personal information is morally valuable and the loss of such control constitutes a health risk (see Chapter 3), then the notion that the mere existence of such a database is not morally problematic is suspect. Furthermore, I am certain that such a tool would eventually be misused. Well-meaning government officials have been and will be tempted to set aside reasonable safeguards in times of emergency or crisis. For example, just think how such a database would have been used during the McCarthy era. From doctoring the information found in the database to changing the access requirements during a perceived crisis—"We have a moral obligation to stop those communists, homosexuals, Jews, or Muslims"—to how the rich or powerful might be spared such monitoring (think of the black-market antimonitoring products that would be produced), the risks are hardly negligible.[52]

THE NOTHING TO HIDE ARGUMENT

A counterpart to the "just trust us" view is the nothing to hide argument.[53] According to this argument we are to balance the potential for harm of

50. One could cast Taylor's argument as a version of the old "guns don't kill people, people kill people" view. An important difference between these two positions is that almost everyone can own a gun while only a few will be able to access the database. Power in the gun case is more or less equalized—whereas power in the database access case is not.

51. See, for example, McCahill and Norris, "CCTV in London," 20.

52. Other risks include regime change and hacking by other nations. Also, if this technology is available to the best of governments, it would also, sooner or later, be available to the worst of governments. I suppose the United States would then pursue a "nonproliferation" strategy so that our secrets could be kept safe while we had access to everyone else's.

53. For a more rigorous analysis of this argument, see Daniel Solove's "I've Got Nothing to Hide and Other Misunderstandings of Privacy," *San Diego Law Review* 44 (Fall 2007): 745–72.

data mining and the like with the security interests of detecting and preventing terrorist attacks. I suppose we could weaken this further by merely referencing "security interests," which would include, but not be limited to, "terrorist attacks." A formal version of the argument might go something like this:

P1. When two fundamental interests conflict, we should adopt a balancing strategy, determine which interest is more compelling, and then sacrifice the lesser interest for the greater. If it is generally true that one sort of interest is more fundamental than another, then we are warranted in adopting specific policies that seek to trade the lesser interest for the greater interest.

P2. In the conflict between privacy and security it is almost always the case that security interests are weightier than privacy interests. The privacy intrusions related to data mining or NSA surveillance are not as weighty as our security interests in stopping terrorism, and so on—these sorts of privacy intrusions are more of a nuisance than a harm.

C3. So it follows that we should sacrifice privacy in these cases and perhaps adopt policies that allow privacy intrusions for security reasons.

One could easily challenge premise 2—there are numerous harms associated with allowing surveillance that are conveniently minimized or forgotten by the "nothing to hide" crowd. Daniel Solove notes that "privacy is threatened not by singular egregious acts but by a slow series of small, relatively minor acts, which gradually begin to add up."[54] Solove also points out, as I have already highlighted, that giving governments too much power undermines the mission of providing for security—the government itself becomes the threat to security. The point was put nicely by John Locke: "This is to think, that Men are so foolish, that they take care to avoid what Mischiefs may be done them by *Pole-Cats*, or *Foxes*, but are content, nay think it Safety, to be devoured by *Lions*."[55] It is also important to note the risk of mischief associated with criminals and terrorists compared to the kinds of mischief perpetrated by governments—even our government. In

54. Ibid., 769.
55. John Locke, *The Second Treatise of Government,* ed. C. B. Macpherson (Indianapolis: Hackett, 1980), chap. 5, sec. 93.

cases where there is a lack of accountability provisions and independent oversight governments may pose the greater security risk.

Consider a slight variation of a "nothing to hide" argument related to what I have called physical privacy. Suppose there was a way to complete body cavity searches without harming the target or being more than a mere nuisance. Perhaps we search the targets after they have passed out drunk. Would anyone find it plausible to maintain a "nothing to hide" view in this case? I think not—and the reason might be that we are more confident in upholding these rights and policies that protect these rights than we are of almost any cost/benefit analysis related to security. Whether rights are viewed as strategic rules that guide us to the best consequences as Mill would argue, or understood as deontic constraints on consequentialist sorts of reasoning, we are more confident in them than in almost any "social good" calculation. I am not saying that rights are absolute—they are just presumptively weighty. This line of argument is an attack on the first premise of the "nothing to hide" position. In essence, it is the view that rights are resistant to cost/benefit or consequentialist sort of arguments. Here we are rejecting the view that privacy interests are the sorts of things that can be traded for security.

Another problem for the "nothing to hide" argument has to do with justice and the distribution of harms. The distribution aspect is highlighted when surveillance policies pick targets based on appearance, ethnicity, or religion. If the burden of surveillance policy and the corresponding harms fall on one portion of society, we may have a problem of justice. Jeremy Waldron writes, "If security-gains for most people are being balanced against liberty-losses for a few, then we need to pay attention to the few/most dimensions of the balance, not just the liberty/security dimension. . . . We are not balancing the rights of the innocent against the rights of the guilty. We are balancing the interests in life or liberty of the one innocent man against the security interests of those of the rest of us . . . that will be served if . . . criminals are convicted by procedures that lead to a violation of an innocent."[56]

Balancing arguments that seek to justify trading privacy for security are typically based on the assumption that privacy and security are measurable values that can be compared and traded. But it is not at all clear how these trade-offs should work or how these items should be measured. For example, we may agree that there is no amount of ice cream that we would

---

trade for our arms and legs.[57] Ice cream may be tasty, but it is not on the same scale as having arms and legs. Or suppose we were faced with the choice of living normally for a year and then dying or having a brain operation and living in a vegetative state for thirty years.[58] It is not at all clear that any amount of "vegetative" existence is worth one year of normal living. James Griffin is not so sure and argues that if dessert consumption was not subject to diminishing marginal utility (roughly meaning the more you have of something the less valuable it is), had value, and we could contemplate the large numbers involved, there may be a trade-off point. In addition, Griffin claims that living a long life in a vegetative state may have no value, so the second case has little force.

While I think it is clear that most of us would trade privacy for a certain level of security and vice versa, we must not lose sight of the risks involved. In any case, coming up with a way to compare or rank-order privacy and security would be difficult—especially when such calculations are related to rules or legislation.[59]

To conclude the critique of the "nothing to hide" view, balancers rarely discuss the consequences of the surveillance policy they are promoting or whether an alternative might exist that better protects both privacy and security.[60] Consider, just for example, almost any predominately developed "isolationist" country—perhaps Switzerland. My guess is that these sorts of countries do not have much terrorist activity and likely do not have higher crime rates than the United States.[61] The point here is that one way to obtain more security would be to change our selectively interventionist policies—in this way security and privacy could be protected.

THE "SECURITY TRUMPS" VIEW

While it has been assumed that security is a fundamental value, we might inquire about how this view might be justified.[62] At the most basic level

---

57. This case comes from Laurence Tribe, "Policy Science: Analysis or Ideology?" *Philosophy and Public Affairs* 2 (Fall 1972): 90; cited in James Griffin, "Are There Incommensurable Values?" *Philosophy and Public Affairs* 7 (1977): 44.

58. This case comes from Griffin, "Are There Incommensurable Values?" 47.

59. For more about incommensurability, see Ruth Chang, ed., *Incommensurability, Incomparability, and Practical Reason* (Cambridge: Harvard University Press, 1997).

60. Waldron, "Security and Liberty," 13–14.

61. See http://www.nationmaster.com/country/sz-switzerland/ter-terrorism (accessed April 8, 2009).

62. For a defense of the security trumps view, see Ken Himma, "Privacy vs. Security: Why Privacy Is Not an Absolute Value or Right," *San Diego Law Review* 45 (Spring 2007): 857.

security affords individuals control over their lives, projects, and property. To be secure at this level is to have sovereignty over a private domain—it is to be free from unjustified interference from other individuals, corporations, and governments. At this level it would seem privacy and security come bundled together.

At a second level, security protects groups, businesses, and corporations from unjustified interference with projects and property. Corporations need to be secure from industrial espionage, theft, and the like. Without this kind of control, businesses and corporations could not operate in a free market—not for long anyway. In any case, if we ask the question, "Why do we care about corporations and free markets?" we are quickly led back to security at the individual level. We value security at the level of groups, businesses, and corporations because these entities are intertwined with security at the personal level. It is through these groups that many of us pursue lifelong plans and projects and order our lives as we see fit. Few would maintain that these groups are valuable independent of their impact on individual lives. Privacy and security come bundled together at this level as well, although in a different way. Through the use of walls, guards, and fences, groups are able to secure a private domain that may be necessary for the continued existence of groups and group activities.

There is also national security to consider. Here we are worried about the continued existence of a political union. Our institutions and markets need to be protected from foreign invasion, plagues, and terrorism. But again it seems that we value national security, not because some specific political union is valuable in itself, but because it is a necessary part of protecting individual liberty. Armed services, intelligence agencies, police departments, public health institutions, and legal systems provide security for groups, businesses, and, at the most fundamental level, individuals.

According to what might be called the "security trumps" view, whenever privacy and security conflict, security wins—that is, security is more fundamental and valuable than privacy. However, it is not clear why a "security trumps" view should be adopted over a "privacy trumps" view. Privacy or perhaps self-ownership seems at least as fundamental or intuitively weighty as security.

In some cases, privacy enhances security and vice versa. Suppose that rights afforded their holders specific sorts of powers. For example, Fred's privacy rights generate in him a god-like power to completely control access to his body and to information about him. If we had such powers, we would also have increased security. Furthermore, if we had complete security in our bodies and property—including informational security—we would have secured privacy as well. The tension between privacy and security arises because these values cannot be protected by individuals acting alone. Nevertheless, it is important to note again that as these services are contracted out to other agents, like governments, we grant these parties power over us—power that may undermine security and privacy.

It also seems odd to maintain that any increase in security should be preferred to any increase in privacy or any decrease in privacy is to be preferred to any decrease in security. Such a view would sanction massive violations of privacy for mere incremental and perhaps momentary gains in security. Also, given that security will be provided by others and power is likely a necessary part of providing security, we have strong prudential reasons to reject the security trumps view. If those who provide security were saints, then perhaps there would be little to worry about. The cases already presented are sufficient to show that we are not dealing with saints.[63]

TURNING SECURITY ARGUMENTS ON THEIR HEADS

It is false to claim that in every case more privacy means less security or more security entails less privacy. Security arguments actually cut the other direction in some cases—it is only through enhanced privacy protections that we can obtain appropriate levels of security against industrial espionage, unwarranted invasions into private domains, and information warfare or terrorism.

Carnivore (now called DCS 1000) is a physical device, something like a small computer, designed to allow law enforcement agents to monitor electronic communications such as e-mail.[64] After obtaining the appropriate legal permission the device can be connected to the hardware of a target's

---

63. Isaiah Berlin points to a different worry related to safety arguments and governmental paternalism. "Paternalism is despotic, not because it is more oppressive than naked, brutal unenlightened tyranny, nor merely because it ignores the transcendental reason embodied in me, but because it is an insult to my conception of myself as a human being, determined to make my own life in accordance with my own . . . purposes, and, above all, entitled to be recognized as such by others." Isaiah Berlin, "Two Concepts of Liberty," in *Isaiah Berlin: Liberty*, ed. H. Hardy (Oxford: Oxford University Press, 2002), 202.

64. I am indebted to Griffin Dunham's presentation in, "Carnivore, The FBI's E-mail Surveillance System: Devouring Criminals, Not Privacy," *Federal Communications Law Journal* 54 (May 2002).

Internet service provider (ISP). Carnivore will then start to search the ISP's traffic and accumulate packets of the suspect's communications.

What I am interested in here is not the ease with which Carnivore can be legally deployed, but rather accountability provisions across two dimensions. The "black box" and the program, which together make up the Carnivore device, are not open for public scrutiny. FBI and DOJ assurances amount to nothing more than these agencies saying, "Just trust us"— obviously not a robust accountability provision. Moreover, the system, we are told, can be programmed with different search parameters depending on the type of surveillance being conducted, and there is no auditing function. There is no user accountability built into the system—nothing that records which agents configure the system or conduct the surveillance. As with the lack of sunlight provisions related to FISA courts we may ask why. Individual security from rogue agents, overzealous law enforcement officials, and the potential for programming errors would seem to necessitate accountability. Accountability, civilian oversight, and sunlight provisions in turn protect individual privacy. Finally, given the widespread availability of strong encryption, the use of Carnivore will not likely affect the sorts of terrorists capable of posing a credible threat to national security.[65]

A more salient example of how privacy protections enhance security comes from the debate over encryption standards for electronic communications and computer networks.[66] Although the National Security Administration's position is that the widespread use of encryption software will allow criminals a sanctuary to exchange information necessary for the completion of illegal activities, consider how easily this security argument can be stood on its head. National security for government agencies, companies, and individuals actually *requires* strong encryption. Spies have admitted to "tapping in" and collecting valuable information on U.S. companies—information that was then used to gain a competitive advantage.[67] A report from the CSIS Task Force on Information Warfare and Security notes that "cyber terrorists could overload phone lines . . . disrupt air traffic control . . . scramble software used by major financial

65. See Stephen W. Tountas, "Carnivore: Is the Regulation of Wireless Technology a Legally Viable Option to Curtail the Growth of Cybercrime?" *Washington University Journal of Law and Policy* 11 (2003): 351.

66. Some of the following draws from material published in Adam D. Moore, "Privacy and the Encryption Debate," *Knowledge, Technology, and Policy* 12 (2000): 72–84.

67. Jonathan Wallace and Mark Mangan, *Sex, Laws, and Cyberspace* (New York: Henry Holt, 1997), 51.

institutions, hospitals, and other emergency services . . . or sabotage the New York Stock Exchange."[68] Related to information war, it would seem that national security requires strong encryption, multilevel firewalls, and automated detection of attacks.

BALANCING PRIVACY AND SECURITY WHILE MAINTAINING ACCOUNTABILITY

Suppose that there was good evidence that an attack was about to happen in a private domain. In this case we may be more confident that security interests outweigh privacy interests and allow the intrusion. To avoid the travesties already mentioned we need a set of policies or rules that adequately protect privacy and security.

With probable cause, a warrant issued from a judge, and sunlight provisions opening up the warrant and the procedure to public scrutiny, we can be confident that security concerns may be addressed with minimal impact on individual privacy. The requirement of probable cause puts the burden of proof in the appropriate place—invasions of private domains must be justified. The official seeking the warrant would highlight the security risks involved along with the privacy interests at stake. Judicial oversight inserts an outside element into the process, providing a check on the enthusiasm of law enforcement officials. In any event, the question of when security should override privacy would not be left to the subjective judgment of one individual or a small group of individuals with similar interests. Finally, sunlight provisions provide public oversight of the entire process including the reasons for the warrant and the judicial ruling. In this way, at each step, public accountability is ensured. Consider the following table that measures privacy interests across several dimensions.

First, if the subject has consented to the surveillance, then the magnitude, context, and security dimensions become irrelevant—such monitoring would be justified. Short of consent, if the magnitude is slight, the context was clearly "public," and the security threat high, the burden of proof for overriding privacy would be low. Sliding to the other extreme, if the magnitude of the invasion is profound, the context clearly "private,"

---

68. Cited in Christopher Jones, "Averting an Electronic Waterloo," *Wired Magazine* Online News Flash (February 1999). See also Eric Jensen, "Computer Attacks on Critical National Infrastructure: A Use of Force Invoking the Right of Self-Defense," *Stanford Journal of International Law* 38 (Summer 2002).

Table 2. Guidelines to be followed when balancing privacy and security

	Invasion of privacy for security reasons justified	Invasion of privacy for security reasons not justified
Magnitude*	*Slight* A one-time wire-tap of a cell-phone conversation.	*Profound* Total surveillance, to include data mining and the monitoring of electronic communications and physical movements.
Context	*Little expectation of privacy* The subject will be monitored in "public"—perhaps as he or she walks down the street.	*Reasonable expectation of privacy* The subject will be monitored at his or her primary residence.
Consent	*Consented to surveillance* The subject consents to the surveillance.	*Evaded surveillance* The subject actively avoids the surveillance.
Public security	*Of great public importance* There is credible evidence that lives are at stake.	*Of little public importance* A pacifist alliance plans to have a bake sale to raise funds.

*Concept of magnitude includes duration, extent, and means.

and the security threat low, then the burden for overriding privacy would be high. Finally, if there is a substantial security threat backed by clear and credible evidence, then independent of the magnitude, context, or consent, the burden for overriding privacy would be low. For example, if a police officer has good evidence that a murder will take place tomorrow afternoon at a suspect's home, then a warrant would be justified.

In addition, there will be justifiable exceptions to the rule of requiring probable cause and warrants. There may be instances when law enforcement officials need to act quickly and do not have the time to secure a warrant or provide an argument for probable cause—suppose a police officer hears a scuffle and someone shouts for help. Provided that law enforcement officers act in "good faith" and can articulate reasonable grounds for entering private domains after the fact, they should be given some leeway in these cases. Perhaps internal and civilian oversight committees could review such cases to determine if appropriate action was pursued. Thus even in "emergency" situations where privacy is traded for security without a warrant or judicial oversight, we may insist on sunlight provisions and accountability.

Security concerns related to mass transportation or large public gatherings may also warrant an exception to the probable cause rule—individuals may be searched without evidence that they will commit a crime in these cases. Nevertheless, there are at least two important controls that should be noted. First, individuals, in many instances, consent to these sorts of minimal intrusions. If you don't want to have your bag searched, then stay home and watch the ballgame on television. Note that the more voluntary the activity the more robust the consent. Second, in cases where the activity is less voluntary—flying on an airplane for example—we insist on stronger justifications for more intrusive searches. Moreover, judicial and civilian oversight are still appropriate mechanisms for establishing the correct balance between privacy and security in these cases. Few would sanction body cavity searches at airports for the minimal gains in security that could be obtained.

It should be clear from the preceding just how far we have strayed from the baseline of probable cause, judicial oversight, and public accountability. We should be alarmed about legislation that sanctions secret courts, gag orders, sneak, peek, and grab searches, and has few or no provisions for governmental accountability. For the sake of argument, suppose that secret courts and gag orders are indeed necessary for certain cases dealing with sensitive matters related to national security. Why are there no sunlight provisions—ever? Since 1978 the FISC judges have considered more than fourteen thousand FISA applications for surveillance (not including Patriot Act Section 215 orders). "Of these applications, the FISC summarily approved without modification all but five, and it did not reject even one."[69] The American Civil Liberties Union noted that in May 2002 the FISC judges unanimously rejected a Department of Justice application for expanded powers to conduct electronic monitoring under the Patriot Act. This ruling was overturned by an appeals court that had never before convened.[70] In addition, over a thousand individuals have been taken into federal custody without being charged.[71] Some have been U.S. citizens. Most, if not all, of those detained were Muslims of Arab descent. Late 2001 and early 2002 over eight thousand Muslim immigrants were interviewed by law enforce-

---

69. ACLU, "Unpatriotic Acts," 3.

70. Ibid.

71. "Six days after the terrorist attack, Ashcroft effectively canceled the 'Great Writ' of habeas corpus with a decree announcing that the government would henceforth lock up suspected aliens for a 'reasonable period.' Over one thousand 'special interest' detainees were jailed in the months after 9/11. . . . More than six hundred were deported after secret trials. When a New Jersey judge denounced the government's refusal to release the names of detainees as 'odious to democracy,' Ashcroft responded by issuing an emergency regulation trumping the state court decision." Bovard, *Terrorism and Tyranny*, 3.

ment agents. "The Attorney General Ashcroft also announced a massive new program to fingerprint over 100,000 Arab and Muslim immigrants suspected of no wrongdoing."[72]

In this final chapter I have argued that balancing tests that purport to justify invasions of privacy in the name of security often go awry and attempt to trade values that are difficult to measure. The cases already presented along with numerous others are sufficient to support this claim. It has also been argued that in trading privacy for security we should insist on establishing probable cause, judicial oversight, and accountability. Probable cause sets the standard for when security interests override privacy rights. Judicial oversight, sensitive to case-specific facts like the context and magnitude of the proposed intrusion, introduce an "objective" agent into the process. Sunlight provisions allow for a public discussion of the merits of specific searches and seizures. All of this promotes accountability by ensuring that the reasons for a search and the actions of government officials are open to public scrutiny. A further benefit is that such policies engender trust and confidence in public officials.

Two recently abandoned programs also deserve mention. The Terrorist Information and Prevention System (TIPS) proposed by President George W. Bush threatened to circumvent Fourth Amendment protections against unreasonable searches by turning postal workers, utility employees, and the like into surveillance agents of the federal government. These individuals, who have access to private places, were to report "suspicious" activity directly to the DOJ.

A second program, originally entitled Total Information Awareness (TIA), sought to "imagine, develop, apply, integrate, demonstrate and transition information technologies, components and prototype, closed-loop, information systems that will counter asymmetric threats by achieving total information awareness useful for preemption; national security warning; and national security decision making."[73] The idea was to create a database

72. ACLU Report, "Insatiable Appetite: The Government's Demand for New and Unnecessary Powers After September 11" (April 2002), 7.

73. Taken from the TIA Web site before it was removed. TIA was originally headed up by John Poindexter. "[Poindexter] was convicted in 1990 of five felony counts of lying to Congress, destroying official documents and obstructing congressional inquiries into the Iran-contra affair, which involved the secret sale of arms to Iran in the mid-1980s and diversion of profits to help the contra rebels in Nicaragua. . . .

"Poindexter . . . was the highest-ranking Reagan administration official found guilty in the scandal. He was sentenced to six months in jail by a federal judge who called him 'the decision-making head' of a scheme to deceive Congress. The U.S. Court of Appeals overturned that conviction in 1991, saying Poindexter's rights had been violated through the use of testimony he had given to Congress after being granted immunity." Robert O'Harrow Jr., "U.S. Hopes to

of information that approached total information awareness about citizens and visitors to the United States. In part, this was to be achieved by accessing numerous private and public sector databases, including education records, tax filings, purchasing profiles, medical records, and criminal files.

Through the use of administrative subpoenas the government gathers information necessary for the maintenance of the state. A critic of the proposed view of requiring probable cause, judicial oversight, and sunlight provisions may argue that these rules are too strong. Governments must be able to require disclosures from individuals and corporations for taxing purposes or for licensing without going before a judge.[74] Nevertheless, there is a vast difference between requiring citizens and corporations to file yearly tax returns and creating a database on each of us that attempts total information awareness. A required disclosure for tax information without showing probable cause seems reasonable—assuming that such information is accessed and used only by the IRS. Beyond such specific purposes and uses related to the administrative state, we should insist on probable cause, judicial oversight, and accountability. For example, if the tax records of a suspected criminal are relevant to an investigation, then the investigators should go before a judge, show probable cause, and if appropriate, acquire access.

CONCLUSION

In this work I have argued that individuals have privacy rights. Defined as a right to control access to and uses of places, bodies, and personal information, privacy is valuable and necessary for human flourishing. Beyond being morally valuable, privacy rights protect bodies, places, and personal information from unwanted access and manipulation. If legal systems are to reflect important moral norms, then privacy protections must be codified in the law. More specifically, the tort of intrusion should be strengthened to protect private domains from the prying eyes and ears of neighbors, corporations, and media interests. When privacy interests are at stake, I have argued that "right to know" or free speech considerations should be recast in terms of "what kinds of information are necessary for the continued existence and stability of democratic institutions." We have been will-

Check Computers Globally: System Would Be Used to Hunt Terrorists," *Washington Post*, November 12, 2002.

74. For an analysis of subpoenas, see Slobogin, "Subpoenas and Privacy," 805.

ing to place content-based restrictions on speech—for example, obscene pornography, hate speech, sexual harassment, and threats. I have proposed that we consider a privacy-based restriction on speech.

Additionally, individuals have privacy rights in both private and public places. It does not follow that just because someone is accessible they have no rights to control access to their body or to personal information—free access views defended by digital natives are not compelling. This is also true in the workplace. Employee drug testing unjustifiably invades private domains and should be replaced, when necessary, with impairment testing. Finally, I have argued that balancing tests that trade privacy for security are problematic and typically lead to decreases in both.

A transparent society is not inevitable. Privacy at the personal level can be secured through custom and social pressure.[75] Privacy related to big media, corporate interests, and the state can be guaranteed by law and also be grounded in customs and social practices. On the other hand, transparency is an essential component of good government in the sense that those in power can be held accountable for their actions. Justice Douglas, in *Osborn v. United States* noted,

> The time may come when no one can be sure whether his words are being recorded for use at some future time; when everyone will fear that his most secret thoughts are no longer his own, but belong to the Government; when the most confidential and intimate conversations are always open to eager, prying ears. When that time comes, privacy, and with it liberty, will be gone. If a man's privacy can be invaded at will, who can say he is free? If his every word is taken down and evaluated, or if he is afraid every word may be, who can say he enjoys freedom of speech? If his every association is known and recorded, if the conversations with his associates are purloined, who can say he enjoys freedom of association? When such conditions obtain, our citizens will be afraid to utter any but the safest and most orthodox thoughts; afraid to associate with any but the most acceptable people. Freedom as the Constitution envisages it will have vanished.[76]

Douglas paints a grim picture, and we should heed his warning. We have good reason to resist traveling toward a Watcher society. Moreover, it is

---

75. See, for example, Schoeman's analysis in *Privacy and Social Freedom,* chaps. 5 and 6.
76. William Douglas, *Osborn v. United States,* 385 U.S. 323 (1966) at 353–54.

within the walls of privacy that we find the moral space to order our lives as we see fit, experiment with new ways of living, and pursue lifelong goals and projects. For the sake of freedom, autonomy, and human flourishing we should resist becoming a society of the Watchers and the Watched. Socrates once said that "the unexamined life is not worth living"—but neither is the life examined by government agents or corporations, or the life open to inspection by anyone for any reason.[77]

77. Paraphrasing John Silber in "Masks and Fig Leaves," in *Privacy: Nomos XIII*, ed. J. Roland Pennock and John W. Chapman (New York: Atherton Press, 1971), 234.

SELECT BIBLIOGRAPHY

Ackrill, J. L. "Aristotle on Eudaimonia." In *Essays on Aristotle's Ethics*, ed. A. Rorty. Berkeley and Los Angeles: University of California Press, 1980.

Adams, Robert. *Finite and Infinite Goods: A Framework for Ethics.* Oxford: Oxford University Press, 1999.

Alderman, Ellen, and Caroline Kennedy. *The Right to Privacy.* New York: Knopf, 1995.

Allee, W. C. *The Social Life of Animals.* Boston: Beacon Press, 1958.

Allen, Anita. *Why Privacy Isn't Everything: Feminist Reflections on Personal Accountability.* Lanham, Md.: Rowman and Littlefield, 2003.

Ariès, Philippe, and Georges Duby, et al., general editors. *A History of Private Life.* 5 vols. Trans. Arthur Goldhammer. Cambridge: Belknap Press of Harvard University Press, 1987–91.

Barlow, John Perry. "Private Life in Cyberspace." *Communications of the ACM* 34 (1991): 23–25.

Barnum, Darold, and John Gleason. "The Credibility of Drug Tests: A Multi-Stage Bayesian Analysis." *Industrial Relations Review* 47 (July 1994): 610–21.

Beauchamp, Tom L. "The Right to Privacy and the Right to Die." *Social Philosophy and Policy* 17 (2000): 276–92.

Becker, Lawrence. *Property Rights, Philosophic Foundations.* London: Routledge and Kegan Paul, 1977.

Benn, Stanley, and G. Gaus, eds. *Public and Private in Social Life.* New York: St. Martin's Press, 1983.

Berlin, Isaiah. "Two Concepts of Liberty." In *Isaiah Berlin: Liberty*, ed. H. Hardy. Oxford: Oxford University Press, 2002.

Black, Hugo L. "The Bill of Rights." *New York University Law Review* 35 (1960): 865–81.

Bloustein, Edward. "Group Privacy: The Right to Huddle." In *Individual and Group Privacy*, ed. Edward J. Bloustein, 123–86. New Brunswick: Transaction Books, 1978.

Bok, Sissela. *Secrets: On the Ethics of Concealment and Revelation.* New York: Vintage Books, 1984.

Bovard, James. *Terrorism and Tyranny: Trampling Freedom, Justice, and Peace to Rid the World of Evil.* New York: Palgrave Macmillan, 2003.

Brandeis, Louis. *Other People's Money, and How the Bankers Use It.* New York: Frederick A. Stokes, 1914.

Brandt, Richard. *A Theory of the Good and the Right.* Oxford: Clarendon Press, 1979.

Branscomb, Anne Wells. *Who Owns Information?* New York: Basic Books, 1994.

Brenner, Susan. "The Privacy Privilege: Law Enforcement, Technology, and the Constitution." *Journal of Technology Law and Policy* 7 (December 2002): 123–94.

Bush, Tom. "Comment: A Privacy-Based Analysis for Warrantless Aerial Surveillance Cases." *California Law Review* 75 (1987): 1767–1808.

Calhoun, John. "The Study of Wild Animals Under Controlled Conditions." *Annals of the New York Academy of Sciences* 51 (1950): 113–22.

Cate, Fred. *Privacy in the Information Age.* Washington, D.C.: Brookings Institution Press, 1997.

Christian, John. "Phenomena Associated with Population Density." *Proceedings of the National Academy of Science* 47 (1961): 428–49.

Cohen, G. A. "The Pareto Argument for Inequality." *Social Philosophy and Policy* 12 (1995): 160–85.

Cooley, Thomas M. *A Treatise on the Constitutional Limitations Which Rest upon the Legislative Power of the States of the American Union.* Boston: Little, Brown, 1903.

———. *A Treatise on the Law of Torts.* Chicago: Callaghan, 1880.

———. *A Treatise on the Law of Torts.* 2nd ed. Chicago: Callaghan, 1888.

Cox, Verne, Paul Paulus, and Garvin McCain. "Prison Crowding Research: The Relevance of Prison Housing Standards and a General Approach Regarding Crowding Phenomena." *American Psychologist* 39 (1984): 1148–60.

Crouch, Denis, et al. "A Critical Evaluation of the Utah Power and Light Company's Substance Abuse Management Program: Absenteeism, Accidents, and Costs." In *Drugs in the Workplace: Research and Evaluation Data,* ed. S. Gust and J. Walsh. Rockville, Md.: National Institute on Drug Abuse, 1989.

Curtis, Michael Kent. "Democratic Ideals and Media Realities: A Puzzling Free Press Paradox." *Social Philosophy and Policy* 21 (2004): 385–487.

Daniels, Roger, Sandra Taylor, and Harry Kitano, eds. *Japanese Americans, from Relocation to Redress.* Salt Lake City: University of Utah Press, 1986.

Davis, Frederick. "What Do We Mean by 'Right to Privacy'?" *South Dakota Law Review* 4 (1959): 1–24.

DeCew, Judith Wagner. "Drug Testing: Balancing Privacy and Public Safety." *Hastings Center Report* 24 (1994): 17–25.

———. *In Pursuit of Privacy: Law, Ethics, and the Rise of Technology.* Ithaca: Cornell University Press, 1997.

———. "The Scope of Privacy in Law and Ethics." *Law and Philosophy* 5 (1986): 145–73.

Dickenson, Donna. *Property in the Body: Feminist Perspectives.* Cambridge: Cambridge University Press, 2007.

Dittrich, David, and Ken Himma. "Hackers, Crackers, and Computer Criminals." In *The Handbook of Information Security,* vol. 2, ed. H. Bidgoli. Hoboken, N.J.: John Wiley and Sons, 2005.

Dunham, Griffin. "Carnivore, The FBI's E-mail Surveillance System: Devouring Criminals, Not Privacy." *Federal Communications Law Journal* 54 (May 2002): 543–66.

Dworkin, Ronald. *Law's Empire.* Cambridge: Belknap Press of Harvard University Press, 1986.

———. "Rights as Trumps." In *Theories of Rights,* ed. J. Waldron. New York: Oxford University Press, 1985.

———. *Taking Rights Seriously.* Cambridge: Harvard University Press, 1977.

Ely, John. "The Wages of Crying Wolf: A Comment on *Roe v. Wade.*" *Yale Law Journal* 82 (1973): 920–49.

Englehardt, H. Tristram, Jr. "Privacy and Limited Democracy." *Social Philosophy and Policy* 17 (Summer 2000): 120–40.

Etzioni, Amitai. *The Limits of Privacy.* New York: Basic Books, 1999.

Fabre, Cecile. "Justice, Fairness, and World Ownership." *Law and Philosophy* 21 (May 2002): 249–73.

Farrington, David, and Christopher Nuttal. "Prison Size, Overcrowding, Prison Violence and Recidivism." *Journal of Criminal Justice* 8 (1980): 221–31.

Feinberg, Joel. "Autonomy, Sovereignty, and Privacy: Moral Ideas in the Constitution?" *Notre Dame Law Review* 58 (1983): 445–92.

———. "Grounds for Coercion: Hard Cases for the Harm Principle." In *Applied Social and Political Philosophy*, ed. E. Smith and H. G. Blocker. Englewood Cliffs, N.J.: Prentice Hall, 1994.

———. *Rights, Justice, and the Bounds of Liberty.* Princeton: Princeton University Press, 1980.

Feldman, Fred. "The Good Life: A Defense of Attitudinal Hedonism." *Philosophy and Phenomenological Research* 65 (2002): 604–28.

———. "Hyperventilating About Intrinsic Value." *Journal of Ethics* 2 (1998): 339–54.

———. "Some Puzzles About the Evil of Death." *Philosophical Review* 100 (April 1991): 205–27.

Finnis, John. *Natural Law and Natural Rights.* Oxford: Clarendon Press, 1980.

Floridi, Luciano. "The Ontological Interpretation of Informational Privacy." *Ethics and Information Technology* 7 (2005): 185–200.

Foot, Philippa. *Natural Goodness.* Oxford: Oxford University Press, 2001.

Francis, William, and Robert Collins. *Cases and Materials on Patent Law: Including Trade Secrets, Copyrights, Trademarks.* 4th ed. St. Paul, Minn.: West Publishing, 1995.

Frankfurt, Harry. "Coercion and Moral Responsibility." In *Essays on Freedom of Action*, ed. T. Honderich. London: Routledge and Kegan Paul, 1973.

Freund, Paul. "Privacy: One Concept or Many?" In *Privacy: Nomos XIII*, ed. J. Roland Pennock and John W. Chapman, 182–98. New York: Atherton Press, 1971.

Frey, R. G. "Privacy, Control, and Talk of Rights." *Social Philosophy and Policy* 17 (2000): 45–67.

Froomkin, A. Michael. "The Death of Privacy." *Stanford Law Review* 52 (May 2000): 1461–1543.

Fuller, Theodore D., J. Edwards, S. Vorakitphokatorn, and S. Sermsri. "Chronic Stress and Psychological Well-Being: Evidence from Thailand on Household Crowding." *Social Science Medicine* 42 (1996): 265–80.

Gasquet, Abbot. *Lord Acton and His Circle.* London: G. Allen, 1906.

Gauthier, David. *Morals by Agreement.* Oxford: Oxford University Press, 1987.

Gavison, Ruth. "Information Control: Availability and Control." In *Public and Private in Social Life*, ed. Stanley Benn and G. Gaus, 113–34. New York: St. Martin's Press, 1983.

Gerstein, Robert S. "Intimacy and Privacy." *Ethics* 89 (October 1978): 76–81.

Gert, Bernard. "Rationality, Human Nature, and Lists." *Ethics* 100 (January 1990): 279–300.

Gormley, Ken. "One Hundred Years of Privacy." *Wisconsin Law Review* (1992): 1335–1441.

Graham, Charles J., Rhonda Dick, Vaughn I. Rickert, and Robert Glenn. "Left-handedness as a Risk Factor for Unintentional Injury in Children." *Pediatrics* 92 (December 1993): 823–26.

Grant, Ruth. *John Locke's Liberalism.* Chicago: University of Chicago Press, 1987.

Griffin, James. "Are There Incommensurable Values?" *Philosophy and Public Affairs* 7 (1977): 39–59.

———. *Well-Being: Its Meaning, Measurement, and Moral Importance.* Oxford: Clarendon Press, 1986.

Gross, Hyman. "Privacy and Autonomy." In *Privacy: Nomos XIII,* ed. J. Roland Pennock and John W. Chapman, 169–81. New York: Atherton Press, 1971.

Grove, Walter, and Michael Hughes. *Overcrowding in the Household.* New York: Academic Press, 1983.

Hall, Edward. "Proxemics." *Current Anthropology* 9 (1968): 83–108.

Halpern, Sheldon, David Shipley, and Howard Abrams. *Copyright: Cases and Materials.* St. Paul, Minn.: West Publishing, 1992.

Harris, John. "The Marxist Conception of Violence." *Philosophy and Public Affairs* 3 (1973–74): 192–220.

Hart, H. L. A. *The Concept of Law.* Oxford: Clarendon Press, 1961.

———. *Essays in Jurisprudence and Philosophy.* New York: Clarendon Press, 1983.

———. *Essays on Bentham.* New York: Clarendon Press, 1982.

———. *Law, Liberty, and Morality.* Oxford: Oxford University Press, 1963.

Henkin, Louis. "Privacy and Autonomy." *Columbia Law Review* 74 (1974): 1410–33.

Hettinger, Edwin. "Justifying Intellectual Property." *Intellectual Property: Moral, Legal, and International Dilemmas,* ed. A. Moore. Lanham, Md.: Rowman and Littlefield, 1997.

Himma, Ken. "Justifying Intellectual Property Protection: Why the Interests of Content-Creators Usually Win Over Everyone Else's." In *Information Technology and Social Justice,* ed. E. Rooksby. Hershey, Pa.: Idea Group, 2006.

———. "Privacy vs. Security: Why Privacy Is Not an Absolute Value or Right." *San Diego Law Review* 45 (Fall 2007): 857–919.

Hubin, Don, and Mark Lambeth. "Providing for Rights." *Dialogue* 27 (1988): 489–502.

Inness, Julie. *Privacy, Intimacy, and Isolation.* New York: Oxford University Press, 1992.

Johnson, Deborah G. *Computer Ethics.* Upper Saddle River, N.J.: Prentice Hall, 1994.

Kagan, Shelly. *The Limits of Morality.* Oxford: Oxford University Press, 1989.

Kahn, Jonathan. "Privacy as a Legal Principle of Identity Maintenance." *Seton Hall Law Review* 33 (2003): 371–410.

Kasl, S. V. "Stress and Health." *Annual Review of Public Health* 5 (1984): 319–41.

Kharkhordin, Oleg. "Reveal and Dissimulate: A Genealogy of Private Life in Soviet Russia." In *Public and Private in Thought and Practice,* ed. J. Weintraub and K. Kumar. Chicago: University of Chicago Press, 1997.

Kleinig, John. "Good Samaritanism." *Philosophy and Public Affairs* 5 (1975–76): 382–407.

Korsgaard, Christine. "The Reasons We Can Share: An Attack on the Distinction Between Agent-Relative and Agent-Neural Values." In *Altruism,* ed. Ellen Frankel Paul, Fred Miller Jr., and Jeffrey Paul. Cambridge: Cambridge University Press, 1993.

———. "Skepticism About Practical Reason." In *Moral Discourse and Practice,* ed. S. Darwall, A. Gibbard, and P. Railton. Oxford: Oxford University Press, 1997.

———. "The Sources of Normativity." In *Moral Discourse and Practice,* ed. S. Darwall, A. Gibbard, and P. Railton. Oxford: Oxford University Press, 1997.

Kozinski, Alex, and Stuart Banner. "The Anti-History and Pre-History of Commercial

Speech: A Problem in the Theory of Freedom." *Iowa Law Review* 62 (1976): 747–75.

———. "Who's Afraid of Commercial Speech." *Virginia Law Review* 76 (1990): 627–53.

Lee, Dorothy. *Freedom and Culture.* Englewood Cliffs, N.J.: Waveland Press, 1959.

Lee, Laurie Thomas. "The USA Patriot Act and Telecommunications: Privacy Under Attack." *Rutgers Computer and Technology Law Journal* 29 (2003): 371–403.

Lessig, Lawrence. "Privacy as Property." *Social Research* 69 (2002): 247–69.

Levy, Leonard. *Legacy of Suppression.* Cambridge: Belknap Press of Harvard University Press, 1960.

Lilly, Jacob. "National Security at What Price? A Look into Civil Liberty Concerns in the Information Age Under the USA Patriot Act of 2001 and a Proposed Constitutional Test for Future Legislation." *Cornell Law Journal* 12 (2003): 447–71.

Lomasky, Loren. *Persons, Rights, and the Moral Community.* Oxford: Oxford University Press, 1987.

Lyons, David. *Forms and Limits of Utilitarianism.* Oxford: Clarendon Press, 1965.

———. *Rights, Welfare, and Mill's Moral Theory.* Oxford: Oxford University Press, 1994.

———. "Welcome Threats and Coercive Offers." *Philosophy* 50 (1975): 425–36.

MacCormick, Neil. *Legal Right and Social Democracy: Essays in Legal and Political Philosophy.* Oxford: Clarendon Press, 1982.

Mack, Eric. "Bad Samaritanism and the Causation of Harm." *Philosophy and Public Affairs* 9 (1979–80): 230–59.

———. "Causing and Failing to Prevent Harm." *Southwestern Journal of Philosophy* 7 (1976): 83–90.

———. "Gauthier on Rights and Economic Rent." *Social Philosophy and Policy* 9 (1992): 171–200.

———. "Moral Individualism: Agent-Relativity and Deontic Restraints." *Social Philosophy and Policy* 7 (1989): 81–111.

———. "Self-Ownership, Marxism, and Egalitarianism." *Politics, Philosophy, and Economics* 1 (2002): 237–76.

Macpherson, C. B. "Elegant Tombstones: A Note on Friedman's Freedom." In *Theory: Essays in Retrieval.* Oxford: Oxford University Press, 1973.

Maltby, Lewis. "Drug Testing: A Bad Investment." ACLU Report, 1999, 1–29.

Marx, Gary. "Privacy and Technology." *Whole Earth Review,* Winter 1991, 91–95.

McCain, Garvin, Verne Cox, and Paul Paulus. "The Effect of Prison Crowding on Inmate Behavior." Washington, D.C.: U.S. Department of Justice, 1980.

McClurg, Andrew. "Bringing Privacy Law Out of the Closet: A Tort Theory of Liability for *Engblom v. Carey,* 677 F.2d 957 (2d Cir. 1982)." *North Carolina Law Review* 73 (1995): 989–1088.

McGinley, Phyllis. "A Lost Privilege." In *Province of the Heart.* New York: Viking Press, 1959.

McNulty, Patrick J. "The Public Disclosure of Private Facts: There Is Life After *Florida Star.*" *Drake Law Review* 50 (2001): 93–158.

Megargee, E. I. "The Association of Population Density, Reduced Space, and Uncomfortable Temperatures with Misconduct in a Prison Community." *American Journal of Community Psychology* 5 (1977): 289–98.

Meiklejohn, Alexander. "The First Amendment Is an Absolute." *Supreme Court Review* (1961): 245–66.

Mizutani, Masahiko, James Dorsey, and James H. Moor. "The Internet and Japanese Conception of Privacy." *Ethics and Information Technology* 6 (2004): 121–28.

Montague, Phillip. "Two Concepts of Rights." *Philosophy and Public Affairs* 9 (1980): 372–84.

Moor, James. "Towards a Theory of Privacy in the Information Age." *Computers and Society* 27 (1997): 27–32.

Moore, Adam D. "Employee Monitoring and Computer Technology: Evaluative Surveillance v. Privacy." *Business Ethics Quarterly* 10 (2000): 697–709.

———. "Intangible Property: Privacy, Power, and Information Control." *American Philosophical Quarterly* 35 (October 1998): 365–78.

———. *Intellectual Property and Information Control: Philosophic Foundations and Contemporary Issues*. New Brunswick, N.J.: Transaction Books, 2001.

———. "Intellectual Property, Innovation, and Social Progress: The Case Against Incentives-Based Arguments." *Hamline Law Review* 26 (2003): 602–30.

———. "Personality-Based, Rule-Utilitarian, and Lockean Justifications of Intellectual Property." In *Information and Computer Ethics*, ed. H. Tavani and K. Himma. New York: John Wiley and Sons, 2008.

———. "Privacy and the Encryption Debate." *Knowledge, Technology, and Policy* 12 (2000): 72–84.

———. "Privacy: Its Meaning and Value." *American Philosophical Quarterly* 40 (Fall 2003): 215–27.

———. "Toward a Lockean Theory of Intellectual Property." In *Intellectual Property: Moral, Legal, and International Dilemmas*, ed. A. Moore. Lanham, Md.: Rowman and Littlefield, 1997.

———. "Values, Objectivity, and Relationalism." *Journal of Value Inquiry* 38 (Fall 2004): 75–90.

Moore, Barrington, Jr. *Privacy: Studies in Social and Cultural History*. New York: M. E. Sharpe, 1984.

Morris, Desmond. *The Human Zoo*. New York: McGraw Hill, 1969.

Murdock, George. "The Universals of Culture." In *Readings in World Anthropology*, ed. E. A. Hoebel, J. D. Jennings, and E. R. Smith. New York: McGraw-Hill, 1955.

Nagel, Thomas. *The View from Nowhere*. Oxford: Oxford University Press, 1986.

Nelkin, Dorothy. *Science as Intellectual Property*. New York: Macmillan, 1984.

Nissenbaum, Helen. "Protecting Privacy in an Information Age: The Problem of Privacy in Public." *Law and Philosophy* 17 (1998): 559–96.

Normand, Jacques. *Under the Influence? Drugs and the American Workforce*. Washington, D.C.: National Academy Press, 1994.

Normand, Jacques, Stephen D. Salyards, and John J. Mahoney. "An Evaluation of Preemployment Drug Testing." *Journal of Applied Psychology* 75 (1990): 926–39.

"Note: Privacy, Photography, and the Press." *Harvard Law Review* 111 (1998): 1086–1103.

Nozick, Robert. *Anarchy, State, and Utopia*. New York: Basic Books, 1974.

———. "Coercion." In *Philosophy, Science and Method*, ed. S. Morgenbesser, P. Suppes, and M. White. New York: St. Martin's Press, 1969.

Nussbaum, Martha. "Human Functioning and Social Justice: In Defense of Aristotelian Essentialism." *Political Theory* 20 (May 1992): 202–47.

O'Harrow, Robert. *No Place to Hide.* New York: Free Press, 2006.

O'Rourke, P. J. *Parliament of Whores.* New York: Grove Press, 1991.

Ortiz, Daniel R. "Privacy, Autonomy, and Consent." *Harvard Journal of Law and Public Policy* 12 (1989): 91–97.

Palfrey, John, and Urs Gasser. *Born Digital: Understanding the First Generation of Digital Natives.* Philadelphia: Basic Books, 2008.

Parent, W. A. "Privacy, Morality, and the Law." *Philosophy and Public Affairs* 12 (1983): 269–88.

Parker, Richard B. "A Definition of Privacy." *Rutgers Law Review* 27 (1974): 275–329.

Paton-Simpson, Elizabeth. "Privacy and the Reasonable Paranoid: The Protection of Privacy in Public Places." *University of Toronto Law Journal* 30 (Summer 2000): 305–46.

Paulus, Paul, Verne Cox, and Garvin McCain. "Death Rates, Psychiatric Commitments, Blood Pressure, and Perceived Crowding as a Function of Institutional Crowding." *Environmental Psychology and Nonverbal Behavior* 3 (1978): 107–16.

Peikoff, Amy. "No Corn on This Cob: Why Reductionists Should Be All Ears for Pavesich." *Brandeis Law Journal* 42 (2004): 751–92.

Pennock, J. Roland, and John W. Chapman, eds. *Privacy: Nomos XIII.* New York: Atherton Press, 1971.

Porporino, Frank. *An Analysis of the Effects of Overcrowding in Canadian Penitentiaries.* Ottawa: Research Division, Programs Branch, Solicitor General of Canada, 1984.

Posner, Richard. *An Economic Analysis of Law.* Boston: Little, Brown, 1972.

Pound, Roscoe. "Interests in Personality." *Harvard Law Review* 28 (1915): 343–92.

Prosser, William. "Privacy." *California Law Review* 48 (1960): 383–422.

Quinn, Warren. *Morality and Action.* Cambridge: Cambridge University Press, 1993.

Rachels, James. "Why Privacy Is Important." *Philosophy and Public Affairs* 4 (1975): 323–33.

Rader, Melvin. *False Witness.* Seattle: University of Washington Press, 1979.

Rainbolt, George. "Rights as Normative Constraints on Others." *Philosophy and Phenomenological Research* 53 (1993): 93–112.

Rawls, John. *A Theory of Justice.* Cambridge: Harvard University Press, 1971.

Raz, Joseph. *The Morality of Freedom.* Oxford: Oxford University Press, 1986.

Reiman, Jeffrey H. "Privacy, Intimacy, and Personhood." *Philosophy and Public Affairs* 6 (1976): 26–44.

Richards, David. *Sex, Drugs, Death, and the Law: An Essay on Human Rights and Overcriminalization.* Lanham, Md.: Rowman and Littlefield, 1982.

Rickless, Samuel. "The Right to Privacy Unveiled." *San Diego Law Review* 44 (2008): 773–99.

Roberts, John, and Thomas Gregor. "Privacy: A Cultural View." In *Privacy: Nomos XIII,* ed. J. Roland Pennock and John W. Chapman, 119–225. New York: Atherton Press, 1971.

Rosen, Jeffery. *Naked Crowd.* New York: Random House, 2004.

Rosenberg, Alexander. "Privacy as a Matter of Taste and Right." *Social Philosophy and Policy* 17 (2000): 68–90.

Ross, David. *The Right and the Good.* London: Oxford University Press, 1930.

Rothenberg, Lance. "Re-Thinking Privacy: Peeping Toms, Video Voyeurs, and the Failure of the Criminal Law to Recognize a Reasonable Expectation of Privacy in the Public Space." *American University Law Review* 49 (2000): 1127–65.

Sandel, Michael. *Democracy's Discontent: America in Search of a Public Philosophy.* Cambridge: Belknap Press of Harvard University Press, 1998.

Scanlon, Thomas. "Thomson on Privacy." *Philosophy and Public Affairs* 4 (1975): 315–22.

Schmidtz, David. *Rational Choice and Moral Agency.* Princeton: Princeton University Press, 1995.

Schoeman, Ferdinand D. *Privacy and Social Freedom.* New York: Cambridge University Press, 1992.

Schwartz, Barry. "The Social Psychology of Privacy." *American Journal of Sociology* 73 (1968): 741–52.

Seale, Darryl. "Why Do We Do It If We Know It's Wrong?" In *Ethical Issues of Information Systems,* ed. A. Salehnia. London: IRM Press, 2002.

Shapiro, Ian. "Resources, Capacities, and Ownership: The Workmanship Ideal and Distributive Justice." *Political Theory* 19 (February 1991): 47–72.

Simmons, A. John. *The Lockean Theory of Rights.* Princeton: Princeton University Press, 1992.

Slobogin, Christopher. "Public Privacy: Camera Surveillance of Public Places and the Right to Anonymity." *Mississippi Law Journal* 72 (2002).

———. "Subpoenas and Privacy." *DePaul Law Review* 54 (2005): 805–45.

Solove, Daniel. "I've Got Nothing to Hide and Other Misunderstandings of Privacy." *San Diego Law Review* 44 (Fall 2007): 745–72.

Spinello, Richard. "Interview with a Hacker." *Case Studies in Information and Computer Ethics,* ed. R. Spinello. Upper Saddle River, N.J.: Prentice Hall, 1997.

Spiro, Herbert. "Privacy in Comparative Perspective." In *Privacy: Nomos XIII,* ed. J. Roland Pennock and John W. Chapman, 121–48. New York: Atherton Press, 1971.

Spitz, Rene. "The Derailment of Dialogue." *Journal of the American Psychoanalytic Association* 12 (1964): 752–75.

Spooner, Lysander. *The Law of Intellectual Property; or, An Essay on the Right of Authors and Inventors to a Perpetual Property in Their Ideas.* In *The Collected Works of Lysander Spooner,* ed. C. Shively. Weston, Mass.: M and S Press, 1971.

Steiner, Hillel. *An Essay on Rights.* Oxford: Blackwell, 1994.

Strossen, Nadine. "Protecting Privacy and Free Speech in Cyberspace." *Georgetown Law Journal* 89 (2001): 2103–15.

Talbott, William J. *Which Rights Should Be Universal?* Oxford: Oxford University Press, 2005.

Tavani, Herman. "Philosophical Theories of Privacy: Implications for an Adequate Online Privacy Policy." *Metaphilosophy* 38 (2007): 1–22.

Taylor, James Stacey. "In Praise of Big Brother: Why We Should Learn to Stop Worrying and Love Government Surveillance." *Public Affairs Quarterly* 19 (July 2005): 227–46.

———. "Privacy and Autonomy: A Reappraisal." *Southern Journal of Philosophy* 40 (2002): 587–604.

Taylor, Paul. "Happiness and Intrinsic Value." In *Ethical Theory: Classical and Contemporary Readings,* ed. Louis Pojman. Belmont, Calif.: Wadsworth, 1989.

Thomson, Judith Jarvis. "The Right to Privacy." *Philosophy and Public Affairs* 4 (1975): 295–314.

Turkington, Richard, and Anita Allen. *Privacy Law: Cases and Materials.* 2nd ed. St. Paul, Minn.: West Group, 2002.

Tushnet, Mark. "Legal Conventionalism in the U.S. Constitutional Law of Privacy." *Social Philosophy and Policy* 17 (2000): 141–64.

"Unpatriotic Acts: The FBI's Power to Rifle Through Your Records and Personal Belongings Without Telling You." ACLU Report, July 2003.

U.S. Senate. *Final Report of the Select Committee to Study Governmental Operations with Respect to Intelligence Activities of the United States Senate.* 94th Cong., 2nd sess., 1976. Archived at http://www.archive.org/details/finalreportofselo2unit.

Van den Haag, Ernest. "On Privacy." In *Privacy: Nomos XIII,* ed. J. Roland Pennock and John Chapman, 149–68. New York: Atherton Press, 1971.

Veyne, Paul, ed. *A History of Private Life.* Vols. 1–3. Cambridge: Harvard University Press, 1987.

Volokh, Eugene. "Freedom of Speech and Information Privacy: The Troubling Implications of a Right to Stop People from Speaking About You." *Stanford Law Review* 52 (2000): 1049–1124.

Waldron, Jeremy. "Rights in Conflict." *Ethics* 99 (April 1989): 503–19.

———. "Security and Liberty: The Image of Balance." *Journal of Political Philosophy* 11 (2003): 191–210.

Wallace, Jonathan, and Mark Mangan. *Sex, Laws, and Cyberspace.* New York: Henry Holt, 1997.

Warren, Samuel, and Louis Brandeis. "The Right to Privacy." *Harvard Law Review* 4 (1890): 193–220.

Wasserstrom, Richard. "Privacy: Some Arguments and Assumptions." *Philosophical Law,* ed. R. Bronaugh. Westport, Conn.: Greenwood Press, 1978.

Weinstein, W. L. "The Uses of Privacy in the Good Life." In *Privacy: Nomos XIII,* ed. J. Roland Pennock and John Chapman, 27–55. New York: Atherton Press, 1971.

Weintraub, Jeffrey. "The Theory and Politics of the Public/Private Distinction." In *Public and Private in Thought and Practice,* ed. J. Weintraub and K. Kumar. Chicago: University of Chicago Press, 1997.

Wertheimer, Alan. *Coercion.* Princeton: Princeton University Press, 1987.

Westin, Alan F. *Privacy and Freedom.* New York: Atheneum, 1967.

White, Amy E. *Virtually Obscene: The Case for an Uncensored Internet.* Jefferson, N.C.: McFarland, 2006.

Whitman, James. "The Two Western Cultures of Privacy: Dignity Versus Liberty." *Yale Law Journal* 113 (2004): 1151–1221.

Wilson, James Q. "Against the Legalization of Drugs." *Commentary* 89 (February 1990): 21–28.

Wolf, Clark. "Contemporary Property Rights, Lockean Provisos, and the Interests of Future Generations." *Ethics* 105 (1995): 791–818.

Zimmerman, David. "Coercive Wage Offers." *Philosophy and Public Affairs* 10 (1981): 121–45.

Zimmerman, Diane L. "False Light Invasion of Privacy: The Light That Failed." *N.Y.U Law Review* 64 (1989): 364–453.

———. "Requiem for a Heavyweight: A Farewell to Warren and Brandeis's Privacy Tort." *Cornell Law Review* 68 (1983): 291–365.

Zwerling, Craig, James Ryan, and Endel John Orav. "The Efficacy of Preemployment Drug Screening for Marijuana and Cocaine in Predicting Employment Outcomes." *Journal of the American Medical Association* 264 (1990): 2639–43.

FURTHER READINGS

Agre, Philip E. "The Architecture of Identity: Embedding Privacy in Market Institutions." *Information, Communication, and Society* 2 (1999): 1–25.

———. "Surveillance and Capture: Two Models of Privacy." *Information Society* 10 (1994): 101–27.

Agre, Philip E., and Marc Rotenberg. "Technology and Privacy: The New Landscape." *Journal of the American Society for Information Science* 50 (1999): 631–33.

Alfino, Mark. "Information Ethics in the Workplace: Misplacing Privacy." *Journal of Information Ethics* 10 (2001): 5–8.

Alfino, Mark, and G. Randolph Mayes. "Reconstructing the Right to Privacy." *Social Theory and Practice* 29 (2003): 1–18.

Allen, Anita L. "Coercing Privacy." *William and Mary Law Review* 40 (1999): 723–57.

———. "Cyberspace and Privacy: A New Legal Paradigm? Gender and Privacy in Cyberspace." *Stanford Law Review* 52 (2000): 1175–1200.

———. "Is Privacy Now Possible? A Brief History of an Obsession." *Social Research* 68 (2001): 301–6.

———. "Lying to Protect Privacy." *Villanova Law Review* 44 (1999): 161–88.

———. "Privacy and Equal Protection as Bases for Abortion Law: Citizenship, Gender, and the Constitution." In *Having and Raising Children*, ed. Uma Narayan. University Park: Pennsylvania State University Press, 1999.

———. *Uneasy Access: Privacy for Women in a Free Society*. Totowa, N.J.: Rowman and Littlefield, 1988.

———. "The Virtuous Spy: Privacy as an Ethical Limit." *Monist: An International Quarterly Journal of General Philosophical Inquiry* 91 (January 2008): 3–22.

———. "Women and Their Privacy: What Is at Stake." In *Beyond Domination*, ed. Carol C. Gould, 233–49. Ottowa: Rowman and Allanheld, 1984.

Anderson, Scott A. "Privacy Without the Right to Privacy." *Monist: An International Quarterly Journal of General Philosophical Inquiry* 91 (January 2008): 81–107.

Andre, Judith. "Privacy as a Value and as a Right." *Journal of Value Inquiry* 20 (1986): 309–17.

Arneson, Richard J. "Egalitarian Justice Versus the Right to Privacy?" *Social Philosophy and Policy* 17 (2000): 91–119.

Austin, Lisa. "Privacy and the Question of Technology." *Law and Philosophy* 22 (2003): 119–66.

Baker, Edwin. "Autonomy and Informational Privacy, or Gossip: The Central Meaning of the First Amendment." *Social Philosophy and Policy* 21 (2004): 215–68.

Beck, Robert N. "The Right of Professional Privacy." *Personalist* 55 (1974): 145–50.

Benn, Stanley. "Private and Public Morality: Clean Living and Dirty Hands." In *Public and Private in Social Life*, ed. S. Benn and G. Gaus, 155–82. New York: St. Martin's Press, 1983.

————. "Protection and Limitation of Privacy." *Australian Law Journal* 52 (1978): 601–12.

Benn, Stanley, and G. Gaus. "The Liberal Conception of the Public and the Private." In *Public and Private in Social Life*, ed. S. Benn and G. Gaus, 31–66. New York: St. Martin's Press, 1983.

Bier, William, ed. *Privacy*. New York: Fordham University Press, 1980.

Bierman, A. K. "Spying, Liberalism, and Privacy." *Journal of Social Philosophy* 5 (1974): 11–14.

Bishop, Nicole. "Trust Is Not Enough: Classroom Self-Disclosure and the Loss of Private Lives." *Journal of Philosophy of Education* 30 (1996): 429–39.

Bloche, M. Gregg. "Managed Care, Medical Privacy, and the Paradigm of Consent." *Kennedy Institute of Ethics Journal* 7 (1997): 381–86.

Bloustein, Edward. *Individual and Group Privacy*. New Brunswick, N.J.: Transaction Books, 1978.

————. "Privacy as an Aspect of Human Dignity: An Answer to Dean Prosser." *New York University Law Review* 39 (1964): 962–1007.

Boetzkes, Elisabeth. "Privacy, Property, and the Family in the Age of Genetic Testing: Observations from Transformative Feminism." *Journal of Social Philosophy* 32 (2001): 301–16.

Boone, C. Keith. "Privacy and Community." *Social Theory and Practice* 9 (1983): 1–30.

Borna, Shaheen, and Stephen Avila. "Genetic Information: Consumers' Right to Privacy Versus Insurance Companies' Right to Know a Public Opinion Survey." *Journal of Business Ethics* 19 (1999): 355–62.

Boyle, James. *Shamans, Software, and Spleens*. Cambridge: Harvard University Press, 1996.

Branscomb, Anne W. "Law and Culture in the Information Society." *Information Society* 4 (1986): 279–311.

Brenkert, George G. "Privacy, Polygraphs, and Work." *Business and Professional Ethics Journal* 1 (1981): 19–36.

Brennan, Geoffrey. "The Economy of Privacy: Institutional Design in the Economy of Esteem." *Monist: An International Quarterly Journal of General Philosophical Inquiry* 91 (January 2008): 23–51.

Brill, Alida. *Nobody's Business: Paradoxes of Privacy*. Reading, Mass.: Addison-Wesley, 1990.

Brin, David. *The Transparent Society*. New York: Perseus Books, 1998.

Brown, William S. "Technology, Workplace Privacy, and Personhood." *Journal of Business Ethics* 15 (1996): 1237–48.

Chambers, Jean E. "Privacy, Sex, and Norms: An Indirect Control Definition." *Journal of Information Ethics* 9 (2000): 10–25.

Claeys, Eric R. "The Private Society and the Liberal Public Good in John Locke's Thought." *Social Philosophy and Policy* 25 (Summer 2008): 201–34.

Cohen, Julie E. "Privacy, Visibility, Transparency, and Exposure." *University of Chicago Law Review* 75 (Winter 2008): 181–201.

Corlett, J. Angelo. "The Nature and Value of the Moral Right to Privacy." *Public Affairs Quarterly* 16 (2002): 329–50.

Cranford, Michael. "Drug Testing and the Right to Privacy: Arguing the Ethics of Workplace Drug Testing." *Journal of Business Ethics* 17 (1998): 1805–15.

Danna, Anthony, and Oscar H. Gandy Jr. "All That Glitters Is Not Gold: Digging

Beneath the Surface of Data Mining." *Journal of Business Ethics* 40 (2002): 373–86.

Davidson, Dan. "Employee Testing: An Ethical Perspective." *Journal of Business Ethics* 7 (1988): 211–17.

DeCew, Judith Wagner. "Alternatives for Protecting Privacy While Respecting Patient Care and Public Health Needs." *Ethics and Information Technology* 1 (1999): 249–55.

———. "Constitutional Privacy, Judicial Interpretation, and 'Bowers versus Hardwick.'" *Social Theory and Practice* 15 (1989): 285–303.

———. "Defending the 'Private' in Constitutional Privacy." *Journal of Value Inquiry* 21 (1987): 171–84.

———. "The Priority of Privacy for Medical Information." *Social Philosophy and Policy* 17 (2000): 213–34.

———. "Privacy and Policy for Genetic Research." *Ethics and Information Technology* 6 (2004): 4–14.

Diffie, Whitfield, and Susan Landau. *Privacy on the Line: The Politics of Wiretapping and Encryption.* Cambridge: MIT Press, 1998.

Dromm, Keith. "Love and Privacy." *Journal of Applied Philosophy* 19 (2002): 155–67.

Dworkin, Ronald. "Privacy and the Law." In *Privacy,* ed. John Young, 113–36. New York: John Wiley and Sons, 1978.

Elwood, John P. "Outing, Privacy, and the First Amendment." *Yale Law Journal* 102 (1992): 747–76.

Engstrom, Timothy H. "Corporate Appropriation of Privacy: The Transformation of the Personal and Public Spheres." *Ethics and Behavior* 7 (1997): 239–52.

Epstein, Richard A. "Deconstructing Privacy: And Putting It Back Together Again." *Social Philosophy and Policy* 17 (2000): 1–24.

Etzioni, Amitai. "A Communitarian Perspective on Privacy." *Connecticut Law Review* 32 (2000): 897–905.

———. "The First Amendment Is Not an Absolute Even on the Internet." *Journal of Information Ethics* 6 (1997): 64–66.

———. "Identification Cards in America." *Society* 36 (1999): 70–76.

———. "Medical Records: Enhancing Privacy, Preserving the Common Good." *Hastings Center Report* 29 (1999): 14–23.

Floridi, Luciano. "Four Challenges for a Theory of Informational Privacy." *Ethics and Information Technology* 8 (2006): 109–19.

Forester, Tom, and Perry Morrison. "Computer Crime: New Problem for the Information Society." *Prometheus* 8 (1990): 257–72.

Francis, Huw W. S. "Of Gossips, Eavesdroppers, and Peeping Toms." *Journal of Medical Ethics* 8 (1982): 134–43.

Francis, Leslie Pickering. "Privacy and Confidentiality: The Importance of Context." *Monist: An International Quarterly Journal of General Philosophical Inquiry* 91 (January 2008): 52–67.

Freedman, Warren. *The Right of Privacy in the Computer Age.* Westport, Conn.: Quorum Books, 1987.

Fried, Charles. "Privacy." *Yale Law Journal* 77 (1968): 475–93.

Friedman, Batya. "Social Judgments and Technological Innovation: Adolescents' Understanding of Property, Privacy, and Electronic Information." *Computers in Human Behavior* 13 (1997): 327–51.

Friedman, David. "Privacy and Technology." *Social Philosophy and Policy* 17 (2000): 186–212.

———. "A World of Strong Privacy: Promises and Perils of Encryption." *Social Philosophy and Policy* 13 (1996): 212–28.

Garfinkel, Simson. *Database Nation*. Sebastopol, Calif.: O'Reilly and Associates, 2000.

Garrow, David J. *Liberty and Sexuality: The Right to Privacy and the Making of* Roe v. Wade. New York: Macmillan, 1994.

Gaus, Gerald. "Public and Private Interests in Liberal Political Economy, Old and New." In *Public and Private in Social Life,* ed. S. Benn and G. Gaus. New York: St. Martin's Press, 1983.

Gavison, Ruth. "Privacy and the Limits of Law." *Yale Law Journal* 89 (1980): 421–71.

Gerber, Scott D. "Privacy and Constitutional Theory." *Social Philosophy and Policy* 17 (2000): 165–85.

Gerstein, Robert S. "Privacy and Self Incrimination." *Ethics* 80 (1970): 87–101.

Gilliom, John. *Surveillance, Privacy, and the Law: Employee Drug Testing and the Policies of Social Control*. Ann Arbor: University of Michigan Press, 1996.

Ginsberg, Robert. "The Right to Privacy vs. Government Need to Know." *Journal of Social Philosophy* 4 (1973): 5–8.

Gould, James. "Abortion: Privacy Versus Liberty." *Journal of Social Philosophy* 21 (1990): 98–106.

Grcic, Joseph M. "The Right to Privacy: Behavior as Property." *Journal of Value Inquiry* 20 (1986): 137–44.

Greenawalt, Kent. "Privacy and Its Legal Protections." *Hastings Center Studies* 2 (1974): 45–68.

Griffin, James. "The Human Right to Privacy." *San Diego Law Review* 44 (Fall 2007): 697–721.

Gross, Hyman. "The Concept of Privacy." *New York University Law Review* 42 (1967): 34–54.

Hallborg, Robert B., Jr. "Principles of Liberty and the Right to Privacy." *Law and Philosophy* 5 (1986): 175–218.

Halper, Thomas. "Privacy and Autonomy: From Warren and Brandeis to 'Roe' and 'Cruzan.'" *Journal of Medicine and Philosophy* 21 (1996): 121–35.

Halpern, Sheldon W. *The Law of Defamation, Privacy, Publicity, and Moral Right*. 3rd ed. Columbus, Ohio: JPM Books, 1995.

Haviland, Leslie, and John Haviland. "Privacy in a Mexican Village." In *Public and Private in Social Life,* ed. S. Benn and G. Gaus, 341–62. New York: St. Martin's Press, 1983.

Hendricks, Evan, Trudy Hayden, and Jack Novik. *Your Right to Privacy*. 2nd ed. Carbondale: Southern Illinois University Press, 1990.

Himma, Ken. "Separation, Risk, and the Necessity of Privacy to Well-Being: A Comment on Adam Moore's 'Toward Informational Privacy Rights.'" *San Diego Law Review* 44 (Fall 2007): 847–57.

Hixson, Richard. *Privacy in a Public Society*. New York: Oxford University Press, 1987.

Horowitz, Irving Louis. *Communicating Ideas*. New York: Oxford University Press, 1986.

Hudson, Stephen D., and Douglas N. Husak. "Benn on Privacy and Respect for Persons." *Australasian Journal of Philosophy* 57 (1979): 324–29.

Inness, Julie. "Information, Access, or Intimate Decisions About One's Action? The Content of Privacy." *Public Affairs Quarterly* 5 (1991): 227–42.

Introna, Lucas D. "Privacy and the Computer: Why We Need Privacy in the Information Society." *Metaphilosophy* 3 (1997): 259–75.

Introna, Lucas D., and Athanasia Pouloudi. "Privacy in the Information Age: Stakeholders, Interests, and Values." *Journal of Business Ethics* 22 (1999): 27–38.

Johnson, Jeffery L. "Constitutional Privacy." *Law and Philosophy* 13 (1994): 161–93.

———. "Privacy and the Judgment of Others." *Journal of Value Inquiry* 23 (1989): 157–68.

———. "Privacy, Liberty, and Integrity." *Public Affairs Quarterly* 3 (1989): 15–34.

———. "A Theory of the Nature and Value of Privacy." *Public Affairs Quarterly* 6 (1992): 271–88.

Krygier, Martin. "Publicness, Privateness, and 'Primitive Law.'" In *Public and Private in Social Life*, ed. S. Benn and G. Gaus, 307–40. New York: St. Martin's Press, 1983.

Kukathas, Chandran. "Cultural Privacy." *Monist: An International Quarterly Journal of General Philosophical Inquiry* 91 (January 2008): 68–80.

Kupfer, Joseph. "Privacy, Autonomy, and Self Concept." *American Philosophical Quarterly* 24 (1987): 81–89.

Lane, Frederick S. "The Naked Employee: How Technology Is Compromising Workplace Privacy." *Knowledge, Technology, and Policy* 16 (2003): 108–9.

Langer, Richard. "Abortion and the Right to Privacy." *Journal of Social Philosophy* 23 (1992): 23–51.

Levy, Steven. *Hackers: Heroes of the Computer Revolution.* New York: Dell Publishing, 1984.

Lieberstein, Stanley H. *Who Owns What Is in Your Head? Trade Secrets and the Mobile Employee.* New York: Hawthorne Books, 1979.

Lippke, Richard L. "Work, Privacy, and Autonomy." *Public Affairs Quarterly* 3 (1989): 41–55.

Loch, Karen D., Sue Conger, and Effy Oz. "Ownership, Privacy, and Monitoring in the Workplace: A Debate on Technology and Ethics." *Journal of Business Ethics* 17 (1998): 653–63.

Lund, William R. "Communitarian Politics, the Supreme Court, and Privacy: The Continuing Need for Liberal Boundaries." *Social Theory and Practice* 16 (1990): 191–215.

Lusky, Louis. "Invasion of Privacy: A Clarification of Concepts." *Political Science Quarterly* 87 (1972): 192–209.

Lyons, David. *The Electronic Eye: The Rise of Surveillance Society.* Oxford: Blackwell Publishers, 1994.

———. *Surveillance Society: Monitoring Everyday Life.* Buckingham, U.K.: Open University Press, 2001.

Machan, Tibor R. "The Right to Privacy Versus Uniformitarianism." *Journal of Social Philosophy* 23 (1992): 75–84.

MacKinnon, Catharine. "Privacy v. Equality: Beyond *Roe v. Wade.*" In *Feminism Unmodified.* Cambridge: Harvard University Press, 1987.

Manning, Rita C. "Liberal and Communitarian Defenses of Workplace Privacy." *Journal of Business Ethics* 16 (1997): 817–23.

Marshall, Sandra E. "Public Bodies, Private Selves." *Journal of Applied Philosophy* 5 (1988): 147–58.

Martin, Kirsten, and R. Edward Freeman. "Some Problems with Employee Monitoring." *Journal of Business Ethics* 43 (2003): 353–61.

Marx, Gary T. "Murky Conceptual Waters: The Public and the Private." *Ethics and Information Technology* 3 (2001): 157–69.

———. *Undercover: Police Surveillance in America*. Berkeley and Los Angeles: University of California Press, 1988.

Matheson, David. "A Distributive Reductionism About the Right to Privacy." *Monist: An International Quarterly Journal of General Philosophical Inquiry* 91 (January 2008): 108–29.

———. "Unknowableness and Informational Privacy." *Journal of Philosophical Research* 32 (2007): 251–67.

Matthews, Steve. "Privacy, Separation, and Control." *Monist: An International Quarterly Journal of General Philosophical Inquiry* 91 (January 2008): 130–50.

May, Larry. "Privacy and Property." *Philosophy in Context* 10 (1980): 40–53.

McArthur, Robert L. "Reasonable Expectations of Privacy." *Ethics and Information Technology* 3 (2001): 123–28.

McCarthy, J. T. *The Rights of Publicity and Privacy*. New York: Clark Boardman, 1987.

McCloskey, H. J. "The Political Ideal of Privacy." *Philosophical Quarterly* 21 (1971): 303–14.

———. "Privacy and the Right to Privacy." *Philosophy* 55 (1980): 17–38.

McLean, Deckle. *Privacy and Its Invasion*. Westport, Conn.: Praeger Publishers, 1995.

Meeler, David. "Is Information All We Need to Protect?" *Monist: An International Quarterly Journal of General Philosophical Inquiry* 91 (January 2008): 151–69.

Meslin, Eric M., et al. "The Ethical, Legal, and Social Implications Research Program at the National Human Genome Research Institute." *Kennedy Institute of Ethics Journal* 7 (1997): 291–98.

Michelfelder, Diane P. "The Moral Value of Informational Privacy in Cyberspace." *Ethics and Information Technology* 3 (2001): 129–35.

Mill, John Stuart. *On Liberty*. New York: Penguin, 1976.

Miller, Seumas, and John Weckert. "Privacy, the Workplace, and the Internet." *Journal of Business Ethics* 28 (2000): 255–65.

Montague, Phillip. "A Child's Right to Privacy." *Public Affairs Quarterly* 2 (1988): 17–32.

Moor, James H. "Using Genetic Information While Protecting the Privacy of the Soul." *Ethics and Information Technology* 1 (1999): 257–63.

Moore, Barrington, Jr. "Privacy." *Society* 22 (1985): 17–27.

Mossholder, Kevin W. "Information Privacy and Performance Appraisal: An Examination of Employee Perceptions and Reactions." *Journal of Business Ethics* (1991): 151–56.

Nagel, Thomas. "Concealment and Exposure." *Philosophy and Public Affairs* 27 (1998): 3–30.

Nelkin, Dorothy, and Lori Andrews. "DNA Identification and Surveillance Creep." *Sociology of Health and Illness* 21 (1999): 689–706.

Nelkin, Dorothy, and Laurence Tancredi. *Dangerous Diagnostics: The Social Power of Biological Information*. New York: HarperCollins, 1989.

Neville, Robert. "Various Meanings of Privacy: A Philosophical Analysis." In *Privacy*, ed. William Baier, 22–34. New York: Fordham University Press, 1980.

Nissenbaum, Helen. "The Meaning of Anonymity in an Information Age." *Information Society* 15 (1999): 141–44.

———. "Privacy as Contextual Integrity." *Washington Law Review* 79 (2004): 119–58.

———. "Toward an Approach to Privacy in Public: Challenges of Information Technology." *Ethics and Behavior* 7 (1997): 207–19.

Nunan, Richard. "Militant Gays, Gays in the Military, and Privacy as Social Freedom." *Law and Philosophy* 13 (1994): 481–92.

O'Brien, David M. *Privacy, Law, and Public Policy.* New York: Praeger Publishers, 1979.

O'Neill, Onora. "Between Consenting Adults." *Philosophy and Public Affairs* 14 (1985): 252–77.

Ottensmeyer, Edward J., and Mark A. Heroux. "Ethics, Public Policy, and Managing Advanced Technologies: The Case of Electronic Surveillance." *Journal of Business Ethics* 10 (1991): 519–26.

Parent, W. A. "A New Definition of Privacy for the Law." *Law and Philosophy* 2 (1983): 305–38.

———. "Recent Work on the Concept of Privacy." *American Philosophical Quarterly* 20 (1983): 341–56.

Parmet, Wendy E. "Legal Rights and Communicable Disease: AIDS, the Police Power, and Individual Liberty." *Journal of Health Politics, Policy, and Law* 14 (1989): 741–71.

Paul, Ellen Frankel, Fred D. Miller Jr., and Jeffrey Paul, eds. *The Right to Privacy.* Cambridge: Cambridge University Press, 2000.

Persson, Anders J., and Sven Ove Hansson. "Privacy at Work: Ethical Criteria." *Journal of Business Ethics* 42 (2003): 59–70.

Posner, Richard A. "Orwell Versus Huxley: Economics, Technology, Privacy, and Satire." *Philosophy and Literature* 24 (2000): 1–33.

———. "Privacy, Secrecy, and Reputation." *Buffalo Law Review* 28 (Winter 1979): 1–56.

———. "The Right of Privacy." *Georgia Law Review* 12 (1978): 393–422.

Regan, Priscilla M. *Legislating Privacy: Technology, Social Values, and Public Policy.* Chapel Hill: University of North Carolina Press, 1995.

Reiman, Jeffrey H. "Driving to the Panopticon: A Philosophical Exploration of the Risks to Privacy Posed by the Information Technology of the Future." *Santa Clara Computer and High Technology Law Journal* 11 (1995): 27–44.

Rosen, Jeffrey. "Out of Context: The Purposes of Privacy." *Social Research* 68 (2001): 209–20.

———. *The Unwanted Gaze: The Destruction of Privacy in America.* New York: Vintage Books, 2001.

———. "Why Privacy Matters." *Wilson Quarterly* 24 (2000): 32–38.

Rössler, Beate, ed. *Privacies: Philosophical Evaluations.* Stanford: Stanford University Press, 2004.

———. *The Value of Privacy.* Trans. Rupert D. V. Glasgow. Cambridge: Polity, 2005.

Rubel, Alan. "Privacy and the U.S.A. Patriot Act: Rights, the Value of Rights, and Autonomy." *Law and Philosophy* 26 (March 2007): 119–59.

Rubenfeld, Jed. "The Right of Privacy." *Harvard Law Review* 102 (1989): 737–807.

Ruiz, Blanca R. "The Right to Privacy: A Discourse Theoretical Approach." *Ratio Juris* 11 (1998): 155–67.

Rule, James. *Privacy in Peril: How We Are Sacrificing a Fundamental Right for Security and Convenience.* Oxford: Oxford University Press, 2007.

Ryan, Alan. "Private Selves and Public Parts." In *Public and Private in Social Life,* ed. S. Benn and G. Gaus, 135–54. New York: St. Martin's Press, 1983.

————. "Public and Private Property." In *Public and Private in Social Life,* ed. S. Benn and G. Gaus, 223–48. New York: St. Martin's Press, 1983.

Saunders, John Turk. "In Defense of a Limited Privacy." *Philosophical Review* 78 (1969): 237–48.

Saxonhouse, Arlene. "Classical Greek Conceptions of Public and Private." In *Public and Private in Social Life,* ed. S. Benn and G. Gaus, 363–84. New York: St. Martin's Press, 1983.

Schauer, Frederick. "Can Public Figures Have Private Lives?" *Social Philosophy and Policy* 17 (2000): 293–309.

Schneider, Carl. *Shame, Exposure, and Privacy.* Boston: Beacon Press, 1977.

Schoeman, Ferdinand D. "AIDS and Privacy." In *AIDS and Ethics*, ed. Frederic G. Reamer. New York: Columbia University Press, 1993.

————. *Philosophical Dimensions of Privacy: An Anthology.* Cambridge: Cambridge University Press, 1984.

————. "Privacy and Criminal Justice Policies." *Criminal Justice Ethics* 3 (1983): 71–84.

————. "Privacy: Philosophical Dimensions." *American Philosophical Quarterly* 21 (1984): 199–214.

Shils, Edward. *The Torment of Secrecy.* New York: Free Press, 1956.

Singleton, Solveig. "Privacy and Twenty-First-Century Law Enforcement: Accountability for New Techniques." *Ohio Northern University Law Review* 30 (2004): 417–50.

Soifer, Eldon, and Bela Szabados. "Hypocrisy and Privacy." *Journal of Philosophical Research* 27 (2002): 601–18.

Solove, Daniel J. *The Digital Person: Technology and Privacy in the Information Age.* New York: New York University Press, 2004.

————. "A Taxonomy of Privacy." *University of Pennsylvania Law Review* 154 (2006): 477–560.

————. *Understanding Privacy.* Cambridge: Harvard University Press, 2008.

————. "The Virtues of Knowing Less: Justifying Privacy Protections Against Disclosure." *Duke Law Journal* 53 (2003): 967–1065.

Solove, Daniel J., and Neil Richards. "Privacy's Other Path: Recovering the Law of Confidentiality." *Georgetown Law Journal* 96 (2007): 123–82.

Sykes, C. J. *The End of Privacy.* New York: St. Martin's Press, 1999.

Tavani, Herman T. "Informational Privacy, Data Mining, and the Internet." *Ethics and Information Technology* 1 (1999): 137–45.

————. "KDD, Data Mining, and the Challenge for Normative Privacy." *Ethics and Information Technology* 1 (1999): 265–73.

————. "Privacy Enhancing Technologies as a Panacea for Online Privacy Concerns: Some Ethical Considerations." *Journal of Information Ethics* 9 (2000): 26–36.

Tavani, Herman, and Frances S. Grodzinsky. "Cyberstalking, Personal Privacy, and Moral Responsibility." *Ethics and Information Technology* 4 (2002): 123–32.

Townsend, James B., and Robert J. Paul. "Employee Privacy Rights." *Business and Public Affairs* 16 (1990): 16–21.

Tunick, Mark. "Does Privacy Undermine Community?" *Journal of Value Inquiry* 35 (2001): 517–34.

Van den Hoven, Jeroen. "Privacy and the Varieties of Informational Wrongdoing." *Australian Journal of Professional and Applied Ethics* 1 (1999): 30–43.

Wacks, Raymond. *Personal Information: Privacy and the Law.* Oxford: Oxford University Press, 1989.

————. *The Protection of Privacy*. London: Sweet and Maxwell, 1980.

Walton, Anthony. "Public and Private Interests: Hegel on Civil Society and the State." In *Public and Private in Social Life*, ed. S. Benn and G. Gaus, 249–66. New York: St. Martin's Press, 1983.

Weinreb, Lloyd L. "The Right to Privacy." *Social Philosophy and Policy* 17 (2000): 25–44.

Westin, Alan F. "Intrusions: Privacy Tradeoffs in a Free Society." *Public Perspective* 11 (2000): 8–19.

————"Privacy and Personnel Records: A Look at Employee Attitudes." *Civil Liberties Review* 4 (1978): 28–34.

————. "Social and Political Dimensions of Privacy." *Journal of Social Issues* 59 (2003): 431–53.

Wiesenthal, David L., and Neil I. Wiener. "Privacy and the Human Genome Project." *Ethics and Behavior* 6 (1996): 189–202.

INDEX

abortion, 7 n. 8, 102, 111–12, 112 n. 54, 114–15. See also *Roe v. Wade*

accountability, 3–4, 9–10, 99, 108, 111, 139, 189, 201, 204, 208–14

Allen, Anita, 106

American Civil Liberties Union (ACLU), 134, 161, 197, 211

anonymity 3, 103–04, 115–16, 134, 199

appropriation tort, 13, 17, 23, 101, 120–21

Aristotle, 11, 32, 40, 44 n. 26, 181

association, rituals of, 6, 11, 52–55, 53 n. 57, 87

Atkinson v. Detroit Free Press Company, 152

autonomy, 2–4, 13, 17, 19 n. 28, 33, 42, 63, 68–72, 76, 78 n. 42, 83–84, 115, 142, 146, 151, 215

Barlow, John Perry, 94

Barns v. Glen Theater, 149

Bartnicki v. Vopper, 118–19

baseline of comparison, 9, 60, 62–67, 75, 179

Berger v. New York, 106

Berlin, Isaiah, 207 n. 63

best policy argument, 142–43

Black, Hugo, 136–37

Blackmun, Harry A., 102

Bloustein, Edward, 104

Bok, Sissela, 152

Bowers v. Hardwick, 112–13

Brandeis, Louis, 13, 100–101, 193

Briscoe v. Reader's Digest Association, Inc., 117

Brownie Miller et al. v. National Broadcasting Co. et al., 95–96, 130–31

Burger, Warren, 197

Cape Publications, Inc. v. Bridges, 145

Carey v. Population Services International, 102

carnivore, 208

censorship, 139, 141 n. 22, 149

Central Intelligence Agency (CIA), 190–91, 199–200

civil liberties, 9, 15, 193, 200

collective ownership, 85 n. 5

collective rationality, 47, 73–76, 80

Cooley, Thomas, 13, 100, 105, 152

Coolidge v. New Hampshire, 107

Confucius, 51 n. 52

consent argument against privacy, 8, 92, 111, 125–31, 150–53, 158, 165–72, 210–11

constitutional privacy, 100–101, 111–16

contraceptives, 5 n. 7, 102, 161

copyright, 23, 175–77, 177 n. 5, 177 n. 6, 178 n. 8, 185

created information, 2, 42, 65, 68, 83–84, 90, 93, 180

cultural universals, 6, 11, 33, 49–52, 55–56, 87

data mining, 1, 3, 5, 10, 81, 91, 110–11, 146, 152, 189, 191, 197–98, 201–3, 210–13

Davis, Frederick, 15

DeCew, Judith, 14, 19 n. 28, 26, 161

decisional privacy, 5, 101, 112–15

defamation, 120

DeGregorio v. CBS, Inc., 145–46

democracy, 8, 10, 33, 128, 139, 141, 144–51, 196, 214

Department of Justice (DOJ), 116, 200 n. 41, 208, 211–12

desert, 77–78, 86, 183, 188

desires, 34–41, 35 n. 6, 45–46, 60, 66, 96–97, 103, 114, 123, 144, 146

disassociation, rituals of, 6, 11, 20, 52–54, 87

discovered information, 83–84

Douglas, William O., 102, 104, 197, 214–15

due process, 102, 135, 150, 201

Dworkin, Ronald, 166–68

eavesdropping, 100, 105–6

Eisenstadt v. Baird, 102

Electronic Communications Privacy Act (ECPA), 109

Electronic Frontier Foundation (EFF), 94

Ely, John, 115

emergency powers, 193–94

encryption, 2, 28–29, 79, 94, 103, 208–9

eudaimonism, 39–40

expression, 8, 99, 103–4, 133–52, 198, 214

facial recognition technology, 1, 3, 10, 81, 110

Fair Credit Reporting Act of 1970, 108

false light tort, 13, 17, 23, 101, 120–21
Falwell v. Flynt, 120–21
Federal Bureau of Investigation (FBI), 190–96, 199, 200, 208
Feinberg, Joel, 97
Feldman, Fred, 36–37, 37 n. 10, 41
Fifth Amendment, 101–2, 101 n. 7, 114, 135, 196
Finnis, John, 12
First Amendment, 101–4, 115, 118, 120, 134–37, 149, 151, 192, 200 n. 41
Florida Star v. B. J. F., 118–21
flourishing, 2, 6, 12, 33, 40–46, 50, 54, 56, 70–73, 76, 85, 87, 138, 143–44, 165, 213. *See also* well-being
Foot, Philippa, 37, 40, 46
Foreign Intelligence Surveillance Act (FISA), 191–93, 201, 208, 211
Fourteenth Amendment, 102
Fourth Amendment, 7, 101–8, 114–16, 191 n. 8, 212
free access views, 4, 8–9, 99, 176, 180, 184–88, 214
freedom
    of association, 104, 115–16, 214
    of religion, 204
    of speech, 8, 99, 103–4, 133–52, 198, 214

Gates v. Discovery Communications, Inc., 117
Gauthier, David, 58–63, 66, 71
genetic enhancement, 43, 49, 65, 180
genetic information, 10, 19, 81, 98
Gerstein, Robert, 54
Gert, Benard, 46–47
Gill v. Hearst Publishing Company, 117–18, 121
global positioning systems, 189
gossip, 30–31, 147
Griswold v. Connecticut, 102, 104, 112, 115
Gormley, Ken, 107

hacking, 4, 9, 99, 175–76, 180, 184, 186–88
harassment, 8, 137, 147, 151, 155, 198, 214
Health Insurance Portability and Accountability Act of 1996, 109, 111
Henkin, Louis, 115
Hobbes, Thomas, 15
homosexuality, 112, 147, 202
Hubin, Don, 61
human nature, 41–49, 66, 83
Hume, David, 45–46

information assault, 31
Inness, Julie, 13
intellectual property, 5, 9, 16, 22–23, 95–96, 135, 175–88

intimacy, 5 n. 7, 13–14, 17, 19, 31, 47, 54–55, 214
intrusion tort, 7, 13, 17, 23, 101, 109, 120–31
isolation, 26, 51, 86

Japanese-American internment, 194–95
Jefferson, Thomas, 177
judicial oversight, 9, 116, 191, 204, 209–13
justice, 11, 54, 57, 72 n. 30, 129, 202, 204

Katz v. United States, 105–6
Korematsu v. United States, 194
Korsgaard, Christine, 46 n. 30, 72 n. 31, 73–74

Laird v. Tatum, 197
Lawrence et al. v. Texas, 112–15
libel, 120
liberty, 5 n. 7, 11, 14–20, 32, 52, 61, 70–71, 75–76, 92, 102, 114–15, 135, 138–39, 142–43, 147, 150–57, 165, 173, 189, 193, 198, 204, 206, 214
Lincoln, Abraham, 181, 193–94
Locke, John, 9, 58, 63, 84, 178–81, 187–88, 203
Loving v. Virginia, 102

marriage, 89, 102, 113, 199
medical records, 5, 90, 94, 116, 148, 184, 213
McCarthy, Joseph, 195–96, 202
Meiklejohn, Alexander, 137, 139
Melvin v. Reid, 117–22
Mill, John Stuart, 10, 15, 137–43, 204
monitoring, 2–3, 69, 92, 94, 99, 108–11, 125, 155, 159–60, 165–71, 189–90, 192, 197, 200–202, 208, 210–11. *See also* surveillance
Moore, Kim, 127 n. 106

NAACP v. Alabama, 104
National Security Administration (NSA), 190–93, 201, 203, 208
Ninth Amendment, 102, 114
"no harm, no foul" rule, 6–7, 10, 47, 58, 61–62, 67, 72, 84–85, 98, 178, 185–88
noninterference, duties of, 77, 78 n. 42
non-zero-sum, 73–74, 80
"nothing to hide" argument, 167, 169, 203–5
Nozick, Robert, 18 n. 27, 69, 85 n. 5
nudity, 145, 149

objectivity (values), 34–39, 144
obscenity, 113, 214
Olmstead v. United States, 105–6, 193
Orchemenos, Greece, 89
original acquisition, 58, 63, 84–86, 85 n. 5, 178–79
Orwell, George, 90
Osborn v. United States, 214

Parent, William, 13–21, 20 n. 30, 27, 52 n. 55
Pareto-based proviso, 62–79, 72 n. 30, 84–85, 143
patents, 176–77, 185
paternalism, 113, 165, 207 n. 63
Patriot Act (U.S.), 10, 111, 191–92, 200, 200 n. 41, 211
Paulsen v. Personality Posters, 146
Peeping Tom, 96–98, 109, 159 n. 9, 185, 188
pen registers, 190
photography, 25, 30, 100, 109–10, 117–18, 122–26, 130, 145, 149–50, 191
Plato, 11, 32, 53 n. 57
pornography, 102, 116, 134, 147, 149, 214
privacy
    interest view of, 5, 15, 24, 31, 97, 106, 111, 119, 121, 134, 146, 184, 188, 203–4, 209, 214
    normative and non-normative views of, 11–21, 26–27, 32
    property view of, 22–25, 30
    psychological need for, 51–56
    reductionist/nonreductionist views of, 14–16, 22
    reproductive, 5 n. 7, 7, 102, 111–15
    tort, 7, 13, 17, 23, 101, 109, 116, 118, 120–31
    trespass view of, 96, 100, 105–6, 106 n. 23, 121, 128–30, 176, 186, 192
    waiving claims of, 8, 28–29, 117, 156, 165, 168
    zones of, 14, 23, 28, 30, 176
Privacy Act of 1974, 108–11
private facts tort, 13, 17, 23, 101, 116, 118, 120, 121
property rights, 1–2, 5, 7, 11, 14, 16–19, 22–25, 28–32, 60, 78–79, 82–87, 90, 92–98, 135–36, 144, 150, 152, 191, 206–7. See also intellectual property
Prosser, William, 13, 17, 23, 101, 117, 120, 122
public domain, 19, 90, 92, 117–18
public/private distinction, 51 n. 52, 87

Quinn, Warren, 46

Rachels, James, 52, 54 n. 62
Rader, Melvin, 196
Rand, Ayn, 195
rational basis for regulation, 112, 114
rationality, 36, 39, 40–47, 63, 68, 72–76, 80
rational project pursuit, 44, 63, 76
Rawls, John, 44, 72 n. 30, 144–45, 150–51
reasonable person, 14, 121–25
recidivism, 56, 98
relationalism (values), 6, 34, 38–40, 43, 55, 63
reputation, 120, 198

risk, 7, 69–70, 86–92, 96–98, 156, 160, 171, 175, 186–88, 202, 204–5, 209
Roe v. Wade, 5 n. 7, 7, 102, 111–15

Scalia, Antonin, 112–14
Scanlon, Thomas, 23–24
Schenk v. United States, 195
Schmidtz, David, 74, 74 n. 36
Schwartz, Barry, 52–54
seclusion, 26, 33, 47, 121
secrecy/secrets, 2, 10, 19, 115, 65, 95–98, 110, 115
security, national, 4, 7, 9, 116, 184–86, 206–12
separation, 26, 33, 47–48, 54, 86, 97
sexual harassment, 8, 137, 147, 155, 214
Shulman v. Group W. Productions, 121–22
sickle-cell anemia, 89
Sipple v. San Francisco Chronicle Inc., 147
Socialist Workers Party v. Attorney General, 199
solitude, 1, 3, 13, 31, 122
Solove, Daniel, 203
Spooner, Lysander, 182 n. 16, 183
subjectivism (values), 34–42, 35 n. 6, 55, 59–62, 66, 72, 97, 144
subpoenas, 111, 116, 190, 196, 213
sunlight provisions, 9–10, 139, 198, 208–13. See also transparency
Supreme Court (U.S.), 104–8, 112, 118–20, 139, 146, 194–97
surveillance, 1, 3, 10, 51, 81, 88–91, 105–10, 116, 128, 148, 153, 155, 159, 165–69, 189–93, 197–205, 208–12. See also monitoring

Taylor, James Stacey, 201–2
Taylor, Paul, 40–42
terrorism, 2, 9, 108, 186, 189, 189 n. 1, 192, 200, 200 n. 41, 203–9
Terrorist Information and Prevention System (TIPS), 212
Thomson, Judith Jarvis, 14–15, 21–24
tolerance, 142
torture, 150, 201 n. 45
Total Information Awareness (TIA), 212, 212 n. 73
trade secrets, 7, 137, 147, 149, 176–77, 185
transparency, 3, 214. See also sunlight provisions
trespass, 96, 100, 105–6, 106 n. 23, 121, 128–30, 176, 186, 192

Urofsky v. Gilmore, 104
utilitarianism, 9, 66 n. 30, 138, 143, 177–78

values
    objectivity of, 34–39, 144

subjectivity of, 34, 35, 35 n. 6, 36–42, 55, 59–62, 66, 72, 97, 144
relationalism and, 6, 34, 38, 39, 40, 43, 55, 63
veil of ignorance, 144–50
video surveillance, 1–3, 10, 61, 81, 90, 92, 109–11, 123, 124–30, 148, 159, 185, 189
Video Voyeurism Prevention Act of 2004, 109–11, 130

waiving privacy claims, 8, 28–29, 117, 156, 165, 168

Waldron, Jeremy, 18 n. 27, 204
Warren, Samuel, 13, 100–101
Weintraub, Jeff, 87
well-being, 2, 6, 12, 21, 32, 40, 44, 46, 49–50, 56, 61–67, 64 n. 18, 85, 96–97, 138, 143, 179
Westin, Alan, 13, 47, 49, 51
wiretapping, 108–9, 199

X-ray, 20 n. 30, 21–25, 30

zero-sum/non-zero-sum, 73–74, 80
zone of privacy, 14, 23, 28, 30, 176